Battling the Bay

Battling the Bay

by Jordan Zinovich

The publisher:
Lone Pine Publishing
206, 10426-81 Avenue
Edmonton, Alberta, Canada
T6E 1X5

Canadian Cataloguing in Publication Data
Zinovich, Jordan, 1955-
    Battling the Bay

    Includes bibliographical references.
    ISBN 0-919433-96-0

    1. Nagle, Ed. 2. Fur traders—Canada, Northern—Biography. 3. Canada, Northern—Biography. 4. Canada, Northern—History. I. Title.
FC3962.1.N32Z56 1991   971.9'02'092   C92-091072-6
F1060.9.N35Z56 1991

Cover illustration: **Don Inman**
Editorial: Gary Whyte, Bev Hills, Elaine Butler, Lloyd Dick
Layout: Elaine Butler, Lloyd Dick
Printing: Hignell Printing Ltd., Winnipeg, Canada

The publisher gratefully acknowledges the assistance of the Federal Department of Communications, Alberta Culture and Multiculturalism, the Canada Council, and the Alberta Foundation for the Arts in the production of this book.

The author gratefully acknowledges financial assistance toward the preparation of this manuscript from the **Alberta Historical Resources Foundation**.

To Winnifred Nagle, Dale Zinovich and Adele Haft-Zinovich. Without the three of you, this could not have been done.

Table of Contents

List of Maps and Figures

Acknowledgements

As is true for all projects of this kind, I owe thanks to many different people. At the outset I extend my sincere apologies to anyone I have overlooked: my memory is sometimes inadequate. First and foremost, I must thank the Nagles. Ted Nagle, Tess Nagle-Felker, Geoff Nagle, and Barry Nagle opened their memories and family records to me; and Frances Kimpton and Mary Nagle-Gallagher gave me more than I could possibly have expected. Of the others who helped, C.H. "Punch" Dickins, F.B. "Ted" Watt, and F.J. "Tiny" Peet were unfailing sources of support and information. Dr. June Helm and Dr. J.G.E. Smith explained key Dené words and concepts and made certain that I read the anthropological sources. Without James Rabesca and the elders of the Rae-Edzo band — Alec Charlot, Elizabeth and Louis Mackenzie, Vital Thomas, and Madeline Zoe — much of the Fort Rae material would be badly skewed. Louis Menez, O.M.I., knows more Fort Resolution history than anyone else on the planet. James Darkes guided my exploration of Smith's Rapids. Shirlee Anne Smith and the staff of the Hudson's Bay Company Archives struggled to help me understand tariffs and Made Beaver currency, and patiently endured the "voice of the opposition." Richard Secord Jr. released Dick Secord's journals to me. Helen Larose helped me in all sorts of ways. And Bev Hills stuck with the project from almost start to finish. Special thanks also to Douglas Cass, Julliette Champagne, Sheryl Dunn, Joanne Frodsham, Harold Haft, Giles Heon, Kathy Kopeck, Lucien Lefrancois, David Leonard, Adam S. Little, Tim Ross, and George Zinovich, who all provided of their time and expertise. Without the assistance of a generous grant from the **Alberta Historical Resources Foundation** I could not have completed my research. Finally, I want to thank Adele: seven years was a long time for us to trudge after Ed.

Preface

My Dear Ed,

I got your letter of 28th Jan. 1883 from Miners' Flatts [sic] yesterday evening, and am Sorry to find you in so miserable a position — Sick & obliged to thresh Barley at only twenty-five cents a Bushel — and much of this hardship brought on by yourself & mismanagement. If you have an established good claim against any of the contracting Surveyors you are, of course, aware that the payment can be enforced — and if you can not do better, make out your amount for work done, Swear to its correctness before a Justice of the Peace, and I will see what I can do for you through the government, but really your best course will be to make it & Send it to G[arrett] James to be Sued at Winnipeg....

I had letters from all the family except you and John at Christmas & John is so busy mining at Hay Island that he should be excused; all were well or passable. Had Parker to Christmas dinner, and wrote you & all others after New Year's, sending your letter to Gerrard for re-direction, seeing that I did not Know your address. You will by this time have received that letter of mine.

...My own condition continues to be a "narrow sufficiency" and my health this winter has been very poor. We have had a hard winter. For a long time the thermometer held from 20 above to 30 below with heavy Snow, & this cold weather confined [me] to the house...

I have just received a letter from Gerrard — Portage la Prairie — in which he mentions having received two letters from you & the Edmonton Bulletin, which he sent me. He mentions your desire that he should go with you to Red Deer River & wishes my opinion, but I know so little about it that I can Scarcely advise — and defer Saying any more about it until I again write to You, which I will in a few days....

affectionately yours,
G.J. Nagle

CHAPTER 1

The Nagles From Ireland
(1823 - 1853)

Québec's cold north winds had already tinted the hardwoods crimson on September 19, 1853, when Gerrard Joseph Nagle first gazed at his wrinkly newborn son. Gerrard was worried about his wife. Edmund Barry was dark-haired Margaret's ninth child. He looked strong, well-formed and healthy, but neither the pregnancy nor the delivery had been easy for Margaret. While she reassured them with pale tired smiles and hugged their new brother close, Gerrard watched his other children gather briefly at his wife's bedside.

It is impossible to exactly establish the sequence of events that had brought Gerrard and Margaret Nagle to their home at Saint Hyacinthe, Québec. The following facts seem clear, however. Gerrard was born in Ireland, near Fermoy town in County Cork. By 1853 he should have been preparing to inherit Rathcormack, the traditional Nagle family stronghold in the Blackwater River valley north of the Nagle Mountains, but a potato famine and the unrest that followed it had changed that. A few years earlier, the family had suffered a reduction in its fortunes when, rather than appointing Gerrard's Irish-born father Garrett Nagle as Fermoy Baronet, in 1815 the British government had bestowed that title on an English branch of the Nagle family.

After the British choice, and with the escalating violence in County Cork, Gerrard's father had grasped the only real opportunity that presented itself to him. A small group of liberal English intellectuals had encountered a problem: to persuade families from southern Ireland to take part in an emigration scheme they were proposing, they needed to assure them that they were not headed for prison colonies. Garrett Nagle was highly regarded both by the Irish in County Cork and the Englishmen involved in the emigration program. In return for passage and assistance for the members of his family who qualified, he had agreed to journey with the Peter Robinson settlers of 1823 into the wilderness of Ramsay Township, in the British colony of Upper Canada.

At the time his father led the Nagles into the Canadian wilderness, Gerrard Nagle was 16 years old. The family had not settled at Shipman's Mills — now called Almonte — as many of the other Robinson settlers did. Instead, they moved seven kilometres farther north, stopping where the Mississippi River cascades over the raw limestone ledges of Norway Pine Falls.

There Gerrard had taken a 70-acre homestead, claiming both the falls and the islands in them. His father had preferred to settle farther away from the noisy cascade, and had laid out his homestead one lot-line north of Gerrard's, on the flat crest of an embankment rising east of the river below the falls. The earth there was a rich, clean mix of clay and sandy loam, covered with a thick forest of tall, straight white pine trees.

Thomas Stevenson, his wife, and his daughter Margaret had also been among the Robinson settlers, and they too had settled near Norway Pine Falls. Together the Nagles and the Stevensons helped pioneer the small town of Blakeney, Ontario: quietly clearing and irrigating fields, building fine frame houses, and tending to their new home. When a group of Orangemen calling themselves the Ballygibblins rioted at Shipman's Mills in 1824, the Blakeney folk had avoided becoming involved.

White pines were the most valuable trees in the Canadian woods at that time. From them came the timbers that framed Britain's tall ships, and English shipyards wanted all they could get. Canadian governments kept careful control of the cutting licences they issued, but Garrett Nagle had maintained his connections. By 1835 he and his sons had terraced one of the small islands in the east side chutes at Norway Pine Falls and built a water-driven sawmill. Rafts of their mast logs and squared timbers were floating down the Mississippi, Ottawa, and Saint Lawrence Rivers bound for the shipyards near Québec City.

Although the early years at Blakeney had been difficult, only one tragedy had affected Gerrard's life. In 1825 Margaret's parents had died, leaving Gerrard's father and mother to assist the orphans. Deep-eyed Margaret was much younger than Gerrard, but during the years following her parents' deaths the two of them grew close. By 1834 romance had flowered between them. They named their first child Sarsfield Barry.

In 1835, when Gerrard was securely in possession of his homestead, the sawmill, and a liquor licence granted him by the government, he had married Margaret. The following year they had purchased his homestead patent.

And if things had remained calm in the Canadas, they might have chosen to grow old at Norway Pine Falls.

However, in 1837 sedition had burst into rebellion in the Canadas. Gerrard had moved to Saint Hyacinthe to help support British efforts to maintain stability in Lower Canada. He was not the only Robinson settler to back the government. William Lyon Mackenzie, one of the most popular rebel leaders, later complained bitterly about the lack of support the Robinson settlers gave to the nationalists. When the uprising subsided Gerrard stood high in the re-

Gerrard Joseph Nagle, photograph copied from tintype.

gard of some of the influential men in Saint Hyacinthe, so he and Margaret decided to stay on there. George Cassimir Dessaulles planned to stretch a retaining weir across the Yamaska River. Saint Hyacinthe would soon have new mills and industry.

Frustratingly, Gerrard's ambitions were not quickly realized; he and Margaret had a growing family to support. When three of his brothers — one of whom was his favourite, Michael Dominic — pressed him to accompany them in search of work on the roads, canals, and railroads edging west across the new American states of Michigan and Indiana, he and Margaret left Saint Hyacinthe. The Nagle brothers stopped briefly at Ypsilanti, Michigan, where Michael Dominic invested in some property, before Gerrard and Margaret continued on toward the newly incorporated city of Chicago. By the time their daughter Mary was born in Michigan City, Indiana, however, a depression had strangled the railroads' western expansion.

Fortunately, when the couple returned to Upper Canada, employment worthy of Gerrard's talents had finally come to him.

Lumbering was booming in the Canadas, and the colonial governments desperately needed capable Superintendents-of-Public-Works. Robert Baldwin's ministry wanted a timber slide built on the Madawaska River, west of Norway Pine Falls. Gerrard's extensive and varied experience qualified him to undertake the project.

By April 25, 1844, Gerrard had had the Madawaska timber slide completed and open to local lumbermen. On the first day of its use, 700 pieces of timber slipped safely down it toward the Ottawa River. Shortly afterwards, Gerrard had followed them. On the strength of his success at Madawaska, he was assigned the task of constructing one of the earliest timber slides on the Ottawa River, near Calumet Island.

After the Ottawa River project was completed, however, he had chosen not to stay on in Upper Canada. Throughout the years between 1837 and 1844, he and Margaret had maintained their belief that, of all the places they had seen, Saint Hyacinthe held the best future for them and their family. The Dessaulles brothers had continued to hold him in high regard. They represented the Seigneury Debartzch at Saint Hyacinthe, and soon after he completed the Ottawa timber slide Gerrard had become Timber Agent for their seigneury.

Edmund Barry Nagle arrived at the moment the Nagles' future looked brightest. Gerrard and Margaret owned their seigneury lot on the south bank of the Yamaska River, near the southern ends of the Dessaulles' weir and Barselou Bridge, and had built a comfortable home in which to house their family. Their two eldest sons were enrolled in the College of Saint Hyacinthe, which was Catholic. And early in 1853 Gerrard had been advanced for the position of Crown Agent for Lands and Forest for the Saint François District. The Saint François District lay within the boundaries of the Seigneury Debartzch, and eight months after Ed's birth his father became the Crown Agent.

Sadly, the Nagles did not savour the full richness of their successes for long. Margaret never fully recovered from delivering Ed, and by August of 1854 she was dead. Although Gerrard loved his children, his wife's death put an unbridgeable gulf between them and him. For a time he threw himself into his work, relying on the elder children to care for their younger siblings.

The Saint François Agency was the largest crown timber agency in Lower Canada. Its 66,305 acres stretched from some heavily

Margaret Stephenson-Nagle, photograph copied from tintype.

forested hills near the confluence of the Magog and Saint François Rivers northwards as far as the Saint Lawrence. Gerrard was responsible for administering and patrolling it, as well as continuing his supervision of the Seigneury Debartzch sawmill.

Gradually, as his distress abated and he became more proficient at his new job, he returned to parenting. He turned to Margaret's sister Mary for companionship and assistance with the children. She soon became an indispensable part of his life, and in 1855 they were married.

Then, as if to further mend the torn fabric of his life, his brother Michael Dominic contacted him again. Michael and his wife were desperate. Since their return from Michigan to Norway Pine Falls, scarlet fever had killed three of their four children. Gerrard insisted that Michael come to settle his family at Saint Hyacinthe, and when his brother arrived he arranged a timber licence for him. The two of them were soon in business together, milling timber for the Québec City markets.

CHAPTER 2

Saint Hyacinthe Boyhood
(1853 - 1870)

Mary Nagle cared for her stepchildren, but did not lavish affection on them, and they received even less of her attention when she began having children of her own. Whether because he associated them with Margaret's memory, or because he considered it a wife's place to tend to children, their father did not spare much time for them either, other than to discipline them.

But despite the emotional gaps between him and his parents, Ed Nagle enjoyed his childhood. Affectionate brothers and sisters surrounded him, and his father's careful first appraisal of him proved astute. As the roots spread beneath the tree Gerrard had planted to commemorate his son's birth, Ed became a healthy, powerful child. On meeting him, people often noticed his intensely clear blue eyes, which he kept steadily fixed on the world around him. Then they discovered his strength of will. From almost the moment he could toddle, Ed was fiercely independent. Once he had explored the gardens and orchard his father and stepmother kept, the white picket fence surrounding the Nagle home no longer served to contain him.

There were few other homes on the south bank of the Yamaska River. South and east of Saint Hyacinthe isolated hills rose up, as if struggling free from the Appalachian mountains farther south. Dense forests of hardwoods and pines covered them and the river banks. Ed's greatest joy came from exploring those forests and wandering the banks of the smooth, clear river. Hours of his young life drifted lazily by while he watched the watery curtain spill over the barrier Senator Dessaulles had stretched across the Yamaska.

The Nagle home in Saint Hyacinthe.

On the north side of the river, Saint Hyacinthe grew almost as rapidly as Ed. From the riverbank he watched twin towers rise above a new cathedral. Many times he must have crossed Barselou Bridge to visit the bustling central market and the huge grey-stone seminary school with the gardens where his brothers and their black-robed teachers mumbled together. On his way to the college he passed the fragile, iron lattice that the Grand Trunk Pacific Railroad was stretching out to bridge the river, and he spent countless hours in the Seigneury sawmill run by his uncle and father.

Of the thirty or so sawmills in and around Saint Hyacinthe, the sawmill managed by the Nagle brothers was one of the largest and best known. Ed was about three years old when his father first encountered a renegade lumberman named Brookes. The exchange between the two men profoundly affected the child, and an incident that occurred during their conflict remained vivid in his memory throughout his life.

Early in 1857, Brookes and some other lumbermen began writing to Gerrard Nagle's superiors. They accused the Crown Agent of a conflict-of-interest, because at the same time as he regulated their lumbering he and his brother managed a sawmill in competition with them. But Brookes went further than merely writing letters: he began cutting unlicensed timber near the Magog River.

Gerrard responded immediately to the charges against him, and quickly moved to apprehend Brookes. Sarsfield, Ed's eldest full brother, went off as a Wood Ranger to shut down the Magog River operation. But Brookes escaped Sarsfield, and when Gerrard sent

19

The Nagle Brothers, circa 1859: (left to right) John Thomas "Jack," Garrett, Edmund, and Parker.

another man to summon him, the renegade drove the messenger off with the threat that he would shoot the next government man who interfered with his business.

Shortly after that violent threat, a fire leveled the seigneury sawmill, making the charges of conflict-of-interest irrelevant. "I own nothing but a few piles of boards," wrote Gerrard to his supervisor. His father's reaction to the sawmill fire so impressed Ed, that many years later he wrote that it had ruined him financially. Whether or not Brookes had anything to do with setting the fire, Gerrard Nagle turned wrathfully to his prosecution. By the time Brookes was sentenced in 1860, Ed had watched his father gain the attention and respect of every lumberman near Saint Hyacinthe.

Ed was then about seven years old, and Saint Hyacinthe had changed substantially from the town into which he had been born. It had become one of the three most important cities in Lower Canada, with a market second only to the one in Montréal in the quality, quantity, and value of the goods traded there. Saint Hyacinthe parishioners worshipped in the newly completed Notre-Dame-du-Rosaire cathedral; The first bunting-festooned Grand Trunk Pacific Railroad engine had steamed eastward across the completed railroad bridge in 1859; and the Seigneury Debartzch sawmill had been rebuilt, farther down the Yamaska River, on the edge of a newly dug canal.

Barselou Bridge, 1874.

In the settlement expanding on the south bank of the river, the Nagle family was changing, too. The collapse of the first seigneury sawmill had not crushed Gerrard's ambitions, but it had moved him along other business avenues. As well as timber agent for the Seigneury and Crown, he now advertised himself as an engineer and undertaker. Although the Saint François agency timber revenues dropped in 1860 and 1861, he remained sufficiently prosperous to purchase an office lot in the heart of Saint Hyacinthe's industrial district, on Rue Cascade. Sarsfield had left to study law in Montréal, but Ed had no shortage of siblings. His half-sister Grace and half-brother Gerrard had both arrived since 1856.

In 1861, most Canadians took more notice of the death of Queen Victoria's consort, Prince Albert, than of any other international news. To Gerrard Nagle and many others, the Canadas seemed perfectly located to assure a continuing peace and prosperity: the treaties of 1812 had stabilized the border with the United States of America; after the 1837 uprising, French-English conflict had ameliorated; the Union Act of 1840 had created a single government for Upper and Lower Canada; and beyond the western frontier of Upper Canada, Hudson's Bay Company fur traders controlled the vast territorial expanse called the northwest.

By 1865, Canadians were debating the nature of dominion status and issues of confederation. There was some heat to the debates, especially in Lower Canada, where politics was not a clear case of advocating one or the other of the dominant secular ideologies. In addition to the Conservatives — among whom Gerrard numbered himself — and the Liberals, the Catholic Church had tossed its miter into the political ring. In 1864, a proclamation from Pope Pius IX had condemned liberalism, socialism and rationalism. Secure in the embrace of Britain's imperial omnipotence, Canadians took little more than marginal interest in the fact that south of them the union of American states was dissolving.

Although the Liberals were the most charismatic politicians in the Saint Hyacinthe area, among French-speaking Lower Canadians Catholicism swayed politics. The Nagles were Roman Catholic, but like most boys Ed hearkened to attitudes that interested him. As the debates ran their course, he gained two insights: that there were always more than two positions in any discussion, and that his own views bent him toward the charismatic Liberals.

By his twelfth year, Ed was already deeply ensnared in his father's plans for his future. He apparently had little difficulty mastering the Irish Gaelic that Gerrard taught him, and easily learned French in addition to English. Although Ed felt most comfortable out of doors and showed an aptitude for sawmill work, Gerrard had fixed on a career in medicine for him. He would study at Saint Lawrence College, but before he could convince his father that he had no interest in college they were both temporarily distracted. The political debates so completely involved most Canadians, that by 1866 they were virtually ignoring their border with the United States. It was an error that could have cost them more dearly than it did.

Irishmen who fled the potato famines had not emigrated only to Canada. Many had settled in the United States, where the most bitter of them had formed the Fenian Brotherhood and vowed revenge on the British. Canada was British territory, so the Fenian General Sweeny took advantage of the chaos following the end of the American Civil War and the assassination of Abraham Lincoln to plan an invasion. From New York City to Vermont's frontier Fenians openly vowed to drive the British from Canada, and to use the liberated territory as their base for retaking Ireland.

Sweeny was a remarkable strategist. He moved his men and supplies north to the Vermont and New York borders with Canada, where he organized commissariats. The two Fenian columns that poured into Canada in 1866 headed towards the frontier towns of Frelighsburg and Huntingdon, in the Eastern Townships. They had three objectives: to cut off the rail and canal lines that supplied Lower Canada, to draw British troops south, and to urge French-speaking Canadians to rise up in support of the invasion.

Like most Canadians, the Nagles were astonished at the news of the Fenian invasion. Saint Hyacinthe lay just 65 kilometres north of Frelighsburg, so during the early stages of the Fenian advance its inhabitants felt particularly vulnerable. The Nagles watched anxiously as the Fenians from Vermont took and defended a secure position on Eccles Hill, near Frelighsburg. Farther west, the Fenian column from New York State was driving startled farmers and settlers from their homesteads in its march towards Huntingdon. When Sweeny judged that sufficient attention was focused on the Eastern Townships, his main force crossed the narrow straits near Detroit, Michigan, and captured Fort Erie, in Upper Canada. Fortunately for the Canadas, French Canadians chose not to join the Irish invaders, and the Fenians were unable to maintain their advances on Frelighsburg and Huntingdon. After fierce fighting at Fort Erie, they were also driven from there, and when they recrossed the border, the Union army subdued them.

Ed Nagle was only 13 years old when the Fenians invaded Canada, but it was all his father could do to restrain him from joining the fight. He celebrated wildly on learning of Canada's victory, and joined his countrymen in lionizing heroes like S.J. Dennis, who had distinguished himself at Fort Erie. After the Fenian invasion, Canadians turned back to their political debates with new resolve and a sense of the larger world surrounding them. The United States was quietly manifesting its intent to control the entire North American continent. Canadians took careful note when, early in 1867, Britain supported the U.S. purchase of Alaska from Russia. And when rumors drifted northward that Americans also planned to annex the Hudson's Bay Company territories, the West's vastness no longer seemed so protective.

Nevertheless, as a result of both the victory over the Fenians and the sense of a continuing threat from its southern neighbour, Canada was experiencing a general sense of unity more powerful than anything that had affected it since 1812. In 1867, Canadian politicians lobbied vigorously for the British parliamentary vote that extended dominion status and responsible self-government to them. After that, they pushed just as actively to attain the Hudson's Bay Company territories that separated them from British Columbia and the Pacific coast.

To celebrate Confederation in 1867, Gerrard Nagle threw a huge party on the south bank of the Yamaska River. Rockets tore apart the night sky over Saint Hyacinthe. More than three hundred people milled around the Nagles' bonfire, while Ed dispensed beer from two large barrels and watched the revellers exult.

By 1869, however, the ferment had waned and Ed was bored with his life. He was an adventurous 16-year-old, with little interest in college. The old loggers in the seigneury sawmill were his real teachers, inspiring him with their stories. According to them, the Bangor Tigers — those river-dancing loggers from Maine whose exploits generated the Paul Bunyan legends — were the greatest of all woodsmen. Joining the Long Drive down the Connecticut River would make him a man.

As Ed would soon learn, however, there were other avenues to manhood. Throughout the spring and summer of 1869, Canadians carefully scrutinized every aspect of the negotiations that would transfer the Hudson's Bay Company territories to them. But as Canada attempted to secure her western frontier, the Métis and Indian inhabitants of the Red River Settlement bluntly injected their opinions into the discussion. Their spokesman, a Métis named Louis Riel, insisted that Canada guarantee native rights before asserting any claim to the land in the Northwest Territories. His people would not allow Canadians into the disputed territory until their rights were assured.

Bewildered easterners read about the situation in newspaper editorials which sometimes hinted that religious fanaticism, murder, and rebellion were Riel's priorities. William McDougall, one of the original Fathers of Confederation and the already-designated lieutenant-governor for the Northwest Territories, was blocked at the northern boundary of the Dakota Territory. McDougall's Conservator of the Peace, the brave S.J. Dennis, retreated ignominiously from Riel's Red River Settlement. But before Canadians could grasp what was unfurling in the West, their attention was again wrenched to their southern frontier.

After the Fenians had driven them from their homes in 1866, the farmers near Frelighsburg had banded together. The government had responded quite quickly to the first invasion, but the 'Missiquoi County home guard' believed that if a second raid came they could react quicker themselves. They had purchased 40 very accurate Ballard sporting rifles, supplied themselves amply with cartridges, and contacted friendly farmers south of the border. And they made a regular habit of practicing with their rifles and asking questions whenever they visited their southern neighbours.

In December of 1869, the home guard had reported that strangely loaded wagons were arriving at Hubbard's farm, near Franklin, Vermont. Earlier in December, in New York City, the Fenian Senate had announced plans for another assault on Canada. General O'Neil had replaced Sweeny. This time the Senate leaders muzzled their more bombastic brethren, but when O'Neil tried slipping north to inspect Hubbard's farm, the sharp-eyed home guard spotted him and notified the Dominion government that trouble was brewing in Vermont.

A call for volunteer Canadian militia units went out on April 11, 1870. Canada was besieged on two fronts — by Riel's Métis in the west and the Fenians in the south — so Ed demanded the right to fight the Fenians. This time Gerrard Nagle did not stand in his son's way. Captain Romuald Saint Jacques — a business associate of Senator Dessaulles and a personal friend of the Nagles' — commanded the Saint Hyacinthe Infantry Company of the Third Provisional Battalion, No. 6 Military District, and Gerrard was willing to entrust responsibility for Ed to him.

Saint Jacques' Infantry Company was one of the first units to respond to the call to arms. By April 12, Ed was marching into Montréal. Three days later he was billeted at the stone fort at Saint-Jean-Sur-Richelieu. Saint Jean rests almost exactly half way between Frelighsburg and Huntingdon, and the military command wanted a mobile force there capable of both protecting the area's canals and railroads and moving south to fight. On the sixteenth of April, Saint Jacques became Major of the Third Provisional Battalion, and Ed's company was ordered to prepare to engage the Fenians.

O'Neil, however, had no intention of immediately moving north. He intended to sting the British by invading on May 24, Queen Victoria's birthday, so in mid-April he returned to New York City. Unaware of the Fenian strategy, the Saint Hyacinthe Company found itself on full alert with no enemy to fight. Mumbling ''humbug,'' Ed and his comrades remained at Saint Jean until April 21; then they and most of the other volunteer units were demobilized and sent home.

After the flag waving and cheers that had greeted him at Montréal, Ed's return to Saint Hyacinthe seemed depressingly inconsequential. But only a month after he returned home a Missiquoi County farmer named S.J. Hunter made a brief visit to a friend in Vermont. Close to Hubbard's farm he stumbled into droves of Fenian soldiers flocking toward Franklin. Hunter returned quietly to Canada to mobilize the home guard, then sent a dispatch off to Montréal.

By the evening of May 24, 1870, Ed was hustling back to Saint-Jean-Sur-Richelieu. There he remained, while the home guard defended Eccles' Hill and the Missiquoi frontier, and another group called the Huntingdon Borderers routed a second Fenian column from Trout River and the Huntingdon border. When his unit was demobilized for good, on June 4, 1870, Ed had still not seen a skirmish. He could and did, however, claim that he had taken part in the first military defense of the Dominion of Canada.

The Dawson Trail West
(1870 - 1874)

Although many Fenian Raid volunteers immediately marched west to face the Red River Métis, Ed was not one of them. His father had shrewdly recognized that he and his brothers were dissatisfied with life in Saint Hyacinthe. Since 1859, Gerrard had liked a piece of land near the Magog River, southeast of Saint Hyacinthe. Shortly after Ed returned from his second trip to Saint-Jean-Sur-Richelieu, Gerrard retired from his government job and put a proposition to his sons: he challenged them to help him pioneer a new settlement. They would call it Rock Forest, after their ancestral Irish estate, and it would be to them what Saint Hyacinthe had become to the Dessaulles family.

Gerrard could not immediately uproot himself from Saint Hyacinthe, and while his father got organized Ed quit college to begin training as a millwright. He worked with the most modern equipment at the lumbering centres in Vermont and then he took a job at Britannia Mills, which was the largest sawmill in the Eastern Townships and the only steam-driven one near Saint Hyacinthe. The workmen there were mostly Irishmen, many of whom had worked on line crews for the Grand Trunk Pacific Railroad. Despite Ed's superior education, they accepted him. By the time he moved to Rock Forest, he was a broadly experienced millwright and lumberman.

When the Nagles started their colony on the Magog River in 1872, the land was raw and undeveloped. They cleared fields, and roads, and dammed the Magog River for saw and flour mills. In spite of the reservations he felt about his father's project, Ed worked hard to become an excellent crew chief. Early on during Rock Forest's construction he acquired the authority to hire his own men, which forced him to begin judging character. He soon learned how fallible he could be.

In one instance, he hired a genial Irish tree feller. An enormous maple tree stood in the road right-of-way, so Ed handed his man an axe. The man worked like a beaver, sharpening the tree like a pencil. When his axeman finally stepped back, Ed casually asked him which way it would fall. "And what do you take me for," was the retort, "a prophet?"

Ed had seen Vermont and some of eastern Canada, and he knew there was a world beyond Rock Forest. The satisfactions he earned during the novel experiment at Rock Forest were insufficient to still a wanderlust that was stirring in him. After 1872, when adventure whirled through eastern Canada in the person of Father Albert Lacombe, Ed's restlessness began to overwhelm him.

The slim, aristocratic-looking Catholic priest swept by on a triumphant eastern lecture tour to support the missions on the western plains. Canada's newspapers soon made him the Dominion's best known adventurer. He had been schooled at Saint Hyacinthe, and had first gone west in 1849 as a missionary to the Indians and Métis beyond the Red River Settlement. He had ministered to Riel's Métis, having joined them on their buffalo hunts and during some battles with the Sioux Indians. He had wandered the grasslands and forests westward to the Rocky Mountains and had learned Indian languages. He had struggled against plagues of whiskey traders and smallpox. He had converted the Cree and Blackfoot, then mediated a tenuous peace between them. His was a resonant voice calling for Catholic settlers that made a deep and lasting impression on Ed's imagination.

Towards the end of 1873, a worldwide economic depression began crippling Rock Forest. By the time the Dominion created the North West Mounted Police, Ed was already thinking increasingly often about the Northwest Territories. The policemen rode off to prevent the lawlessness and Indian wars that were tearing open the western United States from spilling into Canada and, as they went, they improved an overland route from Lake Superior to the Red River Settlement. Ed soon found himself reading advertisements similar to this:

Toronto to Prince Arthur's Landing via Sarnia or Collingwood: adults $5.00; children half-fare; 150 pounds baggage 35 cents; 100 pounds additional baggage $1.00. Prince Arthur's Landing to Fort Gary [sic]: Emigrants $10.00; children half-fare; 200 pounds personal baggage free; extra baggage $2.50 a hundred. Emigrants should take their own provisions.

In 1874 the depression worsened, and Father Lacombe reappeared to call again for adventurous settlers. This time Ed responded. He convinced his elder brother Garrett to emigrate with him to Manitoba. There was little their father could offer to persuade them to remain at Rock Forest, and by late in the summer of 1874 they had their tickets in hand.

Ed and Garrett planned to leave the town of Sherbrooke on September 10, and travel west as far as Sarnia and Point Edwards on the Grand Trunk Pacific Railroad. Thence they would continue to the western end of Lake Superior by steamboat. From Thunder Bay they would follow the route the police had taken to the Red River Settlement.

Although the Nagles had only been two years in the Rock Forest-Sherbrooke area, the gregarious brothers had made many friends. When the community learned that the two of them were emigrating, a local socialite organized their farewell party. Late in the evening of September 10, Ed began the first of many journals he would keep during his adult life with a colourful account of their departure:

[We are on the train] after a very enjoyable evening spent at Mrs. Tom Henry's place with many of our young friends, who had gathered through that evening to give us a good time until train time. They had two barrels of oysters in the shell, and wine galore. Not a single [one of us] being an expert at opening those oysters you should have seen our hands; judging from mine, that were all cut up and did not heal for ten days. The wine, of course, had something to do with it. Anyway, it got the blame.

At 11:30 p.m. we all departed for the station to meet the train that was to take us west to Great Manitoba. After [a] shaking of hands and parting from our Fraulines, we were on board the G[rand] T[runk] P[acific], and with our friends behind us we felt lonely.

The train's first scheduled stop was Saint Hyacinthe, where Ed and Garrett visited the Albion Hotel. When they reached Toronto the following evening, an accident had closed the line ahead. They occupied themselves by exploring the city, which, Ed noted, contained many places of interest, including the Provincial Parliament Buildings. Nonetheless, the delay chafed them, and they were relieved when the train for Point Edwards left from Toronto at 9 p.m., September 12.

Unfortunately, the railroad's western terminus was a disappointing place, made especially so by the unpleasant news that they would have to lay over a full day to await their ship. Point Edwards, which lay at the southernmost tip of Lake Huron, was nothing to speak of, and Sarnia was "a very rum old place." Ed and Garrett diverted themselves with a ferryboat ride to the United States to view the historic fur trading post of Port Huron, then kicked along the Canadian lakeshore until the SS *International* of the Beaty Line allowed them aboard.

Unhappily for Ed, almost immediately after embarking he and a Mr. Star from Banford became violently seasick. However, by the time the *International* passed through the American Locks at the north end of Lake Huron and onto Lake Superior Ed had recovered. On the morning of September 16 he watched intermittently from the ship's rail, while the sky over the lake turned dark and ominous.

Morning [was] very stormy and very large swells [rose on the lake]; very cloudy. At 3:30 snow began falling, and [the] wind blew a perfect hurricane. When night came, all the passengers excepting the crew and myself were heaving all over the place .... It got so bad that the hatches had to be nailed down on the 800 passengers in the hole [sic].

The captain was obliged to run for Marquette — out of our course — the second mate handling the wheel. All our dishes were then broken, as well [as] many of the state-room windows.

I was standing at my state-room door when another gentleman [stood] across the dining table from me. When the boat pitched and rolled in the trough [he] went clean over the table and headfirst into an elderly lady's cabin, who was also very sick.

At 11:30 that night we made Marquette harbour. It was so dark and foggy, with snow falling thick, that we were obliged to feel our way in, as the breakwater was not to be seen — the lighthouse being our only guide. We finally made the entrance safely, and steamed to the pier.

You talk about overjoyed people, they were on that boat. Everybody slept well that night, after getting their supper on shore at the steamboat's expense.

Marquette, a renowned harbour on the south shore of Lake Superior, had been named after the famed explorer-interpreter Father Marquette, one of the first white men to explore and map the Mississippi River. The townsite had developed and expanded on the strength

Marquette Harbour, June 1873.

of enormous nearby copper deposits. Several foundries operated within its limits, and the local mines were so productive that there was a railroad line between them and Marquette. The long breakwater and loading pier were designed for large ore ships that hauled away the high-grade concentrates. But the harbour was also a sanctuary from the rocky headlands that lay in either direction along the lakeshore. The Marquette townsfolk regularly provided refuge to boats driven off the lake and their obvious concern helped allay the distress the *International's* passengers felt at the danger they had been in.

Just before he and a still-unsteady Garrett toured the town the following morning, Ed asked how perilous their situation had been during the storm.

> The captain told me that he never expected to get into port, as it (the weather) was so bad, and [we were] running out of their course, and [he had to have] men sounding all the time.

After a day, during which the town's chandlers refitted the ship and Ed and Garrett examined Marquette's smelters and foundries, the *International* steamed back out onto the lake. Lamentably, the captain had badly misjudged the dying storm's violence. As soon as she cleared the Marquette breakwater, the ship was forced to run northwest to another safe haven at Diamond Head. The voyage to Thunder Bay did not really resume again until twilight on the evening of September 18, when the lake became suddenly calm. The rest of the trip was uneventful. By mid-morning on Ed's twenty-first birthday, the *International's* passengers could clearly see a brooding escarpment rising southwest of Thunder Bay. At 4:00 p.m. the *International* slipped behind Isle Royal, rounded Thunder Cape, and nosed into a sheltered moorage protected by the Welcome Islands. Near the Thunder Bay townsite, the sparkling Whitefish River poured into the lake.

The clear waters and the picturesque little community framed against the dark escarpment should have signalled to Ed the start of the safer overland leg of his western journey, but his first impressions of the place distressed him.

What a sight met our eyes, every second house having been burned down for the insurance; the boom having busted. Now we were to leave the boat and take the Dawson Route to Winnipeg. As next morning we were to leave, we sported around town that evening up to a late hour.

The voyageurs and early fur traders who had paddled between the trading posts and the fur trade centres of eastern Canada had never really crossed over into what is now the United States of America. The last of their regular overland routes, the Grand Portage, had lain slightly north of the escarpment Ed could see from Thunder Bay. When Britain and the United States delineated their edges following the War of 1812, the Grand Portage was too close to the frontier. To hint that U.S. settlement of the American prairies must not drift north of the 49th parallel, the Canadas had sent S.J. Dawson to survey a route west from Lake Superior in 1857. The early voyageurs had explored alternatives to the Grand Portage, and Dawson chose one of them as Canada's first government-surveyed western highway.

The Dawson Route followed an overland trail from the Thunder Bay's twin settlements of Port Arthur-Fort William northwest as far as Shebandowan Lake. Thence it crossed a few small lakes and short portages to the height-of-land separating the Great Lakes-Saint Lawrence River watershed from the watersheds that drained west and north into Hudson Bay. At the height-of-land, Dawson's Route left Lac Des Milles Lacs via Baril Bay, following a chain of lakes and short rivers west-southwest to the Rainy River and Lake of the Woods.

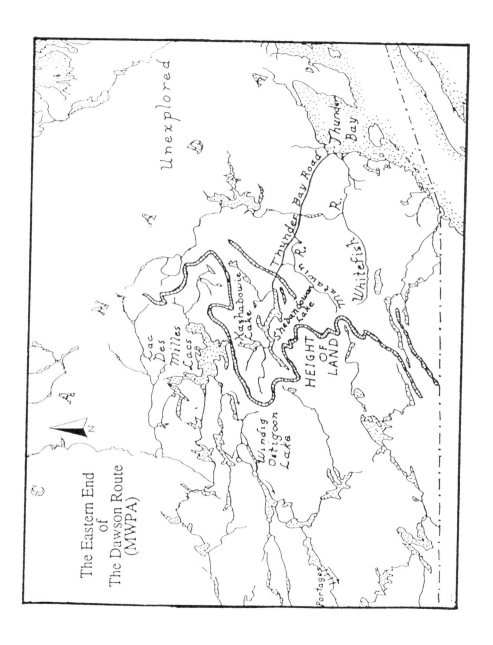

The Eastern End
of
The Dawson Route
(MWPA)

On the western shore of Lake of the Woods, it departed from the voyageurs' route. Dawson chose not to follow the Winnipeg River to its deboucher in Brokenhead Indian territory and swing south, up the Red River to the Red River Settlement. Instead he staked a Canadian claim for that strangely shaped U.S. intrusion called the Northwest Angle, which Peter Pond had aggressively clipped from Hudson's Bay Company territories during the earliest boundary survey. Dawson's Route crossed the Northwest Angle as an overland trail from Lake of the Woods to Saint Boniface and Fort Garry.

After Dawson finished his survey, his route lay dormant until 1868, when Canada's negotiations for control of the Red River Settlement and the Northwest Territories had returned it to prominence. In 1868 Dawson went to resurvey and improve its eastern sections, while C.P. Snow was sent to work on its western terminus at the Red River end. The resurvey was meant to signal clearly to the Red River settlers that defection to the U.S. was not an option available to them.

If Dawson had gone to the western sections, then the resurvey's intended purpose might have been well served. During his initial work with the Red River settlers he had exhibited remarkable tact and diplomacy. Unfortunately, to almost the same degree that Dawson displayed discretion, C.P. Snow blundered. Acting before Canada could say it possessed the Northwest Territories, Snow had blithely ignored the established settlers' concerns. He allied himself with John Christian Schultz — who, although he was actively pro-Canadian and against annexation by the United States, was a man of dubious personal ethics with many enemies in the Red River communities — and began imposing a rectangular-lot survey over the Métis farmers' traditional long, river-fronting lots. The 1869 Red River Uprising can be seen as a direct response to Snow's actions.

When Ed and Garrett reached Thunder Bay, the Dawson Route had been officially open for just one year. Nonetheless, it was widely trumpeted as the best cross-country route to take. It had first been improved by the men who turned westward after the 1870 Fenian Raid, and then by the North West Mounted Police in 1873. Moreover, the government had hired private contractors to put steam tugs on the navigable water, tramways at the portages, and caches of provisions at suitable depots along the way.

Had Ed and his brother known what lay ahead of them, however, they might not even have started overland. The contractors had not performed their tasks well. As recently as July of 1874, guides from Winnipeg had reported that there were no food caches at the way

34

stations. One group of experienced woodsmen had suffered through three full days without food. And one disgruntled band of emigrants was said to have left a slab of bacon, a sack of beans, and a note hanging from a pole at one of the portages. The note had advised subsequent emigrants to abandon all hope of getting through.

Ed and Garrett Nagle were up at 6:30 on the morning of September 20, 1874. The stage they expected to carry them to Lake Shebandowan did not arrive, but they eventually got away in an old lumberjack's wagon. The first overland section of the Dawson Route struck off through thick forest. Occasionally, cleared fields appeared on either side of the road. At boggier places the wagon rattled over stretches of log-corduroy set in the muck, and a short way past Ten-Mile Camp the road crossed Kaministiquia Bridge. Then, for the eight kilometres between the Kaministiquia River and Brown's Lane, the sounds of the Matawan River rapids drifted from the north side of the road. At Sunshine Creek the travellers crossed Matawan Bridge, and the river noises faded behind them. The only sounds they heard during the 66 kilometre ride to McNeil Bay, at the eastern end of Shebandowan Lake, were their own voices and the squeaking wagon wheels.

From McNeil Bay onwards Ed recorded his Dawson Route adventure in his journal:

> Just at dark we arrived at the lake. We had to cook our first meal, Garrett and I having provided ourselves with cooking utensils and grub, as well as blankets: nights were getting cold. We made our bed tender-foot fashion, and what a night was before us! At 10:00 p.m. it started to rain. About thirty were in our party, and from 12:00 p.m. no one slept or even thought of doing so. All [we] could hear was Grouse and Grouse.
> September 21st-
> I managed to sleep a little towards morning. At 5:00 a.m. the little tug whistle blew, and up we had to get and go on board ready to cross the lake .... At 7:00 a.m. we started. We were on board a big, flat scow exposed to the wind and weather. It took us some hours before we reached the other end, a distance of 19 1/2 miles, with stopping to cut wood and cooking our meals.
> We finally made our camp at the first portage, a bare rocky place with no wood except a long way off. We finally got the fire started and got our supper. Such a camp! It was a low swampy country at this place, and we were obliged to make our camp on the flat ledge ....

Garrett would insist on having all the blankets, and of course I protested. So finally, after he had fallen asleep, I got a reef on the blankets and rolled under him and slept quite comfortable. He woke up once during the night, and was giving me fits, but of course he could [not] rouse me.

The tug had carried them along Shebandowan Lake to Kashaboiwe Narrows, then turned sharply north. They were camped at the Lac Des Mille Lacs end of the portage, and had moved there by means of a government tramway.

September 22-

Up at 5:00 a.m. with all bustle! It was fun to listen to the green-horns, who were 20 per cent greener than us, talk about the night they put in. I thought it would finish up with blows, [but] the yell from the tug told us to get ready.

[At] 7:30 a.m. we were off once more. I was made fireman, and in that way I was on the tug warm and nice, while the others were exposed to the wind and rain. As usual, at 12:00 a.m. we landed to give the passengers a chance to get some dinner. [At] 1:30 we pulled out again. Lake Louise this lake is called, after some nice girl who went through some time in the early 18th century.

At 4:30 [we] met a canoe and courier with orders to stop all traffic. [The] lakes ahead were freezing up, and [we] could not get through. Well! We went ashore at the first nice place, which was a bay with good shelter and plenty of dry wood. What a camp we made. [We] had a good supper, having caught 2 nice trout.

September 23 - Lake Louise, Dawson Route

5:00 a.m. up, breakfast, and at 6:00 a.m. off on our back track. As luck would have it, the tug on the other lake was waiting for us. On arriving at the portage we hurried across, and at 11:00 a.m. we started across this lake, arriving at the portage (to Thunder Bay) at 6:00 p.m.; just dark.

Of course [it was] everyone for himself, and the dead take the last one. Garrett and I hurried to a good place as [we felt] we might be obliged to wait two nights: which we did, as the stages did not come until [the] next night. If Old Dawson had been there he certainly would have been invited to more than a meal, as we were all getting short of money.

September 24-

Still on the portage. [I] earned two dollars helping to fix [a] scow which was damaged. [It is the] first money I ever earned [that] was paid by a stranger.

[At] 4:30 p.m. four stages arrived from Thunder Bay to take us back. The drivers having brought a few papers, which they distributed, helped [us] to while away the evening.

September 25-

[It was] snowing some when we got up. Such language as we heard would certainly interest old Satan. Now, at 8:00 a.m. the stages started. [At] 11:30 [we] pulled up at a road house, that we might get a dinner. [It was] sow belly and beans, half-raw, and stale bread with green tea and no sugar or molasses, [for which the] charge [was] 75 cents. At 7:00 p.m. [we arrived] back in Thunder Bay [and] went to the Commercial Hotel.

September 26-

All that day we were out trying to find out what the government intended to do with us. Our tickets called for Winnipeg via the Dawson Route. Now we were up against it.

After three days of waiting, Garrett and I, with several others, [have] made up our minds to go via Duluth, Brainerd, and down the Red River to Winnipeg. We [are] obliged to wait for an American boat to proceed.

Ed and Garrett had crossed the height-of-land and gotten within sight of the high black conical hill at Baril Bay that marks the way onward to Winnipeg. But they were not to be numbered among the 300 emigrants who journeyed the entire length of the Dawson Route in 1874.

However, Dawson's rough track over the pre-Cambrian stone ledges and shimmering muskeg bogs was not the only way west. Since the mid-1800s, trains of Red River Carts had shuttled supplies to Manitoba across the prairie land south of the Canadian border. In fact, the cart trail had become so reliable that by 1870 the Canadian government was using it rather than the Dawson Route for the westbound mails. From Duluth, at the westernmost extremity of Lake Superior, Canadian mail moved overland through U.S. territory to Moorehead on the Red River, then moved northward along the river.

After 1872, when the Northern Pacific Railroad began making regularly scheduled runs between Duluth and Moorehead, an increasing number of emigrants followed the mail. Rather than wintering at Thunder Bay or returning east, the Nagle brothers and other survivors of the abortive Dawson Route excursion had decided to take passage on the Northern Pacific Railroad.

When the *SS International* left Thunder Bay on the morning of September 28, Ed and Garrett were back aboard her. Moving southwest along the lakeshore, she passed the foot of Grand Portage. Beyond Baptism River and the craggy face of Pallisade Head she was sailing outside Canadian territory; by evening she had tied up at Duluth, Minnesota.

Duluth was one of the largest towns on the shores of the western lake. A few grain elevators towered imposingly above the lakeside, and the Northern Pacific was not the only railroad in town: the tracks of the Lake Superior and Mississippi Railroad, which hauled between Duluth and Saint Paul, ran right out on the pier to within a few feet of the mooring cleats. But the four or five long rows of false-front stores, and the family homes clinging to the hillsides rising west of the water did not reassure Ed that Duluth was any more prosperous than the settlements at Thunder Bay.

What a desolate place! Half the houses were burned down, I suppose for the insurance. We put up at the Clark House, a very comfortable Hotel [costing] $2.00 per day. ... after marching around town in pairs we finally returned and [went] to sleep: to sleep the sleep of the just.
September 29-
    Still at Duluth. [We were] invited to the Governor's State Ball, [but] did not go as our decent clothes were on their way to Winnipeg, to arrive before us. We had a (meal?), and a few games of pool, and went to bed.
September 30-
    After breakfast we received word that our money was to be returned, proportionally, charging our tickets only to Duluth. Now we were in a nice fix. We could not wait and fight it, so we had to buy new tickets, which we did. A train was made up of five coaches, a baggage car, and two freight cars, and we started for Broken Head. Leaving this place (Duluth) at 5:30 p.m., with a beautiful snow storm on deck, we travelled all night.

Although it is more open and far less boggy than the muskegs west of Thunder Bay, the land west of Duluth is part of the same vast tract of marshy ground fringing the rock plates of the pre-Cambrian shield. Together, the marsh and the shield make up almost one-third of northern North America. The marshy land west of Duluth is part of what is called the Mississippi Flyway: the north-south migratory route taken each year by enormous flocks of wild birds.

One hundred and twenty-five kilometres west northwest of Duluth, the Mississippi itself rises from the great heart of the marsh. Trickling out the east side of Lake Itasca, the river of steamboats and gamblers flows almost due south for about 40 kilometres, before sweeping southwest in an arc that takes it close to the great plains. Perched on the western edge of that arc was Brainerd, the first Northern Pacific Railroad stop.

While Saint Paul, Minnesota was then considered the farthest north that steamboats should navigate, the caramel-coloured river regularly carried more daring captains as far north as Brainerd. Having left the Dawson Route behind him, Ed regained his good humour.

October 1st-
Still on the train, and at 8:30 a.m. we struck the prairie country with its millions of ducks flying up at every little pond or slough we passed; and we also saw hundreds of prairie chickens. We ran very slow at times.

At 11:00 a.m., when the train was stopped, we got off. We could see the noon stopping place, so we concluded to walk ahead of the train; arriving 30 minutes before her, and having our dinner. When the train arrived we were delayed an hour, waiting until the trainmen could get their dinner.

At 2:30 p.m. we started again, arriving at Brainerd at sun set. This is a wild and woolly town: between lumber-jacks, railroad men, and gamblers. There had been a man shot in a saloon a few hours before we arrived, and that night we had the pleasure of seeing about 50 lumber-jacks take a shack which was filled with gamblers and, with their peavies, pitch the shack into the Mississippi River.

The gamblers jumped out through the windows and commenced shooting and raising hell, but the jacks chased them.

A saloon murder was not an everyday occurrence in Ed's experience, but the lumberjacks and their hard-nosed approach to problems were men he understood. Watching them chase the shysters off, he let his own disappointments and frustrations recede and turned his thoughts

Front Street in Moorehead, Minnesota, 1874.

westward. He would face frontier life without fear; caution and forethought had their places, but not fear. Furthermore, in overcoming the Dawson Route he knew there were alternative ways to attain his blocked objectives.

At Brainerd, Ed and Garrett were still deep in the great marshland. The tall-grass prairie, home of the buffalo, did not begin until the railroad reached the Buffalo River. But then, as now, buffalo and Indians were symbols of the western wilderness. It is easy to imagine the brothers gazing ardently from their carriage window; they could not know that only a few of the shaggy beasts still wandered east of the Red River. After the train stopped briefly to take on wood and water at Wadena and Detroit Lakes, Ed was gazing at prairie similar to the kind that would become his home for the next eight years. When the first rays of sunlight glanced off the hoops the snow had made of the big bluestems and switchgrasses, and lingered on the stray seed clusters scattered over the white blanket, those prairies glowed golden.

October 2 - Brainerd, N.P.R.

At 1:00 a.m. [our] train started again. [This country is] all prairie, except an occasional little lake or swamp. [We ended our journey by] arriving at Broken Head at 9:00 p.m., and what a town [it is]. We had a time getting a bed on the floor of the only boarding house. We were obliged to pay each a dollar, in advance, [and] could not sleep. Fellows kept passing over us, and yelling all night.

40

Moorehead, Minnesota (Ed's Broken Head) was the busiest supply depot on the southern stretches of the Red River, and one of the busiest entrepôts west of the Mississippi. Supplies streamed into town, either to move northwest towards Winnipeg by steamboat, flatboat scow, or wagon; or to cross the river to the Dakota side and move into Indian territory. Traffic rolled incessantly along the muddy main street, mingling outside the standard false-front western structures. Ed and Garrett had arrived at a place every bit as wild as Brainerd, but now they did not have tickets out of town.

October 3-
Up at daylight. [We] rolled up our blankets and took them out of that place. We left them at a Swede's tent, who was camped there waiting for a friend to take him to a homestead somewhere near Abercrombie, Minnesota.
At 8:30 we found a place where we could get some breakfast by paying 75 cents, which we did. After [eating] we went in search of information.

On a small island across a narrow channel from the end of the railroad line, and near the Moorehead steamboat landing, a few mills sawed lumber to float down to Manitoba. Ed headed directly for them. From the railway terminal he and Garrett had seen stacks of green lumber piled along the riverbank. Beside each stack a group of men was building a flat-bottomed scow, and at one of the lumber piles the brothers found the solution to their problem of getting north to Winnipeg.

We struck a crowd of four [men] who were there building a scow to float to Winnipeg with flour sacks. They were anxious to get a couple of good fellows to help them, so we struck a bargain. They agreed to take 1200 lbs. of grub down for us if we would help build the scow. I, being handy with tools, struck in, while Garrett bought our grub and cooked for the gang. Everything fixed, we brought our blankets there and camped, to [better] commence work next morning.

Besides finding transportation, Ed and Garrett were managing to prepare themselves for the coming winter in a way that not many other

Flat boat building on the Red River at Moorehead, Minn., 1874.

emigrants to Manitoba could. During the previous years plagues of grasshoppers had devastated harvests north of the border, driving food prices outlandishly high. The brothers' new companions were speculators on their way north with a shipment of supplies. Taking food with them would mean that Ed and Garrett had only to find themselves a place to live and they would be set to winter at Winnipeg. From the moment they struck their bargain, the Nagle brothers had embarked on the final leg of their western journey.

October 4-
    We were at work on our scow bright and early. About 2000 people are waiting for a steamboat to take them to Winnipeg. A great many toughs are gathered here, in the shape of confidence men, gamblers, and last but not least pick-pockets.

    Our first day's work is over, and my arms are tired from driving big, 4-inch nails. After some sight-seeing we turned into our blankets for the night.

October 5-
    Up and Breakfast over by 6:30 a.m. At work at 7:00 a.m. The day was cold and raw, with quite a frost through the night. Our scow was nearly complete at 6:00 p.m. At 9:30 p.m. we went to bed, as usual. (Big pow wow at a saloon, with chippies dancing.)

October 6-

Quite a bit of ice on the slough this morning. By 10:30 we had our scow calked and pitched, and ready for the water. We finished the oars and sweeps by noon. After dinner, with a crowd helping, we launched her and named her the Last Chance. After filling her with water to soak we went out to purchase our grub for the trip and for the winter. The wind was blowing strong ahead, so we did not load up.

October 7-

At 8:00 a.m. we bailed our scow out and started to load the four of our fleet. At 5:00 p.m. we finished, and moved on board to better enable us to look after them. Pumping them occasionally, we took three hour shifts all night.

October 8-

Early in the morning we pulled out, bidding farewell to Broken Head. We drifted along nicely, keeping clear of sand bars. Passing several farm houses, and even some small towns, that night we took shifts and drifted most of the night.

Talk about coyotes! They seemed to be following us all night. At day break we put ashore for some wood. While the others were getting wood I killed my first chicken and a partridge. Shortly, we pulled out again.

With no high ground to confine it, the Red River snakes back and forth in long meanders. *The Last Chance* and the other three scows in the little flotilla had none of the difficulty that steamboats had with the sharply twisting river. They bobbed nicely along, leaking only when they scraped over sandbars.

Ed and Garrett kept comfortable by staying out of the wind. Although they enjoyed sweeping views of the prairie sky, the willows and squat cottonwoods lining the riverbanks kept the prairie itself from view. At the place the Red Lake River spills into the Red from the east, the *Last Chance* sped down four kilometres of riffles. With Pembina and the Canadian border behind them, Ed and Garrett were soon helping their partners pull toward Winnipeg's Immigrant Sheds, which lay on the north bank of the Assiniboine River near where it flowed into the Red from the west.

CHAPTER 4

Hunting Winnipeg Buffalo
(1874 - 1876)

Ed and Garrett had arrived at a city teetering on the brink of its future. Winnipeg was brand new, boisterous and boozy and overflowing with young men escaping the depression in the East. But jobs were scarce. Work on the Canadian Pacific Railroad had jerked to a halt in 1873, when a corruption scandal toppled John A. MacDonald's Conservatives, and now a luminary from the new government was dismissing it as "two streaks of rust across the wilderness." For two summers, locusts had devastated the prairie crops; so badly in 1874 that a blanket of them ten centimetres deep had covered every flat surface in town. In late 1873 frustrated Winnipeggers had expressed their general displeasure by tarring and feathering the Speaker of the Manitoba Legislature. When Ed reached the city it lacked the restraining presence of the North West Mounted Police, who were trekking westward, and the Métis still awaited a display of Canadian good faith. For the third time since 1870 they had elected Louis Riel as their spokesman; Parliament was debating whether or not to allow him to assume his seat in Ottawa.

Fortunately for them, the Nagle brothers had reached Winnipeg at a peaceful ebb in Manitoba's seasonal round. About October 1, many of the Métis had joined their annual fall buffalo hunt into the Dakota Territories. And most of the other settlers were busily preparing for the onset of the snows that would isolate them until spring. In spite of any anxieties or undercurrents that might have tugged at the people he met on his early walks, Ed's first impressions of the city were pleasant ones. Many years later he would recall:

"... it was all prairie, with just a cart trail where Main Street now stands. There was a single Oak plank [at Brown's Bridge] held in place by wooden pegs, and there were four stores — H.B.C., Stobart and Eaton, A.G.B. Balentine [sic], and Old Garry — that comprised the mercantile solution of then Winnipeg, which was better known as Old Fort Garry. I used to hunt ducks where T. Eaton's store stands."

Ed and Garrett had struggled up the muddy north bank of the Assiniboine River to the Immigrant Sheds, where incoming settlers could find temporary refuge. About 350 metres across a large field west of the sheds, the Hudson's Bay Company's Fort Garry hunkered down behind whitewashed stone walls. A government bonded warehouse rested on the riverbank between the sheds and the fort, overlooking a small ferry servicing the Métis settlement on the south bank of the Assiniboine.

In fact, downtown Winnipeg was not as desolate as Ed later made it seem. To start their search for a house in which to winter, the brothers crossed the field to Fort Garry, where Main Street began. Road right-of-way was clearly not of paramount importance at the intersection of Main Street and Portage Avenue, the heart of a few hundred loosely crowded buildings. One large structure shouldered out from the north-west corner of the intersection into Main Street. George "Dutch" Emmering's oak-log saloon lay beside it. The Red Saloon sat almost in the middle of Portage Avenue, and behind it another small building elbowed out onto the western road. On the southeast corner of the intersection, Devlin's Restaurant catered to the solid appetites of passers-by. The large and respectable McDermot Block — which stood imposingly on the northeast corner — joined with the two churches west of the intersection to gaze balefully at the confusion the saloons caused.

Beyond the crazy attempt to control traffic, Main Street continued northward. In all about 900 buildings housed the population of approximately 3,000 Winnipeggers. Ed and Garrett passed the newly renovated Post Office at Post Office Street, then homes on widely scattered flanking lots. Brown's Bridge crossed a small coulee that marked the southern boundary of Market Place, which was simply a small field. Eventually, they found an empty dwelling and, with six companions, rented it for the winter.

It is not clear exactly what work Ed did after arriving at Winnipeg in the fall of 1874. In fact he may have done nothing but explore the strange little community in which he found himself. He probably returned repeatedly to the banks of the Red River, because east of Main Street, between Matilda and Post Office Streets, Winnipeg's three mills lay on the riverbank. Two more lay across the river in Saint Boniface East, including one that Louis Riel's father had operated on the banks of the Seine River.

The small city was intensely active. Until freeze-up, flatboats and steamers floated steadily north and speculators got whatever prices they asked for the supplies they brought in. News was plentiful, and readily available; two newspapers pursued different editorial policies: *The Nor'wester* spoke for the Canadian party. *The Free Press* was Liberal.

For livelier reports or active debates, however, Winnipeg's young men resorted to their saloons, of which Emmering's was one of the most popular. It had spawned at least one riot, when men favouring annexation by the U.S. had attempted to advance their cause. Another was the Prairie Saloon, which was the threshold to the demimonde. Since at least the time of Winnipeg's incorporation, a string of fine brothels had clung to the banks of Colony Creek, west of the Prairie Saloon.

Saloon conversations ranged widely. The U.S.-Canada border survey was an important topic, as were the recent signing of Treaty Number 4 with the western Indians, the state of the Canadian Pacific Railroad, and the steady arrival of large groups of European immigrants like the Mennonites. But discussions repeatedly returned to and encircled two developing sagas of particular importance. The first was unfolding in the Dakota Territories, and initially seemed to epitomize the differences between Canadian and American attitudes to their western frontiers. As the second ran its course, however, the national distinctions began to blur.

In 1868, the United States government had signed a treaty giving their Plains Indians perpetual rights to sacred Indian lands in and surrounding the Black Hills. By 1872 rumour claimed that there was gold there, and white men were trickling singly or in small groups into the treaty lands. The Indians killed or drove off many of the first prospectors, but enough of them returned to verify the rumours.

In the spring of 1874, without consulting any of the chiefs who had signed the treaty, General George Armstrong Custer had led the U.S. Seventh Cavalry into the Black Hills. In August he returned to announce that the gold there lay just beneath the grass roots. In spite of President Ulysses Grant's proclamation that the treaty must not be broken, newspapers like the *Chicago Inter Ocean* heralded Custer's announcement in bold-face type. When Ed and Garrett had reached Moorehead, droves of prospectors were already moving west. By November, the gold rush news dominated reports from Minnesota, and the Indians on the American plains were preparing themselves for war.

On the surface there was little similarity between the events in the Dakota Territories and the issues facing people in Manitoba. But, in fact, there were distinct resemblances between the way the United States treated its Plains Indians and the way Canadians handled the Métis vis-a-vis Louis Riel. In both the United States and Canada the real question was becoming whether or not eastern power could impose unacceptable conditions on the lives of free western peoples.

Nevertheless, many Winnipeggers claimed that Riel was nothing but a rebel. Some suggested that, in addition to leading the Métis during the incidents of 1869-70, he had supported a Fenian Raid on Manitoba in 1871. Regardless of the fact that he was the legally elected Métis representative, these people and others like them in eastern Canada considered him a malcontent with no claim to Canadian sympathy. By the second week of November it was clear that he would not be allowed to take his parliamentary seat.

The Métis usually returned from their fall buffalo hunt in mid-November, so it is likely that Ed and Garrett experienced some anxious curiosity as they awaited their first glimpses of the plainsfolk. The brothers must have wondered how the Métis would respond to the news that their leader was being exiled to the United States of America.

In spite of what eastern newspapers wrote about them, however, Ed soon recognized that the Métis were neither wicked nor savage. Truly, they seemed impulsive and demonstrative, but Louis Riel was not their only leader. Pascal Breland had tried to have the distinctive Métis culture recognized in the text of Treaty Number 4, and was working closely with the Council of the North West Territories on their behalf. Even when news reached Manitoba that Riel's nerves had shattered, forcing him into a sanitarium in Platsburg, New York, the Métis people resolutely continued trying to secure a parliamentary voice for themselves.

The plainsfolk were proudly and unmistakably different from Manitoba's other citizens. Jet black hair and angular features proclaimed their Indian blood. Their cultural uniforms blazed with emblems of their French heritage: toques or bright bandanas crowned them; scarlet l'assomption sashes wrapped the waists of their blue woollen winter capots; and beaded or silken flowers danced across the tanned leather of their moccasins and the bags filled with the blended tobacco and red-willow bark that the men smoked.

Even the vehicles they drove were distinctly their own. In later years a friend of Ed's would call Red River Carts "scrub oak, shaganappi, and squeals." They were little more than rough wooden boxes perched between a single pair of oversize wheels. Sewn together with strips of raw buffalo hide, they lurched on ungreased axles behind slow-moving oxen or horses.

The Métis Nation had mastered the northeastern plains. Even with the Hudson's Bay Company withdrawing from central Canada, the products from their buffalo hunts continued to feed, cover, and bind together the fragile networks of the Northwest Territories. The twice-yearly arrivals of buffalo hunt caravans were major events at the prairie communities. Ed's capacity with French established a kinship between the Métis and him. As the first waves of Red River Carts towering with loads of meat, pemmican, and buffalo robes lurched into Winnipeg, he may have heard singing. "The Ballad of Frog Plain" commemorated an early Métis battle, and was their cultural anthem. In light of Riel's situation, it was particularly appropriate:

Like men of honor we did act,
Sent an ambassador, in fact,
Asking their governor to wait,
And talk, before it was too late.

Winnipeg's Métis population was not really very large. Most of the Métis lived across the Red River, in Saint Boniface East. Saint Boniface was predominantly French-speaking and very like the communities Ed knew in the Eastern Townships. It is likely that he crossed the river at least a few times during his first winter in Manitoba.

Le Métis was Saint Boniface's French-language newspaper, and the Roman Catholic clergy its dominant presence. It was the centre for the entire Catholic effort in the Northwest Territories. Archbishop Tache's Palace stood right beside the town hall, facing across the Red River towards the Immigrant Sheds. The Catholic hospital stood close at hand, as did an impressive stone cathedral rising to replace a wooden one which had recently been destroyed by fire. Saint Boniface's homes and secular buildings protectively encircled this knot of ecclesiastical propriety.

Although he seldom demonstrated excessive fervor, throughout his life Ed practiced the Catholicism he had learned as a child. At

Winnipeg he did not have to cross the Red River to attend church. Archbishop Taché had designated the new city Saint Mary's Parish, and put up a two-storey church on a plot of land that the Hudson's Bay Company had obligingly donated. The church had been consecrated in May of 1874, and Taché chose its priest specifically to draw Ed and other young immigrants to services.

After returning from his speaking tour of eastern Canada, Father Albert Lacombe had rested briefly at the archbishop's palace in Saint Boniface. But Archbishop Taché refused to keep his star player inactive for long, and assigned him to Saint Mary's Parish in July. During Ed's first winter in Winnipeg he had the opportunity to develop a relationship with the famous missionary.

The long cold winter of 1874-75 revitalized the frontier community's spirit. At Christmas and New Year there were celebrations on the big field near Fort Garry. When the temperature hovered near -39° Fahrenheit for 20 days in January, almost everyone retreated inside to reaffirm old friendships and develop new ones.

The city's population was not impossibly large. In addition to Father Lacombe, other men in the Winnipeg area would play important roles in Ed's future life. No surviving document mentions it, but the winter of 1874-75 may well have seen the first meeting between Ed Nagle and John A. McDougall.

McDougall was a slim, hawk-eyed young fellow who had lived in the city since July of 1873. During the winter of 1873-74 he had attended Kildonan College, a small Presbyterian school that had recently located in Winnipeg. During the past summer he and a partner named Steinhoff had operated a small grocery store and for the winter he was living as a boarder at Brouse House. Like Ed, McDougall enjoyed an occasional drink of whiskey. Even if they only had a passing acquaintance, the two could have met almost anywhere that young men gathered in Winnipeg.

By the time the previous summer's washed-out grasses had risen above the melting snow, Ed and Garrett were set on different courses. Ed was comfortable in Winnipeg. He liked the frontier's attitudes and freedoms and he did not intend to return east before giving Manitoba a real try. Garrett, on the other hand, was fed up. Lacking Ed's manual cleverness he could not get work. Before spring was too far advanced, Garrett had planned his return to Rock Forest. Ed was jobbing as a carpenter when his brother left Winnipeg, which was probably about the time that the first Métis hivernants began arriving from the prairies.

On North America's great plains the Métis Nation recognized two valid but different lifestyles. Hivernants, or winterers, roamed across the prairies hunting and trading throughout the year; other families gathered in small farming communities along the rivers. Twice a year the two kinds joined together to reaffirm their common Métis heritage. The hivernants were lumbering into Winnipeg to trade their furs and re-outfit themselves, before joining the spring buffalo hunt.

The magnitude of the Métis buffalo hunts, and their importance to both Métis culture and the fur trade's provisions systems, had developed them into unparalleled cultural events. The spring hunt was the largest of the two annual hunts. During the fall many farmers stayed on their farms preparing for winter, so spring was the time for the plainsfolk to re-establish the laws by which they guided their lives throughout each year. The men who were elected to enforce the laws and lead the hunts out among the hostile Plains Indian tribes disciplined their fellow Métis and protected their culture.

Ed watched the populations of Winnipeg and her sister communities swell to bursting. By early June the congregation was complete. Hundreds of carts and buffalo-running ponies stood ready among the tents on the edges of town. As the first summer days warmed the bright new blades of grass, the Métis left the Red River communities. Laughter and gaiety rolled with them out of Winnipeg, south towards the Pembina Mountains.

Most of the early summer that year was warm and slow at Winnipeg. With prices for food and supplies remaining high, some young Winnipeggers decided to set off toward their futures. John A. McDougall, for instance, managed to outfit himself as a trader, having had some experience in that line. He had managed to learn the Cree language, and before operating his grocery store he had worked briefly for a Winnipeg fur trader named Henderson. He intended to travel west in search of fur.

But Ed had neither the experience nor the languages required for fur trading. There is no record of him working as a millwright during his first years in Winnipeg nor did he travel to the Dakotas to join the Black Hills gold rush, which by 1875 was in full swing. A few surveyors were leading crews out to survey new townships west of the Red River, but they had brought most of their own men with them. In fact, only one project in Manitoba offered employment to large numbers of men.

The Canadian government still refused to complete the Canadian Pacific Railroad, but it had started work on a short branch line to connect Manitoba to the trunk lines passing through Moorehead. The Pembina Branch would run from Selkirk, where the CPR had established its prairie offices and intended to bridge the Red River, south through Saint Boniface to Emerson on the U.S. border. Strangely enough, there is no record of Ed having worked on the Pembina Branch either. Presuming then, that he was still working as a carpenter, he was probably in Winnipeg when the whole of the Northwest Territories was thrown into a panic in July.

The Métis chased buffalo on two major hunting grounds, so there were said to be two different Métis hunts. The Red River Hunt moved southwest from Winnipeg to the Pembina Mountains, where a column from the White Horse Plains joined it. Then it moved southwest to the prairies between Devil's Lake and the Black Hills in the Dakota Territories. But plainsfolk from west of the White Horse Plains joined what was called the Saskatchewan Hunt, which moved over what is now the southern part of the Province of Saskatchewan. The first indications of the damage that parliament's rejection of Louis Riel had inflicted on the Métis self-image arose among the Saskatchewan hunters.

The Saskatchewan Hunt had elected Gabriel Dumont as its leader. Dumont was one of the greatest plainsmen on the prairies, respected and admired by Métis and Indians alike. One of the most important laws he was elected to enforce was that no hunter or band of hunters chase buffalo before the general order was given. In the spring of 1875, however, a small group of hunters on the Saskatchewan Hunt flagrantly broke that law. Moreover, instead of submitting to the traditional penalties Dumont imposed, the renegades went to Fort Carlton to appeal to the Canadian government for support and justice.

The Hudson's Bay Company representative at Fort Carlton had little understanding of and no sympathy for Métis traditions. Completely misconstruing the incident, he announced to Alexander Morris — Lieutenant Governor of the Northwest Territories — that Dumont's Saskatchewan Hunt was "in open revolt against the authority of the Canadian government," and "had already established a provisional government."

The similarity of the report to the events of 1869-70 was too strong to be overlooked. On July 21, about the time that the Red River Hunt was returning, Winnipeggers read this wildly distorted *Free Press* account of the situation:

Another stand against Canadian government authority in the North-West; a Provisional Government at Carlton; M. Louis Riel again to the front; 10,000 Crees on the warpath; Fort Carlton in possession of the Rebels; a number of Mounted Police killed.

Winnipeggers may have been particularly alarmed by the early reports because they would have had to entrust their safety to Winnipeg's Chief of Police, J.S. Ingram. Ingram's reliability was in such doubt that, as soon as they caught him cavorting in a Colony Creek brothel, the City Council replaced him.

Fortunately, before the brouhaha got out of hand a detachment of North West Mounted Police arrived from Fort Carlton. The police reported that there was no rebellion taking place, and that the renegades' complaints were trivial. When they arrived home, the Red River Métis were completely bewildered by the situation. Riel was in a sanitarium, a fact which they believed everyone knew. Throughout the late summer and early fall *Le Métis* confirmed the police assessment by printing angry denials that any rebellion had been planned.

The spring pageantry of the departing Red River Hunt and the strange account of the attempted Métis rebellion fascinated Ed. By the end of the summer he had resolved to learn more about the plainsfolk, and made arrangements to join the fall hunt of 1875.

On September 9, *Le Métis* mobilized the hunters. An old Métis hivernant had arrived in Saint Boniface from his camp at Wood Mountain to report that a herd of buffalo was on the move. He cautioned the hunters to proceed carefully, however, as the Plains Indians were angry. In July, four Americans from Fort Benton had been massacred, a train of forty wagons had been pillaged and burned, and other freighters had only saved themselves by abandoning the goods they carried. By the time *Le Métis* reported on September 23 that a large herd of buffalo had moved out onto the Devil's Lake prairie, Ed and his companions were already near the Pembina Mountains.

Although only the sketchiest records of Ed's buffalo hunts have survived, it is relatively easy to reconstruct from contemporary accounts some of the wonder and excitement he experienced. During the first few days, as the hunt column moved south and west from Winnipeg, no discipline was enforced. Whenever bunches of long-legged Cabree, the prairie pronghorn antelope, burst away flashing their white rump patches, hunters slipped off after them; often returning with carcasses slung across their saddles. The country was new to Ed. Mesmerized by the rolling prairie grasses, he must have often strayed away from the main party. Beyond the range of the squealing carts, he experienced the Manitoba lowlands at their most glorious.

An Indian summer sun shone warmly, some days so hot that heat waves shimmered above the grass. A few frosting winds had tipped the aspens surrounding the ponds and sloughs with gold. Along the banks of each small stream, the gold gave way to the bronze and scarlet hazes that edged the oak, elm, and ash-leafed maple trees and red willow bushes. Some bunches of yellow flowers still nestled in clumps of buck brush, and from the stream side, brush fluted songs drifted from the last few meadowlarks. Here and there jack rabbits skittered off, and prairie chickens flushed and flew. Overhead, wedges of ducks and geese struck south, and occasional red-tailed hawks rose on the thermals.

In the evenings, when the animals were watered and inside the encircled carts, the hunters gathered at their campfires. A Catholic priest travelled with them, but the plainsfolk were as much Indian as they were French. Their glorious victories over the Indian tribes had made them the masters of the plains, and they perpetuated their heritage in yarns and folk tales. Neither the distant yipping coyotes nor the restless sounds of their animals much bothered the them, but whenever a muttering noise slipped through the night they drew closer to their fires. They claimed it came from a poisonous plant that muttered ceaselessly to itself, stopping only when approached.

By the time his group reached the Pembina Mountains, or Hair Hills as the first rising plateau of the Manitoba Escarpment is sometimes called, Ed must have recognized the importance of the hunt. Many of the Métis families were not well off, and they were not out for a pleasant ramble across the prairie. For some of them, the meat they got on the hunt might be the only sustenance they could rely on through the coming winter.

From Winnipeg, Ed's group had followed a clear trail. Near the United States border, and about 50 kilometres east of the Red River, two other trails joined it. One of them came from Fort Pembina, the other clung to the eastern slope of the Pembina Mountains. The small Métis community of Saint Joseph lay just south of the junction, on the U.S. side of the border. There, on the mixed prairie at the edge of the hunting grounds, the White Horse Plains column joined the Winnipeg group and the laws for the coming hunt were explained.

Though they had been disputed the previous summer, the laws governing Ed's hunt were undoubtedly the traditional Métis ones. A senior hunt captain and several deputies were appointed, to each of whom was assigned ten soldiers to guard and police the camp. Guides were chosen who rotated in their duties, each taking charge of the camp flag in his turn. When the flag was raised, the camp was on the move; when it was lowered, the column had stopped for the day. The guides controlled the column while it moved, but when the flag was down the captains and their soldiers took over. Everything about the camp was organized, even the location for each cart in the circle, and guards were posted each night to watch against attack.

Those were merely the conditions under which the hunters lived until they returned to the safety of Saint Joe. There were other laws that governed the actual hunt, and these, too, were explained: buffalo could not be run on the Sabbath; no small group from the column could leave, lag behind, or proceed the main group without permission; before the senior captain gave the general order, no person or party of hunters could run buffalo. Penalties for infractions were mostly designed to humiliate offenders, and to make them realize the fact that they were endangering the lives and livelihoods of their companions.

Ed had many other things to learn besides the organization and regulations of the hunt. As a boy he had learned to ride and shoot, but he was no match for the Métis. Henry repeating lever-action rifles were not yet available, so he had to learn how to load and fire a muzzle-loader on the run. The loading sequence was difficult enough — pouring a charge of powder from the powder horn, spitting a ball into the muzzle of the gun, then slipping a cap under the hammer — without having to do it while bouncing along on a horse. Nonetheless, by the time he reached the buffalo he had mastered the whole procedure.

He was not accompanying a particularly large hunt. In addition to the carts carrying each family's personal outfit, fifty or sixty others were along to haul meat back to Winnipeg. Because this was a fall hunt, the Métis did not intend to make much pemmican; instead they would take back dried and fresh meat. Experienced hunters reckoned that it took from eight to ten cow buffalo to provide pemmican enough to load a Red River Cart, and dried and fresh meat was bulkier than pemmican. It is likely that Ed's group required only about three hundred buffalo to fill its carts.

However, there were fewer buffalo near Devil's Lake than there had been in previous years. The Métis complained that since the U.S. Cavalry had begun harassing the Sioux, the Indians had herded the buffalo west of the Black Hills, to keep them away from the hunting grounds. Robe hunters were killing unbelievable numbers of buffalo in the south, though, and none of the plainsmen really knew why the herds were vanishing.

By the time the hunt column returned to Saint Joe, the first snow lay on the ground and a rude shock awaited them at the border. The buffalo hunt required excellent horses, so the hunters were in the habit of buying the finest mounts they could find: they often bought horses in the U.S., which they sold when they returned to Winnipeg. But as the Red River hunt crossed the border in 1875, Canadian customs officers halted them. After the 1874 border survey, customs laws had come into effect. Hunters who had gotten horses in the U.S. now had either to pay duty on them, or leave them south of the line. Ed's friends rode back into Winnipeg with the breath of their animals rising in clouds around them.

On returning to Winnipeg, Ed congratulated himself on again having provided for the winter. Nothing was much changed in Winnipeg, except that the City Council had invested $15,000.00 in a new fire hall and fire engine and was boasting that fire was no longer a problem. In the midst of his Christmas celebrations, Ed gathered with his friends to view what the *Free Press* called the "$15,000.00 heap of ashes." And the spirit of that holiday continued right on into the New Year. January 3, 1876 was civic election day. Uncertain exactly how many votes had come to him, Mayor Cornish led a mob raid on the Returning Officer's home and stole the Polling Book. True to its activist traditions, Winnipeg got a mayor with panache.

In spite of the loss of the firehouse, and the extraordinary circumstances of their mayoralty election, Winnipeggers faced a promising new year. Grasshoppers had not ruined the Red River crops in 1875, and work would continue on the Pembina Branch. Moreover, the Northwest Territories Act was finally giving the Métis people a voice on an official Canadian-government council.

All was not well on the plains, however. By early spring, everyone who depended on the buffalo knew that a three-man delegation — one of whom was Father Lacombe — was lobbying in Ottawa for hunting regulations. With the arrival of the first flatboats from Moorehead, the Red River settlers learned that the U.S. government had declared war on the Plains Indians. As a result, Ed did not join the spring Red River Hunt, but got work helping construct a large new building for Timothy Eaton.

After having hunted buffalo, Ed wanted to study their habits more closely. So during the spring of 1876, he likely wandered west of Colony Creek to visit James McKay's Deer Lodge. McKay, better known in Winnipeg as "Tonka Jim," had gotten five live buffalo calves from some passing Indians.

The animals at Deer Lodge eventually became the nucleus for one of the finest captive buffalo herds ever raised on the plains. In time, Colonel S.A. Bedson bought them from McKay and moved them to Stony Mountain, Manitoba. Then Donald Smith bought some as a gift to the Canadian government, and the rest went to the Pablo herd by way of Charles Jesse "Buffalo" Jones. The Pablo herd would become the herd at Wainwright, Alberta, and via Buffalo Jones, the results of Tonka Jim's buffalo husbandry would eventually resurface in Ed's future.

By the fall of 1876 news of the Indian wars was fading, so Ed rejoined the fall Red River Hunt. Until the group reached Devil's Lake everything went much as it had the previous fall. But there were even fewer buffalo there than in the previous year, and as the hunters searched westward they were attacked.

Although Ed and his companions did not know it at the time, Sitting Bull's Sioux Indians had recently annihilated Custer's US Seventh Cavalry at the Little Bighorn River. The furious warriors who attacked the hunt column were trying to rid the plains of all interlopers. Within a few years, Ed would witness some of the tragic consequences of the extremes to which the Sioux had been driven. And late in his life, he would recount fragments of the story of his flight back to Manitoba: with the Métis hunters keeping to the coulee bottoms, their guards and scouts on constant alert.

CHAPTER 5

In the Fringe of the Boreal Forest
(1877 - 1881)

After the fall hunt of 1876, Ed found his elder brother John Thomas waiting for him at Winnipeg. Jack, as the Nagles called him, was an independent spirit like Ed, although more reckless. He would die young — pushed down a mine shaft in Searchlight, Nevada — but when he reached Winnipeg in 1876 he was bubbling with enthusiasm for the frontier.

Jack had fled Rock Forest bearing all the family news with him: Gerrard still ruled as patriarch; Garrett had gotten married; work still crawled ahead at Rock Forest. Because of his recent encounters with the Sioux, the boring and familiar eastern life Jack described held some attraction for Ed. He had no intention of relinquishing his freedom, but he had lost some of his fascination with the boundless frontier.

The Sioux attacks had made Ed acutely sensitive to the Indian presence on the plains. Since 1871, Canadian governments had negotiated with the natives spread across the western prairies. Indians had signed away their rights to southern Manitoba on treaties numbered 1 and 2. In 1873, treaty number 3 had brought the area through which the Dawson Route passed under Canadian control. Treaty number 4, which had been signed in 1874, gave Ottawa southern Saskatchewan. Central and western Manitoba came with treaty number 5 in 1875, and in 1876 treaty number 6 drew what is now the central part of Saskatchewan and Alberta under the government aegis. It was a great relief to feel that there was no immediate threat of an Indian war in Canada.

By the fall and early winter of 1876, two documents were shifting Winnipeg's saloon debates back to the routes connecting the prairies with the outside world. In 1872, Professor John Macoun and Reverend George Grant had accompanied Sandford Fleming's survey of a western line for the Canadian Pacific Railroad. Both men had published versions of their experiences: Macoun's government report and Grant's book, *Ocean to Ocean*, described Fleming's proposal in detail.

From Selkirk the railroad would run northwest, crossing the narrows that linked the north and south parts of Lake Manitoba and skirting the north end of Lake Dauphin. At the northeastern shoulder of the Duck Mountains it would strike west, to cross the South Saskatchewan River and follow the valley of the North Saskatchewan to Fort Edmonton. From about Quill Lakes to Fort Edmonton, Fleming proposed to keep the railroad generally south of the old Carlton Trail. Beyond Edmonton it would slip through the Rocky Mountains by way of the Yellowhead Pass, and twist down the Skeena River valley to a deep Pacific-coast harbour at Cain Island, future site for the town of Prince Rupert.

A telegraph line would soon connect Winnipeg and Edmonton, and Winnipeg's saloon debaters had one immediate suggestion to improve on Fleming's plan. Running the rail line to an eastern harbour on Hudson Bay would avert the need to toss more government dollars into the Dawson Route's muskegs.

Response to the treaties and Fleming's survey provided one necessary benefit to Ed and Jack Nagle: work for the spring of 1877. As soon as the treaties had opened the new areas, settlers began moving into them; the railroad survey now started speculators and entrepreneurs after them. Manitoba's native peoples viewed the influx of white men with alarm. The treaties had assured them protected reservations, so they demanded to know the locations for those reservations and what possession of reservation lands would mean.

Different northern bands were offered the Berens River area on the east shore of Lake Winnipeg, and the Dauphin River area between Lakes Winnipeg and Manitoba. Both places had fine stands of timber, but since as early as 1874 lumbermen had been logging at Fairford, on the Dauphin River site. To prevent trouble, A.H. Whitcher, Manitoba's Inspector of Surveys, was directed to survey reservations at Fairford and Berens River. In July of 1876 he had sent J.P.L. O'Hanly to Berens River, Alphonse F. Martin was heading to Fairford as soon as the snow was off the ground in 1877. Sometime during the winter of 1876-77, the Nagle brothers met Whitcher and arranged to join Martin's survey team.

Christmas in Winnipeg passed without the excitement of the previous winter. The New Year celebration was slightly enhanced by a January 1 proclamation that Queen Victoria was Empress of India. But by late January bad news was trickling into Winnipeg. The *Daily Free Press* reported that a fire had raged through Saint Hyacinthe. And early in February, Ed finally learned about Sitting Bull's encounter with Custer's U.S. Seventh Cavalry. But the worst news of all came on February 20, when the *Daily Free Press* reported smallpox on the plains.

Panic could easily have run through Winnipeg. Two previous smallpox epidemics — the most recent of them in 1870 — had decimated the Indians on the plains. Since about 1838, however, the Hudson's Bay Company had supplied smallpox vaccine to its post factors. Mass vaccination programs had saved lives during the earlier epidemics, so it is likely that as soon as they heard of this latest outbreak Winnipeg's old-timers organized more vaccinations.

Ed and Jack Nagle set off for Fairford with Alphonse Martin on February 24, the same day that Winnipeggers read that the snow had disappeared from the prairies near the Pembina Mountains. Martin did not keep them in the groves of tall spruce for long. By March 8 they were back at Winnipeg and he had paid them off, but their brief northerly excursion had helped them plan for the coming summer.

Having examined the land between Winnipeg and Fairford, the brothers had decided to try homesteading. At the Dominion Lands Office in Winnipeg they entered for two sites near Big Point on Lake Manitoba. Then they visited A.H. Whitcher, to learn which survey regulations would apply to them. Whitcher told them each to claim 160 acres, even if their choices were not on official surveys, but he stressed that they would have to be careful to improve the lands they claimed. They would each have to build and reside in a house of their own.

It took a substantial lump of the brothers' savings to outfit themselves for homesteading. Ed was inclined toward trying to anticipate all the situations they might encounter. Although a partial list of the outfit he amassed is extensive, it probably does not differ appreciably from what every well-prepared homesteader carried into the wilderness. Having provided themselves with three oxen, Ed and Jack filled a new Red River Cart with the following hardware and supplies:

800 lbs. flour
2 sacks pemmican
1 box tea
4 sacks shot
1 small can powder
1 case of matches
1 spade & shovel
1 plough [sic] handle
20 yards of 1/2-inch rope
Assortment of garden seeds
1/2-dozen saddler's needles
1 large bottle black ink
1/2-dozen darning needles
1 box yeast powder
1 plough collar
2 small plough bolts
1 shingle splitter
1 ox-chain staple & ring
2 yoke bolts
2 packs of rivets
4 bands for wheel: 2" X 10" & 2" X 12"
1 whip saw & file
1 lasso rope
10 yards mosquito net for summer
4 pairs shoes
200 lbs. salt & pepper
lime and chalk
1 window & glass
1 cow bell
1 gun
4 pair pants
2 small tea kettles
1 Dutch oven
1 pair of hinges
2 ox bows
1/2-dozen awls & thread
1 ball mould
1 clevis for harrow

About March 9, 1877 they threw a cover over their loaded cart and started west along Portage Avenue. As far as the small community of Gladstone they kept to the Carlton Trail and then they swung north on the Manitoba House Trail. Just beyond Gladstone they noticed the first dark ridges of the Riding Mountain escarpment, rising in steps in the distance to their left. Large patches of open ground separated the last blots of dirty snow. The purple buds of early spring crocuses pierced the green fuzz clinging to the earth. When the trail forked, Ed and Jack turned east and soon found themselves at the white gravel-strewn beaches of Lake Manitoba.

At Big Point, an unpleasant discovery awaited them. A farmer was already settled on their allotted homesteads and had been there at least four years. Noting that most of the best land near the Manitoba House Trail was already settled, the brothers carried on to Manitoba House. Beyond the trading post and Ebb and Flow Lakes, the aspen-grove prairie drew them northward. By the time they reached Turtle River, most of the surveyed country lay far behind them and the first springtime wedges of geese were sweeping the sky overhead.

It was mid-March before Ed and Jack forded the Ochre River and rolled out onto a large meadow on its west bank. The river flowed into the southwest corner of Dauphin Lake. From where they stopped they had a clear view of the ice-covered lake. A few small hay marshes were scattered across the meadow, with a thick stand of large oak and poplar trees due west of it. Tangles of poplar, aspen, and willow rustled along part of the lakeshore. As they unhitched their oxen and set up a permanent camp, the clamor of geese drifted from the open water at the mouth of the Ochre River.

Within a few days the brothers discovered that a party of surveyors was working in the area, blocking out general township outlines. From one of the men they learned that the meadow belonged to the Hudson's Bay Company. However, by chaining due south from one of the new survey markers they found they could establish clear boundaries for claims of their own.

By lining out a north-south boundary and choosing locations for their houses, the brothers set to work proving up their homesteads. They had to make a plow before they could break ground for their garden plots; then they cut pickets and rails for fencing, made flooring, and drew countless loads of firewood from nearby woodlots. Whenever tedium dragged at him, Ed produced a fiddle and played tunes he had learned on the buffalo hunts. The lake absorbed the last shreds of its ice on April 26, and three days later the brothers put their first seeds in the ground.

In mid-May Ed returned briefly to Manitoba House, to collect mail that post factor Henry Martineau was holding for him and Jack. On his way back to Dauphin Lake he visited James Young, one of the Nagles' few close neighbours. By June 10 the bugs were fierce, so the brothers hung their mosquito netting. The following day the first shoots poked from the warm earth in their gardens.

As each new round of Jack's house slipped into its notches, Ed hewed the logs smooth, inside and out. The high point of their summer came on June 10, when a small band of Ojibwa Indians stopped by to admire the work. By August 30, the new dwelling was almost completed, and the brothers were well satisfied with their preparations for the winter. Their gardens had been successful, and they had dried and salted plenty of game birds and fish.

Although Ed and Jack had piled their cart high with provisions, they had not brought enough to keep them through the winter. Ed returned briefly to Winnipeg to supplement what remained of their flour and staples, and arrived to find the city discussing Lord Dufferin's visit to the Northwest Territories. Saloon dialogue also ranged to the telegraph line, which was creeping beyond the northern edge of Dauphin Lake on its stretch westward toward Fort Edmonton.

Despite all their planning and preparations, neither Ed nor Jack were truly primed for the monotony they were about to face. In Winnipeg, friends and news circulated freely. In the small log house at the southwest corner of Dauphin Lake, the brothers were alone. When the leaves dropped and the forests became easier to explore, Ed began spending long periods outside the house.

He had settled in a remarkable area. His homestead lay just 28 kilometres northeast of the Riding Mountain escarpment. The Ochre River was not a large stream: at its mouth it was only one surveyor's chain (about 21 metres) wide, and nowhere were its banks higher than three metres. Its headwaters flowed from a group of small lakes deep in the Riding Mountains. These lakes were stunningly beautiful and so noted for their beavers that the British-born naturalist Grey Owl would later settle there to study the animals. East of the Ochre and Turtle Rivers, Ebb and Flow Lake was part of the Winnipegosis-Manitoba lake system. The southern fringes of the boreal forest brushed its eastern shores.

By mid-winter Ed had tramped widely in all directions, and had cultivated friendships with most of his neighbours, especially with a man named Zlet, who had visited Ochre River the previous summer.

During the spring and summer of 1878, Ed and his brother continued improving their homesteads. After breaking ground for fields, they made at least one trek to Winnipeg, where the saloon debates concerned the wisdom of allowing the Sioux Indians into Canada. Sitting Bull had led his tribesmen to sanctuary in the Cypress Hills, settling them near Fort Walsh. Winnipeg was also abuzz over the arrival of its first locomotive, which had come by steamboat because there were not yet any rails for it.

The brothers obtained a horse then returned to Dauphin Lake to start their second log building. Since Whitcher had insisted that two homes were required to satisfy the homesteading regulations, they had decided to pool their efforts. They had kept their fields and fenced lots side by side. Jack's house had gone up on the northern side of the east-west boundary between the homesteads. For Ed's house, they constructed what was actually a south-side addition to the first building. Although they were a few feet apart, the two buildings acted as a single home straddling the property line.

But by the end of the summer of 1878, Ed and Jack Nagle had grown ambivalent about their experiment at Dauphin Lake. They had reason for cautious optimism: their crops of grain were good, and they had almost satisfied the government's homestead requirements. But they were not certain about the Indian situation. During the summer, a Cree Indian chief named Big Bear had disrupted the 1878 treaty gathering. Not only had he refused to sign the treaty, he or one of his band had fired emphatic rifle shots over the Treaty Commissioner's tent.

For the Christmas holidays, Ed travelled south to Saint Boniface, where his younger sister Louise had become a teacher at Saint Mary's Academy School. After the holiday, she gave him a new journal as a parting gift. And from it, it is evident that he was already trapping in a small way at Ochre River and learning Indian gift-exchange ways.

When he visited Winnipeg again in the spring — after what was an exceptionally severe winter — the city's population had swollen to 7,000. The Red River Settlement eagerly anticipated the arrival of its first CPR rolling stock, which would soon cross a steel bridge planned to span the Red River from Saint Boniface to the Winnipeg side. But out on the far western plains the buffalo had entirely vanished, and the Indians were starving.

As long as they stayed at Dauphin Lake, money was not a problem for Ed and Jack. They could barter garden produce, dried game, or furs for what they needed. For hardware from Winnipeg, however, they had to pay Winnipeg currencies. Furs were good, but since the early 1870s cash money had begun replacing everything else. The brothers were running short of cash for their homesteading, so they welcomed the news of the CPR advances. The passing railroad would make it easier to move things south and would increase land values at Dauphin Lake, making their efforts to pioneer seem worthwhile.

In Winnipeg, Ed sought ways to raise the cash he needed to continue homesteading. There was work at Fort Qu'Appelle for men with oxen and carts of their own. A group of Ed's old friends also suggested he accompany them on a horse-buying trip to Montana. They claimed that $12.00 Montana horses would bring $72.00 in Manitoba. Ed weighed both options before returning with poultry and a cow to help Jack put the crops in. But by the time he reached Dauphin Lake, he doubted that he really wanted to spend the rest of his life farming. A Mr. Pratt needed lumbermen to operate a sawmill at Totogan, and after helping Jack seed the fields Ed returned to millwrighting.

Totogan Mill lay near the confluence of Rat Creek and the White Mud River, close to where the river flowed into the southwestern edge of Lake Manitoba. Pratt was the lumberman who had logged at Fairford, and his mill was one of the finest in the Northwest Territories. During that summer Ed made an effort to meet the steamboat captains calling at the mill. By summer's end he had arranged to have Zlet and the Indian chief at Ebb and Flow Lake cut 85 cords of wood for the boats, providing they also carted them to suitable steamboat landings.

By the early fall of 1879, Ed had earned enough money to ensure at least one more season of homesteading. And Jack had managed to harvest another good crop of grain from their fields. But the brothers were soon forced to recognize how woefully small their dwellings were: on October 1, Garrett arrived from Rock Forest with his new wife and child. Ed summed up the little family's impact on the lives of the bachelor brothers in one wry comment: "Rainy outside, and stormy within house."

He spent much of that winter trapping in the Ochre River's headwaters. And after plowing and seeding his fields in the spring, he returned to Totogan. Garrett was still at Dauphin Lake in the fall, but had done no work on the houses. Ed bucked again at the constraints of close living.

At the beginning of October 1880, he headed back to the solitude of his trap line. He tramped southwest to the top of the Riding Mountain ridge, to camp briefly with an Englishman he knew. As he climbed the ridge, the Ochre River and its aspen parkland fanned out splendidly in the morning light behind him. All of the streams spilling off the main ridge flowed toward Dauphin Lake. Golden aspen swale clung to the Ochre River as it wound northward. Through the crisp morning air he could make out Duck Mountain, nestling against the lake's shining northwest corner.

For six days Ed hunted on the snow-covered ridge top. Then he worked east, slipping down to spend a few days with Jack Otter. Following a brief visit with his brothers, he carried on to the Turtle River. He finally returned home for good on November 4th, bringing 116 muskrat, 6 mink, and 3 skunk pelts through the blizzarding snows with him.

The Dauphin Lake area had proven to be fine homesteading country, with sufficient furs and work available to provide the hard currencies that farming could not. Nevertheless, the spring of 1881 would be the last one that the Nagle brothers spent there. During the winter Garrett decided to leave. Although Ed intended to help Jack put in another crop, heavy rains and spring runoff filled the Ochre River to overflowing. Since the fields were still wet when Garrett was ready to go, Ed and Jack seeded the mud and accompanied their brother as far as Winnipeg.

As they had often done before, on this trip south the Nagles camped at the Whitmore place at Gladstone. Of this final trip it is possible to say only that they must have arrived at Whitmore's in March, and that this particular visit appears to have had far-reaching effects on settlement in the Dauphin Lake area.

Tom Whitmore was one of a group of pioneers having dismal luck at Gladstone. In response to his questions the Nagles reported having taken three good crops from their Dauphin Lake fields. Within a few years Whitmore would lead his Gladstone friends north to check out the area. They would become the pioneers who established the modern town of Dauphin, Manitoba.

The Nagles, however, carried on from Gladstone to Winnipeg. After a short stay in the city, Jack returned to Dauphin Lake. Apparently, until about May, Ed also intended to return, but when the government altered the route for the CPR he changed his mind. Even if their fields did eventually produce grain enough to bring in a little money, how could he and Jack easily move it out of the Dauphin area?

CHAPTER 6

Toward the Shining Mountains
(1881 - 1882)

Winnipeg's population had surged to 9,500 by the spring of 1881, and there had been cause for Jack's optimistic return to Dauphin Lake. Before the Dominion government changed the railroad route, the city was ground zero for an explosive real estate market. Some speculators were buying land along the western trails between Winnipeg, Portage la Prairie, and Brandon. Others invested between Selkirk and Fort Edmonton, gambling that Fleming's initial proposal would hold. Crowds of investors had thronged the streets, and every hotel had its attached real-estate office.

However, after changing the route for the CPR — from Winnipeg across the southern plains to Fort Calgary — the government also announced its intention to re-map the Northwest Territories. The districts of Saskatchewan and Alberta would lie west of Manitoba, with Assiniboia and Athabasca located north of them.

It is not clear how long Ed stayed in Winnipeg that spring. He had family there: Louise still taught at Saint Mary's Academy, and Garrett stayed on in the city for a while. Ed's younger half-brother Gerrard even stopped for a brief visit, on his way toward Portage la Prairie.

Ed could see that development was advancing farther west, but before he made any move himself he needed a new grubstake. In order to raise it he may have worked on one of the construction crews that were tossing up new buildings on every available city lot. By the late fall of 1881, he was on a new saddle horse and drifting west towards Portage la Prairie. Portage was aflame with the same real-estate

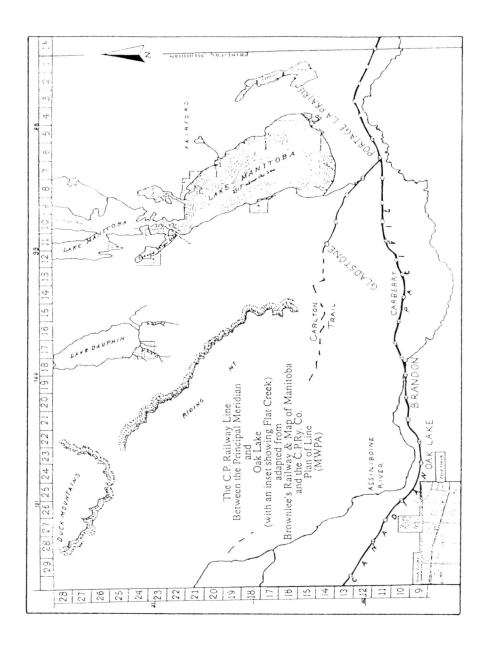

The C.P. Railway Line Between the Principal Meridian and Oak Lake (with an inset showing Flat Creek) adapted from Brownlee's Railway & Map of Manitoba and the C.P.Ry. Co. Plan of Line (MWPA)

speculation that had flared in Winnipeg in the early spring. Moving westward, Ed convinced himself he was searching for another homesteading site; but his search was half-hearted.

In early June of 1882, he turned his back on the tumult at Portage la Prairie and started west toward the CPR's western end-of-steel, which was then at Flat Creek. During those first June mornings, shadows chased a few scudding, flat-bottomed clouds toward him. The afternoon sun shone down warmly. For about 42 kilometres he crossed a flat prairie, then the Saskatchewan Trail twisted upwards among some thickets and knolls dotting the eastern slope of the Manitoba escarpment. The Devil's Lake buffalo grounds lay about 250 kilometres due south.

At the escarpment's crest, in the dip between the Pembina and Riding Mountain highlands, Ed entered the Carberry Sandhills. The dunes — some of which stand anchored firmly by grass while others drift slowly east with the winds — are the remains of the ancient shore of glacial Lake Agassiz. Early summer grasses swirled in waves around the few stands of white spruce etched starkly against them. From Pine Creek to Brandon, Ed had to carry water for his horse.

Brandon lay in the bottom of the Grand Valley of the Assiniboine River. It was a raw place — nothing more than a village way-station for the CPR. Nonetheless, a few river-bottom trees gave it an oasis-like charm. From the valley's eastern lip, Ed could see the dark ridge of the Brandon Hills shimmering in the southern distance. The trail down to the river followed a coulee, bypassing a few elms and poplars that had crept away from the riverbanks.

West of Brandon, he kept to the broad valley bottom. The sun continued shining down. From the marshlands along the riverbanks, cotton grass nodded on breezes heavy with the fragrances of roses and honeysuckles, and silver-berry bushes. Sprays of purple blossoms on tall wands and patches of yellow star grass erupted from the short-grass prairie. Forty kilometres beyond Brandon he rode up the south slope of the Grand Valley.

The river bottom and the end-of-steel contrasted sharply. The tent camp near Flat Creek had ballooned beside some sandy hills at a curve in the railroad bed. In its dusty streets, CPR construction crews rubbed shoulders with gamblers, bootleggers, and confidence men. Whores and chippies welcomed them all to the stifling mobile brothels sweating among the other tents.

Ed did not pause long in the dust. By the first week in July he had joined one of the survey crews coming and going from the tent town, and was moving with a few Red River carts westward toward Fort Qu'Appelle along the old Traders' Road. He had soon forded Pipestone Creek and was gazing into the Qu'Appelle River valley. Until he actually stood at the valley's edge, flat and featureless prairie had seemed to stretch limitlessly ahead of him. Then it had gaped open, displaying the Fishing Lakes strung like four gems on a silver strand of river. Forest covered the valley's southern slopes, opposing the grassy northern hillsides. Beside the water in the valley bottom the air was cool and moist. Huge herons stalked the shallows; goslings popped and bobbed after cruising pairs of geese. Perched kingfishers chattered at the water beneath them, and swallows swept insects from the sky.

By July 24 the surveyor had led Ed's group beyond the Fishing Lakes as far as the Big Arm River. John Palliser had called the country that lay ahead an inland desert. Twenty years later, John Macoun was calling Palliser's Triangle the most fertile part of the North American plains. That night, the surveyors camped at a gently rising plateau called the Eyebrow Hills. Before noon of the following day they had crossed Thunder Creek, a stream about the size of the Ochre River, and started up the slopes of the Missouri Couteau.

As he moved west of the Vermilion Hills, Ed began siding with Palliser's view of the country. He spent his days beneath a skull-bleaching sun. Slick-leafed greasewood plants were the only green he saw, even in the coulee bottoms. The farther west he went the worse the water got until only alkali sloughs remained, glittering centres for concentric encircling bands of brittle red glasswort.

After crossing Swift Current Creek, the surveyor turned to follow the railroad survey line. The seething heat did not begin to abate until July 31, when a brief sun shower cooled the men. But the sunbaked earth quickly sucked in the water and tossed more flames in their faces. By August 2, the party was camped beside the clear runnel of Maple Creek, where they conferred with a surveyor by the name of Madick.

The first westward exploring Frenchmen and Métis had noted the forests of jack pine (cyprés) covering the low range of hills lying southwest of Maple Creek, and called them the "Cypress Hills." They rose above the prairie rather than nestling down into it, but were every bit as attractive as the Fishing Lakes. Water, wood, and game were all plentiful. The Plains Indians — the Blackfoot, Assiniboine, Gros Ventre, and Cree — had considered them a kind of neutral ground, not because they sat near the frontiers of several tribal territories, but because no one was sufficiently powerful to control them.

No alliances had ever maintained the area's neutrality. Violence in the Cypress Hills had affected not only the local Plains Indians, but the whole development of the Canadian west. In 1873 a bunch of wolf hunters from the U.S. armed with Henry and Winchester repeating rifles had slaughtered a large band of Assiniboine Indians, prompting the creation of the North West Mounted Police. Now the police kept the peace on Canada's southern plains from Fort Walsh, which they had built on the northeastern slopes of the Cypress Hills.

From Maple Creek, Ed and his companions passed through Four Mile Coulee and climbed the long hill beyond it to gaze down on the fort. It was one of only a handful of Canadian outposts comparable to the U.S. Cavalry forts south of the border. It was not a trading post, but a strategic fort which existed solely for the protection of the policemen inside it, who lived surrounded by some of the fiercest warriors in North America. The policemen had cleared away and burned any trees and brush that might have provided cover for attackers.

Sitting Bull's tribesmen had pounded the meadow flat outside the stockade, but the Sioux were gone. They had starved when the last large herds of buffalo had finally disappeared during the winter of 1880-81. In July of 1881 they had surrendered to the U.S. Army, and returned to the U.S. side of the line. Although in August of 1882 the fort seemed to rest drowsily in its valley, the fort commander had not relaxed his vigilance. Captain John Cotton and his men had not forgotten that the first Mountie murdered on duty had died in the Cypress Hills.

In November of 1879 Constable Marmaduke Grayburn had been in his early 20s, and had only been with the force for six months. The sole indication that he could have become something more than the first in this new series of NWMP statistics lies in the speed with which he attained proficiency in the Blackfoot language. The police at Fort Walsh, who kept their extra horses pastured in the hills, had assigned Grayburn and five companions to the largest herd, at a place called Horse Camp. Despite a band of Blood Indians that harassed them, the policemen had remained at their picket. But during a mid-November patrol they forgot some tools in the bush, and when Grayburn returned to collect them he had disappeared. Police scouts eventually discovered his horse tied to a tree and shot through the head, and his body in a ravine. A Blood Indian named Star Child was the chief suspect, but when he came to trial in 1881, he was acquitted.

Ed and his companions camped on the meadow outside the palisade walls. They were now very close to the country they had trekked west to survey. From the top of Squaw Mountain, the highest point in the Cypress Hills, they took a visual survey of the country to the north. The next barrier they would encounter was the South Saskatchewan River. In his journal Ed called it "the Bellie."

The CPR had already surveyed a river crossing for itself, near where the town of Medicine Hat would grow up; Ed's survey team crossed the South Saskatchewan there. On August 9 they were camped on the north bank of the river when a sandstorm blew off the western prairie. The surveyor leading the party, who had been compiling a map of the country they traversed, discovered it was lost and the whole team searching for it during the sandstorm.

When the storm died three days later, the men headed north into the heart of what had been the farthest western buffalo range. Ed noted how friable the soil was, crumbling it easily between his fingers. Until they camped in the midst of a field of buffalo bones on the evening of August 12, the only signs he had seen that this had been buffalo country were dry wallows and polished rubbing stones. That evening, when the camp was up and organized, he displayed a prize to his companions. He had taken a large snake with nine rattles on its tail. Two days later he shot another rattlesnake, and on August 18 he glimpsed a small bunch of buffalo trotting east.

The Dominion's surveyors were dividing central Canada along precise lines. They based all their measurements on a Principal Meridian, which had been laid out slightly east of the 98th line of longitude and ran north from the U.S. border. A Second Meridian struck north at 102° west longitude, followed by Third, Fourth, Fifth, and Sixth Meridians at four degree intervals. The meridians were the north-south coordinates for a grid, the baseline of which lay along the Canada-U.S. border. Townships which plugged the space between the meridians were six-miles square and numbered as "ranges" westward from each meridian, and as "lines" northward from a baseline at the border. Since lines of longitude converge as they move north, for accuracy's sake new baselines were surveyed every 36 miles.

Ed and his companions had moved into unsurveyed townships in the area west of the Fourth Meridian near the Third Baseline — on the plains south of the Red Deer River and west of the South Saskatchewan, about 120 kilometres (72 miles) north of the border. After the morning of August 19, when they awoke to find a skin of ice 1/4-inch thick on their wash water, the team began moving over the prairie with mathematical precision. Each east-west or north-south traverse took them along the edge of a range or a line.

As he worked one day Ed saw a few more buffalo moving in the distance, but he could not leave the survey to pursue them. Thankfully, the party's Indian guide did not recognize such restrictions. The survey team returned to their camp that evening to find him roasting the hump of a three-year-old buffalo over the fire.

Ed had enjoyed hunting buffalo in the Dakota Territories, so when he was given August 30 as a day off he rode out in search of game. About mid-day a thin plume of campfire smoke sidetracked him. He sat down to his lunch in company with Sir A.T. Calf and Mr. Bridges (Burgess), the British Columbia Commissioner of Lands.

On September 5, he was back diligently squaring the prairie. A thick pall of smoke drifted over the survey team that afternoon, and the red-orange blaze of the setting sun continued far longer than it should have. Even as the constellations sprang into the settling darkness, flickers lit the western horizon. When the surveyors realized the extent and speed of the prairie fire bearing down on them, they set a fire of their own. Turbulent winds drove it eastward, and the party moved out on to the blackened prairie it left behind. By the time the wildfire reached them, Ed and his companions were on a fire guard extensive enough to protect them.

Ed was stunned by the desolate views that returning daylight brought to him. Bursts of flame continued to flare throughout the day, whenever embers found the few patches of grass remaining in the ashes and soot that stretched off in all directions. The devastation so bewildered the prairie animals that seven days after the fire had passed Ed had no difficulty shooting an aimlessly wandering Cabree.

By mid September, the surveyor felt he had accomplished enough for the season. He had decided to winter at Fort Edmonton, and his group was moving west when a storm of sleet and snow pinned them down. Fortunately, that morning they had not broken camp. Their Indian guide managed to make his way back from the prairie towards evening, but two other men who were caught out when the storm struck spent a night in the open.

Although all the missing men returned safely, the storm heralded the start of a series of near catastrophes for the group. While crossing the Bow River, one man almost drowned when his horse was swept out from under him. Man and horse were saved, but the supplies they had carried vanished into the flood. Fortunately, the survey team was well enough equipped that losing those supplies was not a serious problem.

They plodded on through flurrying rain and snow until early October. Then, during a particularly violent blizzard, their horses broke free and fled. Two members of the party nearly died of exposure during the three days it took to recover them.

At the time of the blizzard Ed and his companions were camped south of Blackfoot Crossing. When it passed they sent one cart and some of the recaptured horses back to the Bow River for firewood. The driver returned with the distressing news that 18 inches of snow lay on the riverbanks.

The surveyors were nearing the limits of their endurance when the weather became milder in the second week of October. Near the valley of the Little Bow River, in a windless storm of large, soft snowflakes, Ed glimpsed his first Bow River range cattle. Concomitant to his stand on Palliser's Triangle, John Macoun was actively promoting the Bow River as the best ranchland in North America. Ed was skeptical, but Bow River ranchers would not learn how treacherous the region's weather really was until the endless freezing blizzards of 1907.

The party had swung north and was near High River when Ed got his first shining view of the Rocky Mountains. For two days he seldom looked at anything else. The sawtooth line of peaks gleamed in the sun's soft morning light and trapped its rose-colored evening rays. The mountain range stretched off into the distant north, scraping the coolly iridescent lower edges of the sky.

Although snow still lay two-feet-deep on the ground, travelling conditions had improved. The snow's thick crust had grown solid enough to bear the carts and horses. Ed and his companions stopped briefly to visit a lonely settler at Sheep Creek, and feasted on trout at Pine Creek before reaching the Elbow River. The Elbow was too wide and swift for them to cross, however, so they moved along its south bank until they reached its confluence with the Bow.

There they camped outside the newly completed stockade walls of Fort Calgary's North West Mounted Police post. The CPR survey was not completed as far as Fort Calgary, and the place was not much of a settlement. Besides the NWMP fort, there was only a sawmill belonging to a Captain Walker, and a store belonging to an American fur trader named I.G. Baker.

During the journey to Fort Calgary the crust on the snow had thinned; beyond the Elbow River the horses began repeatedly breaking through it. It took three days of foundering struggle to travel the 85 kilometres between Calgary and Lone Pine Creek. At Lone Pine Creek, the animals were so exhausted that it was a relief to the travellers to awake to the sound of a blizzard howling outside their tents. Ed and his companions had collected firewood from the banks of the Elbow before starting north. Since their feast of trout at Pine Creek, they had eaten only cold pemmican and trail food, so while they waited for the storm to break they cooked themselves a hot meal.

Despite Ed's belief that the weather had exhausted its bag of tricks, an amazing transformation was taking place outside the tents while he and his friends enjoyed their hot food. Throughout the day the winds gradually warmed, and by the following morning all the snow was stripped away. Although Ed had never before experienced Chinook winds, the surveyor leading the group had. The mild weather held for seven days, during which time he led his team as far as the south bank of the North Saskatchewan River.

The hardships of the trail had worn terribly on Ed. In the eastern logging camps he had contracted a severe form of rheumatism, and ever since the first cold nights had come upon the prairie he had suffered intense pain. At least partly as a result of this affliction, his first view of the lauded Fort Edmonton did not impress him. He was disillusioned by what he had experienced and seen between Flat Creek and the forlorn-looking little outpost, and was convinced that Palliser, not Macoun, had truly judged the nature of the country. On October 28, in a last journal entry, he commented glumly:

Made the long looked for city of Edmonton, and [what] a very great disappointment [it is]. We had poor country for miles around it. [Our] horses [are] all played out. [We] left camp that day, never to return. That ended my misery across the great fertile belt.

75

CHAPTER 7

Scouting a Rebellion
(1883 - 1885)

Draped in a thick tangle of aspens, willows, and spruce trees, the wide valley of the North Saskatchewan River spread out before Ed and his companions. Its north slope climbed up from the river in three distinct steps. The sprawling jumble of a sawmill sat nearest the riverbank, in a small clearing on a flat bench just above the water. A dirt road wound from there up to the palisade walls surrounding the Hudson's Bay Company's trading post on the next level. Some of the homes housing the 275 people who were choosing to gamble on Edmonton's uncertain future lay scattered across the gently sloping plain rising from the stockade to the valley's third level. With the railroad diverted 335 kilometres south of them, the odds seemed formidably stacked against the gamblers.

Unfortunately for Ed, fortune shifted against him, too, shortly after he arrived in Edmonton. When the surveyor for whom he had been working refused to pay him, he had few cards to play. He worked at odd jobs, then moved three and a half kilometres up the North Saskatchewan River to a small community called Miners' Flats. During the last days of November he hunted, and when he had wild meat enough for the winter he attempted to scrape together another grub stake by placer mining.

Many of the grizzled old miners at Miners' Flats were losing their teeth. Whenever they managed to pan a little color from the black sand, they used quicksilver to gather it together. As they steamed off the mercury, the mercury vapor poisoned them. Working among them, mercury vapors slowly took hold of Ed too.

Fort Edmonton, with barricading; Hardisty and Fraser's sawmill in the foreground.

He had left home in 1874 intending to make his way by means of his own skills and initiative and during his years in the Northwest Territories he had been proud of his independence. Now he swallowed his pride and put to the test the slender tie that bound him to his self-esteem. Before he left Rock Forest he had been about to receive $5,000.00, which he had not claimed, but for the first time since 1874 he viewed his situation as critical. Knowing his father must have maintained his government connections, and possibly feeling that he might still speak for his unclaimed legacy, Ed wrote to Gerrard asking him for help.

Letters took a long time to cross Canada, especially during the winter months, but sometime in March or April Ed received his reply.

My Dear Ed,

I got your letter of 28th Jan. 1883 from Miners' Flatts [sic] yesterday evening, and am Sorry to find you in so miserable a position — Sick & obliged to thresh Barley at only twenty-five cents a Bushel — and much of this hardship brought on by yourself & mismanagement. If you have an established good claim against any of the contracting Surveyors you are, of course, aware that the payment can be enforced — and if you cannot do better, make out your amount for work done, Swear to its correctness before a

Justice of the Peace, and I will see what I can do for you through the Government, but really your best course will be to make it & Send it to G[arrett] James to be Sued at Winnipeg.

As to your Rheumatism, it is of an inflammatory [nature], an affair of diseased Blood, and the best Remedy for it is:

Bicarbonate of Potash (Cream of Tartar)	1 Drachm
Acetate of Potash	1/2 Drachm
Solution of acetate of Ammonia	2 Table Spoonfulls [sic]
Water	2 wine Glassfulls [sic]

Mix them in a Tumbler and take one Such every four hours in a State of effervescence [induced] by adding about a little — say about a Scruple, [of] citric acid. Take half a Tumbler of Barley water, or even Flax water, after ea[ch] draft.

Should this not be easily got, Mix up about a Table Spoon full [of] Cream of Tartar to a quart of warm water, add a tea spoon full [of] ground ginger — (Root ginger ground) and drink this during the course of a day together with a tea spoon full of the lye of wood ashes in a cup of milk, before breakfast, before noon, & at going to bed, and continue either of these courses Six days & quit three & commence again & and continue so for 36 days. In the meantime Steep the part affected every night at going to bed with flannel cloths wrung out a Strong Hops tea decoction, to which Salt sufficient to make a brine has been added — continue this for a week and then wear across the small of the back — the seat of the Pain — a plaster of Burgundy Pitch held to its place by an inside belt of doubled flannel: Blue flannel, if you can get it. I do not know the ingredients of which S. Jacobs oil is composed; but would have much mor[e] faith in volatile ointment — that is, Sweet oil with enough Ammonia added to make the oil into the consistence & color of thick cream, and rub the parts affected with it. Keep yourself from exposure to wet. Dress and sleep in (flannels?), and don't touch liquor, that is Spirits.

I had letters from all the family except you and John at Christmas & John is so busy mining at Hay Island that he should be excused; all were well or passable. Had Parker to Christmas dinner, and wrote to you & all others after New Year's, sending your letter to Gerrard for re-direction, seeing that I did not Know your address. You will by this time have received that letter of mine.

You will, of course, have learned from Gerrard every occurrence about Winnipeg: How John is manager of the Reservation Gold mine on Hay Island in Lake of the Woods, & of G. James' Success in the Grocery &ct. And as to things here, Parker is doing well. His Government Salary is $641 per annum, no great affair in itself but it gives him an opportunity to Speculate for more than four times the amount. Parker is making money & Spends little. My own condition continues to be "a narrow sufficiency" and my health this winter has been very poor. We have had a hard winter. For a long time the Thermometer held from 20 above to 30 below with heavy Snow, & this cold weather confined [me] to the house. Kate is well, & Rose is also. She teaches Rock Forest School for a pittance of $15 per month & boards at home.

I have just received a letter from Gerrard — Portage la Prairie — in which he mentions having received two letters from you & the *Edmonton Bulletin*, which he sent me. He mentions your desire that he should go with you to Red Deer River & wishes my opinion, but I know so little about it that I can Scarcely advise — and defer Saying any more about it until I again write to You, which I will in a few days.

Rose and Kate join in love to you & the hope & prayer that you may recover your health. I am, My Dear Ed,

affectionately yours,

G.J. Nagle

Mr. Ed Nagle — Edmonton, N.W.T.

Ed had already moved back to Fort Edmonton, and it is fortunate that by the time the letter arrived he had weathered the worst of the problems he faced, because Gerrard's apparent lack of sympathy for his financial predicament seems to have profoundly affected him. As long as his father lived, Ed never again asked him for anything.

The western prairie had experienced an appalling winter. Cold winds had blasted down the valleys of the North and South Saskatchewan Rivers, forcing the Bow River range cattle across the open southern plains and covering the Cypress and Vermilion Hills with ice. The Fishing Lakes had frozen solid. New settlers, who had come to western communities on the strengths of the land booms, shivered and recognized the true face of life in the Northwest Territories.

Hardest hit of all the prairie inhabitants were, of course, the Indians. After the disappearance of the buffalo, necessity had forced most of them onto the reservations assigned them by treaties one through seven. Starving and cold, they threw themselves on the largess and mercy of the government's Indian Department as in former times they had trusted in the compassion of the officers of the Hudson's Bay Company. But the Indian Department was not the Hudson's Bay Company; and the Commissioner of Indian Affairs and some of his assistants, particularly a careerist named Hayter Reed, were systematically betraying the Indians' trust and the articles set down in the treaties.

Hayter Reed had started his career as the Indian Department Agent at Battleford. There he had advanced the notion that severe restrictions be applied to any rations given to the natives. He had a peculiar idea of the role that Indian Agents were to play on the reserves. Regardless of the fact that he had not supplied them with the tools and instruction that the treaties promised, Reed insisted that *his* Indians must work to eat. As he rose in the Indian Affairs Department hierarchy, his notions got wider hearing and credence. And during the winter of 1882-83 the government's Reed-style approach began to change the attitude of some Indian chiefs.

Even if they had never met them, most settlers west of Winnipeg had mental images of the notable Plains Indian chiefs. From the reports in P.G. Laurie's *Saskatchewan Herald* they had learned that Poundmaker was the noblest of them all. He had led his people onto their reserve lands without protest, and urged the other chiefs to follow him in learning to farm. Yet, although Poundmaker's fall harvests proved insufficient to support his people, the Indian Department cut supplies to his reserve. Closer to Edmonton, Chiefs Ermineskin, Bobtail, and Sampson were generally considered friendly and cooperative. But in a letter to the government in January 1883, they too wondered if the Dominion might not be breaking its agreements with them.

Those were chiefs who had faith enough in the government to voice their grievances. Others, like the Blackfoot chief Crowfoot and Big Bear the Cree, were not so disposed. Big Bear, for example, still held to the position he had taken by firing shots over the Treaty Commission tents in 1878. He was a tough, intransigent little man with a trader's business sense, who demanded for his people the right to choose when and where they located their reservation lands.

Neither the winter weather nor Indian dissatisfaction had forced Ed into Edmonton, however. With between 275 and 300 settlers, Edmonton was the centre for the region's population of 800 whites, and several of the settlers had previously been in Winnipeg. Father Albert Lacombe was unquestionably the most influential of Ed's former acquaintances, but the famous missionary was not living full time at Edmonton in the spring of 1883. However, John A. McDougall and the feisty newspaperman Frank Oliver would soon prove almost as important to Ed's future as the priest had been to his past.

After leaving Winnipeg and rolling around the prairies as an itinerant trader, McDougall had risen to become one of the most successful independent merchants on the western plains. He and Louvisa, his wife of five years, were numbered among Edmonton's leading socialites. Frank Oliver was a similarly extraordinary man. His cleanly chiselled features, flowing moustaches and piercing eyes made him a standout and his fiercely outspoken Liberal humanism and vociferous teetotaling made him a presence to be reckoned with. Oliver was a little less concerned with prestige than was McDougall, but every bit as successful in his enterprises.

Ed and Oliver had first met in Winnipeg in 1876, when the newspaperman had been trying to cart a printing press west to Edmonton. He had gotten his press as far as the banks of the North Saskatchewan River, only to lose it when his raft overturned during the river crossing. He had not actually managed to replace the press and print a first issue of his Edmonton *Bulletin* until late 1880, but since then he had added a larger press to his operation.

The *Bulletin* reflected Oliver's attitudes. Despite the bombastic and often eccentric style of his journalism, it was a respected voice in the Northwest Territories. His own evaluation of the *Bulletin's* importance was quite succinct. At the time Ed settled at Edmonton, Oliver flatly claimed that it was the best paper west of Ontario.

Ed shared Oliver's liberal humanism, and appreciated his convictions. The newspaperman was a hospitable fellow, and the friendship he extended during Ed's time of trouble was firm and dependable. In the spring of 1883 Oliver was actively campaigning for the newly created Edmonton Electoral District seat in the Northwest Territories Assembly. If he did not actually assist his friend's spring campaign, Ed certainly encouraged Oliver's eventually successful effort.

That spring Ed was in desperate need of the job he got as millwright at Hardisty and Fraser's jumble of sheds by the river. The millers were expanding their operation: adding a two-storey 20' x 24' addition to their main building. By installing their carpenter shop, slab saw, shingle mill and turning lathe, Ed proved his worth. When the construction was finished he stayed on permanently as Hardisty and Fraser's millwright.

In early 1883, Edmonton's general civic spirit resembled the miasma that lingers over the mud in riverbeds whose waters have been re-routed. The rusty parallel streaks that should have carried the community's future were passing far to the south. Some discouraged settlers were preparing to move away, but the folks who resolved to stay on were a dauntless lot. Once Ed established himself as their associate, the range of his friendships quickly extended.

In addition to McDougall and Oliver, two new friendships would prove especially important to him. Until the spring of 1882, Richard "Dick" Secord had been the schoolteacher at Pakan, a small settlement near Edmonton. He had lost that job by badly injuring one of his arms in a hunting accident. When Ed first met him, Secord was surveying the Fort Edmonton town site. The slim young man with the withered arm enjoyed conviviality.

James Hislop was another man to whom Ed felt especially drawn. In the spring of 1883, Hislop was the book keeper and sales manager at Hardisty and Fraser's mill. He was a clever and charismatic fellow, big and brawling with prodigious appetites for drink and talk. He had grown up on the rolling green hills north of the harbour at Pictou, Nova Scotia, and had studied mathematics and engineering at the Pictou Academy. In 1876 he had left Nova Scotia to work on the Pembina Branch, out of Selkirk, Manitoba and then he had moved to Battleford to help build the new Northwest Territories capital. By the time Ed met him, he knew Cree in addition to the Scottish Gaelic and English he had grown up with.

Edmonton's intrepid little band was not the only group feeling anxious about the future of the Northwest Territories. As spring became summer the Plains Indians sent stronger signals to the men in Ottawa. By closing Fort Walsh in June, the government attempted to disperse Big Bear and the Indians who gathered near the Cypress Hills to speak with him. But when the CPR tried to push across the Blackfoot reserve a short time later, Father Lacombe had to exert all his influence to prevent the Blackfoot warriors from defending their land.

Despite of the unrest, Ed and his friends did not feel any sense of impending danger. They listened to the news about the southern plains and the CPR with interest, and a certain satisfaction. Their own concerns were still focused on reconnecting their community to a railroad. It was good news when a mail stage began running regularly between Edmonton and Calgary in mid-July. The first indicator of events that would soon totally disrupt their lives came on July 23, 1883. From the sawmill Ed may have watched the large band of Indians cross the river and make their way up the winding road to the stockade. The Bears Hills Cree had come to demand the provisions and equipment their treaty had promised them.

When the Indian Agent in Edmonton lied to them, saying he did not have any food for them, the Cree warriors dragged him to the doors of the Hudson's Bay Company post and suggested that he get some. Before long Indians from other bands near Edmonton joined the Bears Hills people, and it became obvious that the warriors in the area were overwhelmingly frustrated. Only the Hudson's Bay Company trader's willingness to advance provisions to them, and the prompt and diplomatic actions of a small detachment of policemen prevented violence.

By late August, more optimistic and myopic western settlers were predicting a complete resolution of the situation. Big Bear brought only one wagon-load of freight to Edmonton, but the most recalcitrant of all the Plains Indian chiefs was said to be intending to establish a freighting business. Moreover, he appeared prepared to accept reserve lands near Fort Pitt, east of Edmonton. Knowledgeable old-timers like Frank Oliver withheld their opinions pending further developments.

In the turmoil of frontier life Ed managed to almost completely forget the crisis which had overtaken him the previous fall; he was probably making a special effort to forget the correspondence that had developed between his father and himself. By delaying his commitment to the Red Deer River homestead scheme, Ed adroitly deflected his father's next overture.

My Dear Ed,

It is now many weeks that I have expected a letter from you respecting the proposed project of colonizing the Nagles somewhere on the Red Deer River or one of its tributaries, but I am yet without it. Do write on receipt — *as to climate, adaptability of the land for mixed farming* — that is for grain growing as well as for Pork & Cattle raising, the *possibility of finding a locality principally prairie* and *well wooded and well watered.* And for my health['s] Sake it is of all things important that *the climate should be milder than it is here.*

If you find a Suitable place you and I will have, apparently, to make a commencement of Settlement, aided by the contributions of John, Garrett Ja[me]s & Gerrard. Parker will come when settlement is made. Gerrard will settle down in time; but I would doubt much that John or G. Jas. would do so. You and I with the assistance of two men & a boy and proper machinery could, I believe, comfortably shape a good "Homestead." I could take in a comfortable outfit and I have no doubt that John, G. Jas. & Gerrard will contribute liberally, and Gerrard and Parker would Join us in the course of about a year.

Matters, things & business here are prosperous. Crops are promising and Hay more than commonly abundant ....

During the fall of 1883, several surveyors arrived at Fort Edmonton to discharge their crews. Although the town was soon flooded with unemployed young men, Ed's job with Hardisty and Fraser was secure. On Christmas Day, Kelly's Saloon did a rousing business. The *Bulletin* noted that more strong liquor was drunk than should have been, but everyone seemed to enjoy the game of soccer on Main Street in spite of the fine snow drifting from the sky.

The really big news that winter came in February, when the *Bulletin* announced that the government had enacted game laws to restrict trapping and big game hunting within an area that extended 35 kilometres north of the North Saskatchewan. Wisely, the government did not propose to regulate the Indians' hunting, although their game sales to settlers would be blocked. Settlers had been accorded seasons during which they could hunt.

There was no shortage of meat in Edmonton during the spring, but on their reserves the Indians' sufferings increased. Big Bear, who had once hunted buffalo professionally, let his judgment on the laws be known: he would not lead his people to any reserve until he saw all the seed, implements, cattle and other items the Indian Department promised him. He commented that white men made many quick promises, which they fulfilled very slowly.

To Frank Oliver, Big Bear was only the most visibly angry of the Indian chiefs. Oliver was now prepared to respond to the optimistic predictions of the previous summer. Throughout the spring and summer of 1884 the *Bulletin* ran a series of increasingly critical articles on the way the Indian Department handled its responsibilities. In June, Oliver condemned the government's incompetence and lack of prescience. Speaking for his many observant readers he stated, "all that is required is the occasion and a leader to land the North-West in a first class Indian war. ...Treaty money is not paid, implements, cattle and rations issued, and the salaries of agents, assistant commissioners, and commissioners paid in order to breed war."

Ed knew that the Métis believed their grievances against the government were as well-founded as those of the Indians. When Louis Riel crossed the Montana border during the second week of July, everyone knew that a leader had arrived. Now only an occasion was required for war.

Riel, however, did not act like the rebel he was said to be. Just the opposite, in fact. After a group of Prince Albert businessmen invited him to speak to them, a story in the Prince Albert *Times* supported the justice of his position and commended his conception of the way the Northwest Territories must approach Ottawa. In a series of public presentations of Métis and Indian viewpoints he was almost considered a moderate, who might finally bring Ottawa's attention to real western problems.

Even Riel's powerful presence could not completely defuse the Indian situation though. Late in August Frank Oliver got a glaring sign of things to come. As he worked in his home one day, he had the uncomfortable feeling he was being watched. When he glanced up, an Indian warrior was standing in his doorway. Oliver's wife was working in their kitchen, and before the Indian vanished he remarked that he would return someday to take her.

In March or April of 1884, Ed had received the news that his father had died at Rock Forest thus freeing him of any obligation to again try homesteading. He remained the millwright at Hardisty and Fraser's mill until August, and when the mill closed down he accepted an invitation to join three Americans who intended to hunt beyond the game law boundaries.

In spite of Oliver's story, Ed and his American companions could not believe that the Indians were a serious threat. They left Edmonton on September 15 to follow the North Saskatchewan upriver as far as Big Island. Two of the Americans decided to winter there, but Ed and a man named Stark carried on upstream. When ice blocked their passage through a canyon in the foothills, they chose the HBC's old Goose Encampment for their winter base camp.

Elk and moose abounded in the nearby woods, and through the early winter Ed's traps yielded a steady harvest of lynx and beaver. By late December he was able to return to Edmonton with fur enough to re-provision himself. On his way he stopped below Big Island at Haney's mine, where he was given some samples of silver-bearing quartz to send out to Winnipeg to be assayed.

Although Christmas was approaching, Edmonton was quiet. Ed got no news about the Indian situation, but he did learn that a telegraph line now connected Edmonton to Father Lacombe's mission at Saint Albert and that a professor of geology named Tyrrell had established that Edmonton was 2,253 feet above sea level. Before returning to his hunting camp, Ed mentioned to the *Bulletin* that he and Stark intended to move through the canyon to trapping grounds above the Goose Encampment. When the hunting partners returned to Edmonton in early May, they had been almost completely alone since late January, and as they neared Lake Wabamun it became plain that something was very wrong: bands of Stony Indians they met pointed weapons at them and were abusive.

An army was encamped at Edmonton, and Canada was at war. From his friends Ed heard a fragmentary version of the way things stood. Hislop had been surveying on the White Mud River until April and was now working in the army commissariat, but Frank Oliver knew more about the situation than anyone else.

Until General Thomas B. Strange had arrived on May 1, bringing the Alberta Field Force from Calgary, the citizens of Edmonton had feared for their lives. Big Bear's Crees had looted and burned the small settlement of Frog Lake: at least seven people, two of them Catholic priests, had died there. The Indians had danced their victory clothed in the priest's vestments, and when they vanished into the bush they had taken two captive white women with them. At Fort Pitt, more Indians had killed a mounted policeman named Cowan.

The Métis, too, were in rebellion against the Dominion. They had driven a detachment of police away from Duck Lake. Caught between the Métis at Duck Lake and the Indians at Frog Lake and Fort Pitt, the police had withdrawn to Fort Carlton, on the North Saskatchewan. Then, deciding that the fort was too difficult for them to defend, they had burned it and retreated to Prince Albert.

Because the Indians and Métis seemed to be fighting alongside each other, Ed briefly faced the dilemma of whether or not he should enlist on the government's side. But, regardless of the friendships he had made on the buffalo hunts and with the Métis at Dauphin Lake, he could ignore neither the women captured at Frog Lake nor the death of the Catholic priests.

When Ed presented himself as a recruit to the Field Force he was immediately accepted for service. General Strange required a small group of experienced bushmen for an especially hazardous duty. Many of his men and most of his supplies would be moving in scows down the North Saskatchewan to Fort Pitt. J. Sinclair, who had been the HBC post factor at Fort Pitt for 12 years, was the flotilla's river pilot, but General Strange needed river scouts willing to drift in canoes ahead of the flatboats.

Ed joined his comrades on the banks of the North Saskatchewan to examine the flatboats they had been assigned to escort. Strange himself had designed them, and they had been specially built in Edmonton during the preceding week. The men and animals would be surrounded by bales and barrels of supplies. Riflemen would fire through loopholes, and oarsmen would be similarly protected. One of the boats had a platform on it for a field gun, and the soldiers were calling it Big Bear. Although the designs were unquestionably innovative, the passengers grumbled that the boats were not watertight.

Telegraph service to Edmonton had been disrupted since March 27, so when the Field Force started off on May 15 General Strange did not know that Louis Riel was preparing to surrender to General Middleton at Batoche. Strange and Major Sam Steele, of the NWMP, ranged eastwards with mounted troops along the north bank of the river. On the water, Ed, James Grant, Dan Macrae, Charles Parley, Charles Rossiter, and a fellow named Osborne slipped their canoes out ahead of the flatboats.

There was not much for the force to worry about until after it reached Fort Victoria, which lay three days' journey down river from Edmonton, but the flotilla travelled under strict discipline. For most occasions the scouts used a system of visual signals to relay information back to Sinclair, but a shot was the signal for all boats to head ashore. Thirty kilometres downstream from Edmonton, at Fort Saskatchewan, Ed and his companions were relieved of one of their responsibilities: when the horse boat filled with water General Strange left it where it sank.

Eight days out of Edmonton, General Strange broke away from the main column and headed north to examine Frog Lake with a small party from Steel's Scouts. The river scouts and flatboats continued down river. As they approached Fort Pitt, Ed and his comrades moved with increasing caution. Ed's canoe was leading the other vessels when he noticed a dark globe bobbing on the river. He soon became convinced he was watching an Indian swim across. At the sound of his shot, the other boats headed for the riverbank. By the time he and his partner found the beaver he had killed, the soldiers were blazing away at the stands of poplar surrounding them.

From where the telegraph line crossed the North Saskatchewan River, the rivermen saw smoke at Fort Pitt. The Frog Lake reconnaissance party had arrived a few hours earlier, and Steele's Scouts had located policeman Cowan's mummified body stretched out on the ground where he had died. His killers had cut out his tongue and heart, and the heart hung impaled on a stake near the body.

Around the evening campfires, the scouts recounted other horrors they had seen. Some of the bodies of the massacred Frog Lake settlers had lain mutilated and decomposing in the open air. Others, with only charred stumps where their hands and feet had been, had to be dragged from the ruins of the burned church.

By the time Ed arrived at Fort Pitt, Sam Steele and a small party of his men had already started off in search of Big Bear's band of Cree Indians. At twilight, they turned back and encountered a party of four men coming up behind them. One of the new men wore a police uniform, so until he whispered something in Cree, Steele's men did not know what to do. In the ensuing gunfight, however, they killed two Indians and recovered policeman Cowan's tunic and Winchester rifle.

While he was camped at the Fort, Ed found a coup stick that one of the Indian warriors had left behind. Throughout his long life, its polished buffalo-horn head and tightly wrapped handle would serve him as a souvenir of this terrible war. Truly, settlers had died horribly at Frog Lake, but the frontier cultures that had been so vital when he first arrived in the Northwest were also in their death throes.

Early the next morning, Steele thundered off with a column of mounted troops towards a landmark called Frenchman Butte. Before following him, General Strange took the field gun off the Big Bear and ordered the river scouts to take the scow and 100 soldiers eight kilometres down river, where they could sweep the northern riverbank and support Steele's flank.

A heavy mist blanketed the water as Ed and his companions guided Sinclair down river. When they reached their position the soldiers debarked and deployed in a skirmish line. The river scouts stayed on the river to relay information among the various groups involved in the action, but as soon as the skirmish line finished its sweep everyone realized that they hadn't been given any further instructions. The soldiers re-embarked and, in an effort to resolve the confusion, Sinclair and the river scouts decided that anchoring the Big Bear farther downstream was the safest thing to do. When they got new orders, Ed and his comrades would return with them to Sinclair.

Unfortunately for the river scouts, Sinclair struck out on his own hook soon after they left him.. When he heard the first distant rumbling thumps of the field gun, he sent a small reconnaissance party ashore.

But when the soldiers peered over the riverbank a single rifle shot whistled above their heads, and the pilot decided the Big Bear was too exposed. Without leaving any signs for the scouts to follow, Sinclair quietly drifted downstream into the fog. At an island a few kilometres east of the Little Red Deer River deboucher, Sinclair dropped anchor again and waited.

It is unclear whether or not the river scouts ever got further orders from General Strange, but when they eventually returned for Sinclair, the Big Bear was gone. Unable to shout for fear of giving away their position, Ed and his companions searched in vain through the thickening fog. They eventually returned to Fort Pitt and reported that the Big Bear and her crew had been lost on the river. Fortunately, before the Field Force had to organize a more extensive search, the *SS Northcote* arrived with supplies from Battleford, and the Big Bear in tow.

For Ed, the rest of the Northwest Rebellion was anticlimactic. The *SS Northcote* had brought the news of Riel's defeat and surrender at Batoche, and by the time Sam Steele returned to Fort Pitt for supplies he had already engaged Big Bear's Cree at Loon Lake. Although Ed and the other river scouts joined the pack train that was organized to support Steele's mounted column, General Middleton soon took over the pursuit of Big Bear. Ed was not present when the women from Frog Lake were rescued. Nor did he ever actually fire shots at any Indians. He spent most of the month of June rolling along in Middleton's wake.

CHAPTER 8

The Boreal Wilderness, Again
(1885 - 1891)

The Northwest Rebellion had two distinct effects on the citizens of Edmonton. Although the settlement's future remained uncertain, those who resolved to stay became inwardly more determined to make something of it while those who had contemplated leaving, soon packed up and left. Ed's friends responded in various ways. Dick Secord had returned to school teaching, his withered arm having prevented him from playing any role in the rebellion. John A. McDougall closed his store, moved his family into a large new home, and retired from business. Frank Oliver lost his seat on the Northwest Territories Council, so he increased the vitriol in his *Bulletin* tirades, and Jim Hislop went to work for the Hudson's Bay Company.

Ed was out of a job when he returned from active service, but the impulse to ramble had seized him. He joined the Ross brothers for a trip to Calgary, to help restock Edmonton's shelves. As they returned north a violent hailstorm wracked the prairie ahead of them. They crossed meadows where the lifeless carcasses of gophers lay strewn about in the torn grass. Dead waterfowl bobbed in ragged disarray on the sloughs and little ponds.

Throughout summer's end, Ed tracked the rebellion's aftermath. He had sympathy for his Métis friends, who would never again freely roam the plains as they once had on their buffalo hunts. Their leader, Louis Riel, was the first man to come to trial.

Even after the rebellion, Louis Riel remained the territories' best card for drawing Ottawa's attention. From a western point of view, it is worth noting that a clement verdict against him would have helped focus attention on the government's inept and insensitive Indian

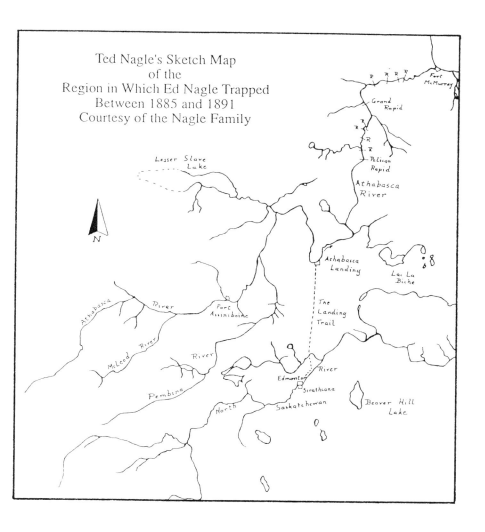

Ted Nagle's Sketch Map
of the
Region in Which Ed Nagle Trapped
Between 1885 and 1891
Courtesy of the Nagle Family

policies. Before the violence, Riel had advanced Métis and Indian claims astutely and with energy. During the rebellion, though, less stable aspects of his personality had emerged. He had claimed to be a prophet, divinely inspired to teach Canadians and he had insisted that the Papal clergy leave Canadian Catholics alone. During his trial many people began considering him mad. And in spite of the insurrection he had led, they wondered whether or not a lunatic should be executed.

Regardless of what anyone else felt about Riel's sanity, the presiding judge did not take long to condemn him to death. The trials of Poundmaker, Big Bear, and the other rebels were decided almost as quickly. The two chiefs were jailed, and the men who had killed settlers at Frog Lake or in smaller-scale incidents were executed.

By the time Riel swung from a scaffold, on November 16, 1885, Ed's winter plans were set. After the Calgary trip he had taken a load of freight north to Athabasca Landing, on the Athabasca River. On his way back to Edmonton he killed a large black bear. Before the rebellion he had been enjoying his life and his encounter with the bear impelled him to return to trapping, this time at Athabasca Landing.

Although Ed's luck was not spectacular that winter, he had one adventure. About half way through the season he began noticing huge wolf tracks along his traplines. He learned from the local Indians that this particular wolf had ranged throughout the area for several years. It stole his baits and catches whenever it could, but never stumbled into any of his traps. Stalking the beast became a challenge of his skill, and his memories of that season are centred the chase.

Ed tracked the wolf from Athabasca Landing as far south as Sturgeon Creek, about 117 kilometres away, then began setting out traps and poisoned bait. Until February 1886, none of his strategies worked. Then one day, as he snowshoed along the Athabasca River, he glimpsed his wolf chasing a coyote over the ice. He missed a shot at it, but poisoned the remains of the dead coyote. When a Hudson's Bay Company trader eventually measured it, from the tip of its nose to the end of its tail, the wolf's skin was eight feet four inches long.

Ed relished bush life. If his notions had not been upended that spring, he might happily have continued trapping on a small scale and millwrighting to outfit himself. But in March of 1886 an independent trader named Peter Pruden arrived at Edmonton. Pruden had wintered somewhere up the Athabasca near Lac La Biche. According to Frank Oliver, the lot of fur he brought to John A. McDougall was worth $6,000.00.

That summer, while working for a lumberman named Lamoureaux, Ed resolved to replicate Pruden's success. Unfortunately, he dreamed more than he should have. Although he was normally a careful workman, in August he caught a hand in Lamoureaux's saw and amputated the tip of one of his fingers.

He had finished at Lamoureaux's mill and was recovering from his accident when his brother Jack blew into Edmonton in late August. Jack crackled with the success that mining at Hay Island had brought him, and liked Ed's plan to trade furs. Within two weeks, Frank Oliver learned that during the winter of 1886-87 the Nagle brothers would take the old Fort Assiniboine trail to the Pembina River, whence they would boat down to the Athabasca. They intended to trap and trade up the Athabasca as far as the McLeod River.

For some reason, though, Jack Nagle could not sustain his enthusiasm: he and Ed got almost as far north as Fort Assiniboine before he decided that the fur trade was not for him. Ed said good-bye to his brother for the last time when they parted company in October. Jack bolted south toward the American mining areas on the eastern slopes of the Rockies, taking his first steps along the road to Nevada. His abrupt departure altered Ed's plans. After building a scow, he drifted down the Pembina River to the Athabasca and back to The Landing.

Athabasca Landing lies 150 kilometres north of Edmonton — at the northern end of the Athabasca Trail — and spreads over a low flat on the south bank of the river. In the fall of 1886 it was a bustling little town: the Hudson's Bay Company (HBC) was closing the Methy Portage-Clearwater River route to the Mackenzie watershed, intending to operate from new facilities at The Landing. In addition to improving the Athabasca Trail, the HBC was constructing an office, warehouse, and shop complex. Of all the places in the Edmonton area, the Company was hardest at work at The Landing.

Throughout that winter, talk at The Landing focused almost entirely on the inroads independent traders (free traders) were making into what many had considered the last great HBC fur reserve. For all its wealth and influence, the HBC was learning that it could not prevent other traders from edging into Canada's northwestern watersheds. Peter Pruden was not the only independent moving north. Freemen like Colin Fraser and Villeneauve (also known as Shot), who were born and raised in the north country, were "free" because they had served out terms with the Company before setting out on their own. Others, like the Elmore brothers and a fellow named McBeth, had only been north a few years.

Athabasca Landing swarmed with all types of men, and rang with their ambitions. It was a place for refugees and adventurers, where the dispossessed and the visionary walked together. As the fur trade had extended into the western north, Métis families had settled there. Now some survivors of the 1885 rebellion were looking northward too, toward the last regions of Canada open to them.

Ed spent most of his winter in the bush. He seriously committed himself to trapping for the first time, coming away that spring with his first respectable lot of fur. Besides actually working his traplines, he visited the Indian camps to get some idea of just how many furs their hunters brought in. At one point he had a frank talk with Jim Hislop. Hislop, who was an employee of the Hudson's Bay Company at Athabasca Landing was tired of working for the Hudson's Bay Company. Like Ed, he saw the potential that lay in independent trading. For the winter of 1887-88, Nagle and Hislop determined to become partners and explore the country that Pruden and the other free traders were working.

Early in April, Ed returned to Edmonton to trade his furs and organize a trading outfit for himself and his new partner. By April ninth he was already on his way back to The Landing, where he spent the balance of his summer. The memory of his accident had probably soured him on his old profession, because there is no record of his working as a millwright. Perhaps he joined one of the Hudson's Bay Company's construction or boat-building crews to raise any extra money he needed.

There were no detailed maps of the north country, and the only options for exploring it lay either in floating off alone or finding suitable guides. Ed and Hislop chose the latter course. They did not intend to winter in the far north but, although they only planned a brief examination of the Fort Chipewyan area, they delayed their departure until extraordinarily late in the season. When Colin Fraser, George Elmore, and J. Favel left The Landing for Fort Chipewyan in September, the new partners joined them.

For some distance below Athabasca Landing the Athabasca River rolled placidly along, but at Grand Rapids it went wild. The west-side channel at Grand Rapids Island appeared to have the most water and fewest boulders, but Fraser guided the boats over to the east bank. While Ed and Hislop portaged some supplies unloaded to lighten their scow, Fraser's pilot ran it down the east-side channel for them.

Two white-faced petroglyphs leered down from the sandstone cliff at the bottom of the rapid where they reloaded their scow. Below Grand

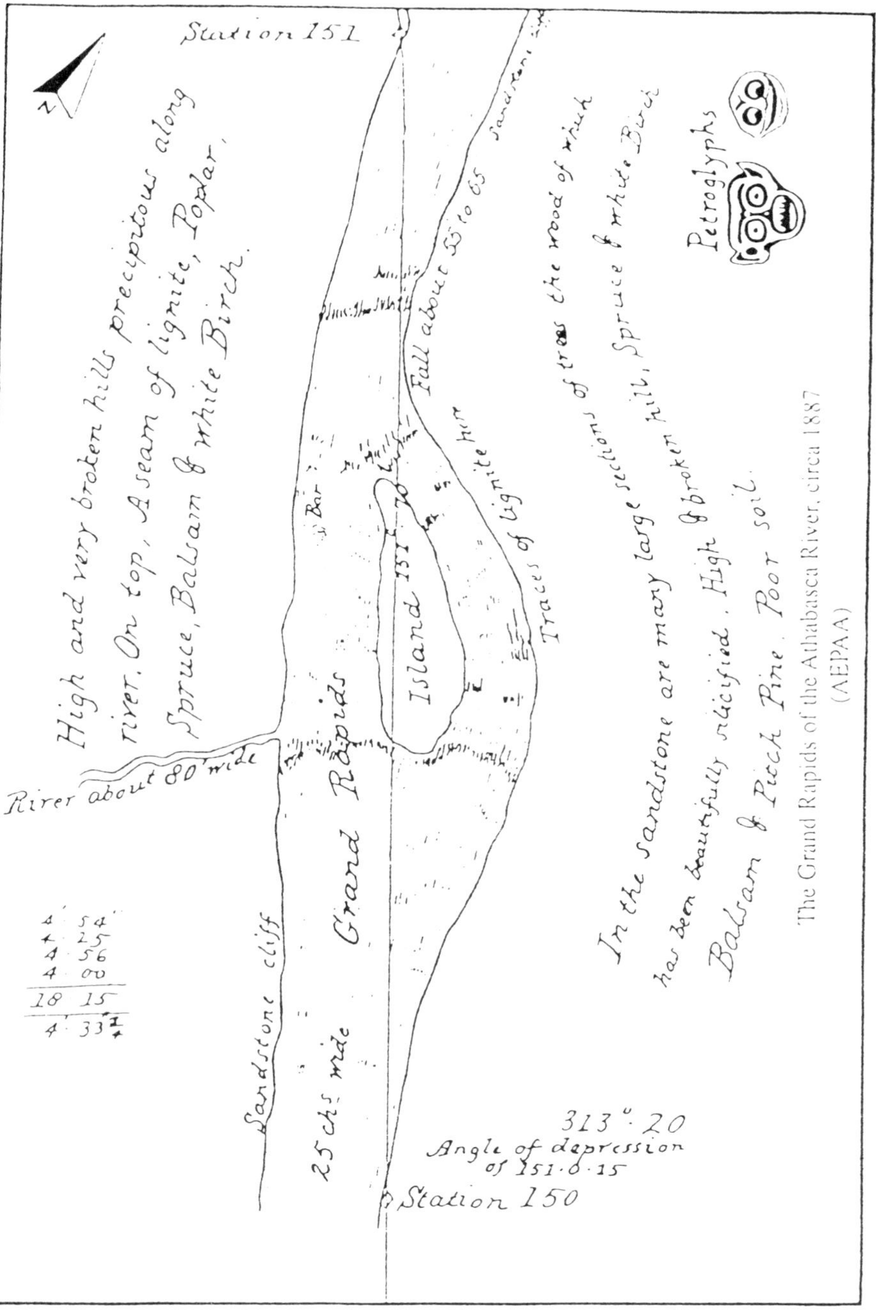

Station 151

N

High and very broken hills precipitous along river. On top. A seam of lignite, Poplar. Spruce, Balsam & white Birch.

River about 80' wide

Fall about 55 to 65

Sandstone

S. Bar

Island 151 to

Grand Rapids

Traces of lignite here

Petroglyphs

In the sandstone are many large sections of trees the wood of which has been beautifully silicified. High & broken hills, Spruce & white Birch

Balsam & Pitch Pine. Poor soil.

The Grand Rapids of the Athabasca River, circa 1887
(AEPAA)

Sandstone cliff

25 chs wide

```
4  54
4  25
4  56
4  00
18  15
4  33 1/4
```

313° 20
Angle of depression
of 151·0·15

Station 150

95

Rapids the river grew narrower and more dangerous. Fraser had no difficulty with the Boiler Rapid, where the Hudson's Bay Company had lost some iron boilers intended for one of its northern steamboats, but at the Big Cascade, Nagle and Hislop were again forced to portage. They could not relax until the riverbanks receded and the Athabasca grew quieter near Fort McMurray.

Without Fraser's help Ed and his partner would have missed the Ambarra River, a small west-side channel branching off the Athabasca a few miles above Lake Athabasca. It cut 15 kilometres from their trip through the Athabasca Delta, and brought them out at a safer place to cross the lake to Fort Chipewyan.

Although its actual location had occasionally shifted since its founding in 1789, Fort Chipewyan had remained at the western end of Lake Athabasca. It was one of the oldest and most important posts in the western north, and it marked the threshold that Alexander Mackenzie had crossed on his way to the Arctic Ocean. Before the Hudson's Bay Company had built Fort Simpson, near the confluence of the Liard and Mackenzie rivers, Chipewyan had been the central supply depot for its entire northwestern trading network.

During the lake crossing Ed could observe Chipewyan's layout. On the north shore of the lake, a small knot of whitewashed buildings crowned the eastern horn of a small bay. The Union Jack and a Hudson's Bay Company flag snapped above a post compound. Behind its low palisade sat the Hudson's Bay Company buildings, with its servants' homes and the Catholic Church buildings crouching outside the walls. Just east of the Company quadrangle stood a small whitewashed tower, built to observe the shoreline to the east. More than a quarter-century earlier, a local Indian medicine man had prophesied that destroying the HBC post would bring other traders bearing more and better goods.

To avoid winter freeze-up, Ed and Hislop should have turned southward soon after they reached Chipewyan. But Colin Fraser was building himself a new trading post, and the partners felt obliged to him for the assistance he had provided during the down-river trip. During the work, Hislop sliced his foot so badly with an axe that it took three weeks to heal. By the time he could move freely again, the ice had set on Lake Athabasca.

The partners made the best use they could of their enforced layover at Chipewyan. They had realized they could not enter the fur trade at Lake Athabasca: they had neither the experience nor the resources to compete against the Hudson's Bay Company, Fraser, the Elmore

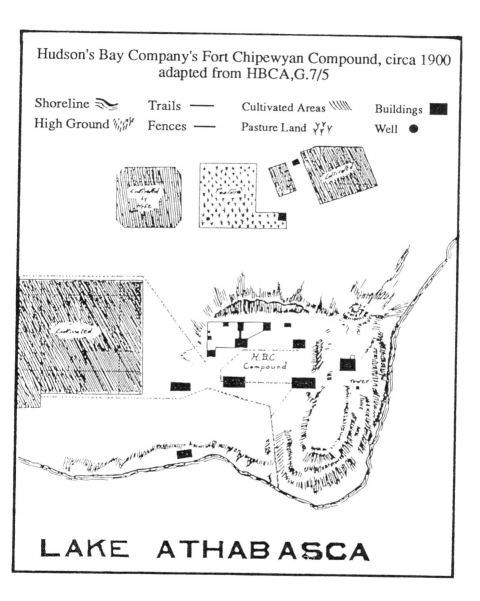

brothers, Peter Pruden, or Shot. But they could begin formulating useful strategies and learning the rules of the game.

The first and most important lesson they learned was that there were two real powers in the north: the Hudson's Bay Company and the Roman Catholic Church. Many of the Indian and Métis trappers were Catholic, and the priests influenced them in various ways. In order to offset the Hudson's Bay Company's economic clout, a successful free trading company would have to gain the priests' support and exploit their influence.

By the time Hislop's foot was healed, he and Ed had built toboggans. The snow was piled in deep drifts on the lake ice, but they relayed their outfit as far as an abandoned HBC post at Fort McKay. About the tenth of December they fitted a fireplace into a new cabin, then settled down to learn the practical business of trading. Unfortunately, the reason that the Hudson's Bay Company had abandoned the post soon became plain. The Strongwoods Cree, who had once traded there, had gradually trapped out the surrounding area and drifted to other trapping grounds. Although the partners managed to trap about $700.00 worth of fur, they did not have much opportunity to trade.

With the onset of spring Ed and Jim faced a calamity: they had placed their cabin high enough above the riverbank that the spring breakup would not sweep it away, but had not reckoned on any flooding. When the spring ice packed and jammed, the river behind it backed up and overflowed. Fortunately, during the winter they had built themselves a canoe. They quickly threw their outfit and themselves into it, and floated safely until they could build a raft large enough to live on. When Colin Fraser passed by Fort McKay on his way upriver to The Landing, Nagle and Hislop had been afloat on the flood for ten days. In return for upstream transport for their outfit, they took places on Fraser's tracking line.

Although "tracking" — dragging boats upriver — is often mentioned by northern travellers, few detail the excruciating drudgery it forced upon the men on the line. Fourteen years after Ed and Jim enjoyed their first unenviable encounter with spring breakup on the Athabasca, an author and poet named Charles Mair recorded this vivid account of a tracker's experience:

> Nothing indeed can be imagined more arduous than this tracking up a swift river against constant head-winds in bad weather. Much of it is in the water, wading up 'snies,' or tortuous shallow channels, plunging into numberless creeks, clambering up slimy banks,

Tracking on the Athabasca River.

creeping under or passing the line over fallen trees, wading out in
the stream to round long spits of sand or boulders, floundering in
gumbo slides, tripping, crawling, plunging, and, finally, tottering
to the camping-place sweating like horses, and mud to the eyes ...

As graphic as his description is, Mair neglects to mention the ice
that floats down the Athabasca throughout its spring flood.

When Ed and Hislop arrived back at Athabasca Landing on July 29,
it was a changed place. The frame and superstructure of a large
steamboat had risen up near the Hudson's Bay Company's new
buildings. The Company already had the SS *Graham* working between
Fort McMurray and the Slave River. When she was finished, the SS
Athabasca would run between Grand Rapids Island and Athabasca
Landing, with stops as far up the Athabasca as the Lesser Slave River.
But the Hudson's Bay Company's new ship was only the most visible
change at The Landing. The partners soon found their way to the
community's newest, and only, trading establishment to be run by a
free fur trader.

Early in 1887, Dick Secord had lost his teaching job. For a time he
had worked with John McDougall in a new store at Edmonton, and
McDougall had recognized his talent for business. Both Secord and
McDougall had known that the Hudson's Bay Company was rerouting
all its northern traffic through Athabasca Landing. They also knew that
the free traders intended to contest the Company in the north. McDougall
had sent Secord to Pakan to learn fur trading, then they had put together
a large and varied trading outfit and moved Secord to The Landing.

Secord had been there since early June of 1888, and his business was booming. In addition to furs, he was collaring most of the cash wages paid to the HBC rivermen and construction workers. Over the years he had come to know many of these men. He knew how powerfully they thirsted. Without breaking any laws he was helping them avoid a trip to Edmonton. He wasn't selling the liquor he kept behind the counter of his new store, but if his friends would trade with him, he gladly shared a drink with them.

After Secord graded and bought their furs, Ed and Jim dissolved their partnership. Hislop wanted to stay in Secord's neighborhood, but Ed did not intend to let his winter's effort trickle away. He had not given up the idea of fur trading. In order to raise himself another grubstake he worked on the new HBC steamer, then became the chief sawyer at Moore and McDowall's sawmill until it closed for the winter of 1888.

When Ed returned to Edmonton, he was in search of a new partner. As usual, the saloons buzzed with various kinds of news: Edmonton had a new Board of Trade; the HBC had finished the SS *Athabasca* and sent her as far north as the Grand Rapids before putting her into winter moorage at The Landing; the beaver north of The Landing were dying from a strange disease; and the geologist who had established that Edmonton was 2,253 feet above sea level had contracted typhoid fever.

These were, however, the more mundane topics of conversation. Most people were also snickering over a recent showdown between the NWMP and Big Nelly Webb. Nelly was well known among the habitués of Edmonton's watering holes: she ran a small brothel, usually a quiet retreat for lonely men. On October 24, three NWMP constables had stopped in Edmonton on their way to Calgary. After a few drinks they had decided to seek out Nelly. In light of the lack of discretion they showed during their subsequent bumbling Odyssey, she had earned most folks' sympathy.

During their search, the policemen had shouldered their way into three respectable homes. Nelly had known they were coming long before they arrived at her doorstep, and in the hope they would pass her by, she had locked her door, but they were nothing if not determined. When they realized she had barred her door to them, they had tried to break it down. As the first splinters shivered off it, Big Nelly had fired a shot at her attackers.

After two of the suddenly sobered constables had arrested her, they helped their bleeding comrade away. But before they left, they had assigned two of Edmonton's policemen to guard Nelly's place. To add insult to NWMP injury, the guards had drunk so much of her booze that they had passed out, and some curious wayfarer had relieved them of their handguns.

Frank Oliver was righteous in his indignation. The *Bulletin* had demanded an explanation for the disgraceful conduct of the "set of men who are supposed to protect the citizens and their property...." But Edmontonians were not without a sense of humour.

Ed spent most of the fall and early winter of 1888-89 searching for a compatible trading partner. By February his efforts had come to Frank Oliver's attention. Ever since the railway had gone south, Oliver had been reassessing Edmonton's potential, so when Ed received a single lot of fifteen letters from Quebec, many of which asked for information about the area, Oliver could not resist a public comment. Always alert for a wagon from which to trumpet Edmonton's virtues, he began a long-running *Bulletin* column devoted exclusively to local immigration.

That winter, the mysterious death of a friend emphasized to Ed his need for a partner. James Haney, who like Ed was of Irish descent and had also grown up in Quebec, had moved west about the same time as Ed, heading for the Black Hills instead of Winnipeg. He had prospected and mined near Edmonton since 1881 and, just before the Northwest Rebellion, had passed Ed some silver samples to send to Winnipeg. During the first week in February, someone discovered him dead in his bunk at the Goose Encampment. Although no one knew how Haney had died, there were countless ways lone men perished in the wilderness.

Towards spring Ed and a fellow named Aubrey teamed up. They made a short trip up the North Saskatchewan River in April, reporting to Frank Oliver that forest fires had stripped the hillsides and the Indians were slaughtering the beaver. Ed was still interested in the far north and was following Oliver's *Bulletin* reports on the free traders. He knew that Matt McCauley had improved the Athabasca Landing Trail for the Hudson's Bay Company, and constructed a new 700-metre tramway at Grand Rapids Island. He had visited Dick Secord's new fur warehouse. More free traders were bringing more fur south from Lake Athabasca, but when Ed and Aubrey left Edmonton in November they were headed towards Fort Assiniboine, not Fort Chipewyan.

Notes scattered throughout Ed's 1889-1890 journals indicate he was developing the opportunistic attitudes essential to successful bushcraft. Whenever the weather was good he travelled, holing up when it turned bad. He never bypassed food, even if it was just an otter-killed jackfish. If the season was changing and he had reached a suitable place, he camped to make the snowshoes or boat he would soon need. Perhaps most importantly, he was expanding his knowledge of the country by speaking with other hunters whenever and wherever he met them.

The winter of 1889-90 was hard. By the end of it, Indians in the area where Ed and Aubrey were trapping had starved. As the partners moved along the Pembina River they encountered harsh evidence of the wilderness' effects on the spiritually unsound. Poling upstream in May of 1890, they passed the site of a tragedy that worked morbidly on Ed.

A few years earlier a fellow named McMullin and his partner had tried to winter on the east bank of the Pembina. Although McMullin was the more experienced of the two, when game got scarce he was the one who snapped. He drove his partner out of their cabin into a small dugout. But even total control of the cabin had not satisfied him. Eventually, in an effort to prevent him from consuming their dwindling supplies, McMullin had murdered his partner. Only the flickering residues of his humanity had kept him from cannibalizing the body.

Haney's death had shaken Ed, and the situation in which McMullan had found himself happened with such regularity that Ed pondered the lunatic's solution to it. It was probably shortly after he passed the tragic camp that he jotted this comment in the back of his journal:

Point of View
  What a thing it is to be cheerful, & to have cheerful people about
  one. Life, except during the pressures of its terrible calamities,
  always has a bright side, & those who look at that side are far the
  wisest.

Ed returned to Edmonton in early July. He had mastered the techniques of trapping with both steel leg-hold traps and the more traditional deadfalls. He had traded with every Indian hunter he had found on the trapping grounds and had gathered together another decent lot of fur, but all his effort was not making him wealthy. His outfit for the season had cost him about $205, and his furs returned him only between $220 and $300. Furthermore, his partnership with Aubrey had broken down.

Late in the fall of 1889, Ed had learned that a railroad spur was finally in place near his old Dauphin Lake homestead. The endless setbacks of the previous years had quickened his reflexes. In the hope that his previous efforts might finally bring him some returns, he hired a lawyer and wrote depositions and statements to regain control of his land. Although his appeals to the government would continue until 1895, they ultimately proved unsuccessful.

Ed was ready to try trading from a large outfit again, but he needed both a grubstake and a partner. By hiring him to run their portable sawmill at Athabasca Landing the Hudson's Bay Company assisted him with his grubstake. He left for The Landing in September with knowledge that must have heightened the allure of the far north. CPR president William Van Horne had promised a railway for Edmonton, which would bring down the prices of trade goods in the settlement. The government had sent R.G. McConnell to explore the geology of the Athabasca River tar deposits near Fort McMurray, which suggested that there might be more than fur down there. Furthermore, during the previous summer HBC work parties had improved the river route as far north as Smith's Rapids, where easy access to the Mackenzie was blocked.

Athabasca Landing was still in transition. Dick Secord had sold his post to the Hudson's Bay Company in May, but Hislop had opened a small post to fill that niche. According to the *Bulletin*, he was doing well and two new independents had successfully wintered on the Athabasca. Ed worked at The Landing until the end of October, and on his return to Edmonton a chance meeting brought him the partner he was seeking.

Dick Secord had gone east during the summer to visit his family and had returned to Edmonton in mid-October accompanied by his brother Jack. Ed had never developed the close friendship with Dick Secord that Hislop had, but he and Jack Secord became fast friends almost from the first moment they met. In early winter of 1890, they headed off trapping together.

Although Ed was much the elder, his partnership with Jack Secord was immediately successful. The younger man was a genial, self-sufficient companion prepared to work hard to learn the skills he needed. Ed kept him close to Athabasca Landing while he learned the arts of trapping and trading. By spring they considered their initial experiment a success, and Ed started work as millwright at Kelly's mill intent on raising his share of their grubstake for the coming year.

On his way to Kelly's mill he stopped to visit Jim Hislop, who gave him a small lot of fur to carry south to Dick Secord. It was through Jack's brother that the new partners would pull their trading outfit together. After selling his post at The Landing, Dick Secord had gone back into partnership with McDougall and was acting as an independent fur buyer in Edmonton. By working closely with Hislop, he had kept a hand in at The Landing. With access to McDougall's wholesale outlets, he was already outfitting Hislop's operation.

At this time Hislop was beginning to grapple with a problem that would soon alter his life, and eventually kill him. Although he had always been an unbridled social drinker, he was now drinking to kill the boredom of life at his trading post. And the liquor was beginning to overwhelm his normal wit and intelligence.

After passing Hislop's fur to Secord and selling a lot of his own, Ed stayed at Kelly's mill until the end of June. Then he returned briefly to Edmonton to talk to his partner. Dick Secord took enormous interest in the trip his brother and Ed were organizing. He arranged to have Hislop build them a scow at The Landing· then he put together an outfit approximating what the Hudson's Bay Company sent north to its posts. And when it became clear that they could not afford to pay outright for everything they needed, he financed more than $2,100.00 for them, over nine months at 2% interest per month.

Having gone into debt for the first time in his life, Ed threw himself wholeheartedly into making his new venture a success. The outfit was so large that it required three wagons to move it. Jack Secord left for The Landing with John Longmore and the first load of goods on August 24; Ed followed the next day with the two other wagons. By the time he reached The Landing, Hislop had a sturgeon-nose scow ready for the downriver trip.

CHAPTER 9

In This Corner

Ed was moving into a northern situation that had not changed appreciably since his winter with Hislop at Fort McKay. The free traders who had nipped at the Hudson's Bay Company's mammoth heels in 1887 were not yet serious challengers to its dominance. Peter Pruden still ranged along the Athabasca and Lac La Biche Rivers. Colin Fraser and Shot still worried Fort Chipewyan. George Elmore still roamed Lake Athabasca and the upper reaches of the Slave River. But they were not coordinating their efforts, and aside from a brief strike at Fort Rae in 1888, no one had penetrated into the region north of Smith's Rapids.

Smith's Rapids block the Slave River approximately 140 kilometres north of Fort Chipewyan, effectively halting navigation northwards to the Arctic Ocean. It was toward the unassailed posts below the rapids that Ed would make his way. It would be there that he became a true player in the northern fur trade. To understand the situations he was about to encounter, one must have some notion of both the the way the Hudson's Bay Company conducted its trade in that region, and the system of relationships developing between white culture and the Indian groups there.

In 1891, the area north of the rapids was still in what anthropologists have called the "Contact-traditional phase." That is to say, in spite of their long interaction with fur traders, the various Indian cultures and populations were still "reacting, adapting, borrowing, and innovating in the face of exposure to elements of European culture."

Although Catholic and Anglican missionaries had been in the area long enough for many natives to be nominally Christian, most priests lived at the trading posts and the Indians were not yet settled in permanent communities. They still maintained their traditional nomadic life style: moving among various bush settings to hunt and fish, and trapping only enough fur to trade for the few non-native items they considered essential.

Half breeds who lived at the posts were mostly Hudson's Bay Company servants. Native groups — families, bands, or regional bands — visited the posts (a process ethnohistorians have called "in-gathering") only to trade, celebrate certain Christian festivals, or, occasionally, when faced with absolute destitution or starvation. Otherwise they stayed in the bush. They had retained their bush-survival skills and technologies, and were perfectly capable of doing without trade goods if they had to. Although they had grown accustomed to having tobacco, tea, metal tools and cooking pots, some manufactured cloth and decorative items, rifles and ammunition, they were not consuming much European-style food, and did not rely on the Hudson's Bay Company for any life-sustaining staples.

Some regional bands, like the Slavey Indians living between Forts Resolution and Simpson, had managed to remain almost totally uninvolved with the fur trade until as late as 1870. They obtained the few metal tools they wanted in the form of gratuities when they visited the posts, and felt absolutely no compulsion to trap furs.

Until 1870, the Hudson's Bay Company was content with its relationships with native trappers in the western subarctic. Changing things would have meant incurring more expenses than were necessary for maintaining its posts, without necessarily guaranteeing larger fur returns. So individual post officers were held accountable for their profits and losses, but left to pursue their own ways of motivating trappers.

However, after the Company transferred its territories to the Dominion of Canada, a serious decline in fur returns from its more easterly trading districts had turned its concentration westward. About 1870, it began instituting and promoting something called the credit-outfit system. Trappers who could be persuaded to trap throughout the winter were encouraged to outfit themselves on credit.

As they attempted to draw trappers away from their traditional bush-oriented lifestyles, HBC policymakers were clever enough not to fix hard and fast times at which the debts had to be repaid. Post managers, however, did make it clear to the trappers that the credit outfits were not gifts. The Company minimized its intrusion into native life by continuing to rely on religious festivals and the traditional transitions from winter to summer hunting and fishing camps to bring trappers back to the posts.

To predispose trappers toward accepting the new system, the HBC had been gradually cutting back on the gratuities offered to natives visiting its posts. By the 1890s, when metal tools and cooking gear, ammunition, tea, and tobacco had become elements in the native life style, the Company had stopped giving the clothing, rifles, and tools that natives had received during the early 19th century. And the amounts of tea, tobacco, and food presented for celebratory feasts to newly arrived trappers had been drastically reduced.

The major flaws inherent in the credit-outfit strategy would not be noticed until free traders began testing it. To a certain extent the Company was innovating at the trappers' expense. The gratuities had partially compensated trappers for the effort they expended in bringing their furs from the trapping grounds. Without emphasizing with gifts its good faith in and satisfaction with its trappers, the HBC risked a certain amount of unpaid credit, or, as the traders called it, "bad debt."

It is true that bad debt arose from various causes. A sudden die-off of fur-bearing animals sometimes left trappers unable to pay back the advances they had received. Or a group that relied on a particular game animal for its survival, like the Caribou-Eater Chipewyans trading at Fort Smith, might be forced by a scarcity of game to spend more time hunting than trapping. But it is also true that by cutting back on the rewards for visiting its posts, the Company was weakening its hold on native loyalty.

As their gratuities were cut back, trappers started changing a few rules of their own. Some tried getting outfits at posts where generous credit was offered, then travelling to others that paid better prices to trade their furs. Northern distances were formidable, however, and most traders recognized the men who had taken credit with them, and were suspicious of well-outfitted trappers who arrived with unusually large "lots" of fur to trade.

Despite its flaws, by the 1880s the credit-outfit system was not only increasing the Company's fur returns, it was also drawing the peripheral Indian groups into the fur-trade mainstream. In order to support a full transition to the new system, the HBC had turned its attention to improving other aspects of its operation in the western north.

Aside from the actual costs of its trade outfits, the largest expense the HBC faced related to its transportation network. While the trade outfits remained relatively small, the Company had used the Methy Portage route that traders had pioneered during the late 1700s. But the portage topography was too rough for wagons, so the goods and furs had to be carried by men. As the size of its northern outfits increased, along with the number and bulk of the returning fur bales, the HBC found the 20-kilometre Methy Portage a major obstacle.

Prior to intensifying its work in the western subarctic, the Company had been extending a system of steamboats westward from Winnipeg along the North Saskatchewan River. (The small tramline constructed to bypass the Grand Rapids of the Saskatchewan was the prototype for the one Matt McCauley installed at the Grand Rapids of the Athabasca in 1889.) Since the steamboats were already in place, the Company decided to shift its whole supply operation farther west; instead of providing outfits from Winnipeg, it made Edmonton its western staging centre. In 1891, when Edmonton finally got its railroad line, the steamboats would be abandoned.

By 1876 the Company had already cleared the Athabasca Trail to bypass the Methy Portage. In a rush of construction during subsequent years it improved its facilities at The Landing and put the SS *Athabasca* on the Athabasca River. Then Matt McCauley placed the tramway at Grand Rapids, and the SS *Graham* began freighting outfits between the bottom of the Athabasca rapids and the head of Smith's Rapids on the Great Slave River. The Smith's Rapids portage road was completed in 1889-90 and became known as Smith Portage, and the Company soon had the SS *Wrigley* steaming between Fort Smith and the Beaufort Sea.

Thus, in less than ten years the Hudson's Bay Company completely revamped its transportation network and fostered regular boat-building crews at The Landing to manufacture the freight scows it required each year. After streamlining its staff of warehousemen, longshoremen, boatmen, steam-engineers, and river pilots, the new system began functioning smoothly.

But there remained some glaring weaknesses in the way the HBC implemented its credit-outfit strategy. Although the revamped transportation network was fully operational by about 1891, it only functioned during open water. From the time the ice set in the fall until break-up in the spring, no furs or goods moved between the posts. Post factors could exchange mail by means of a dog team-drawn packet that the Company had instituted in the early 1800s, but during the winters they were largely isolated from one another.

Jack Secord and Ed Nagle with their dogs.

Dog teams had begun coming into general use in the western subarctic about 1870, at approximately the same time that the credit-outfit system was devised. Initially, the increasing availability of dogs had had only limited impact on the native groups. Many of them were traditionally nomadic. Some cultures, like the Dogrib Indians who commonly traded at Fort Rae on the north arm of Great Slave Lake, even accorded social prestige to their best travellers. Dog teams helped them increase their winter mobility, but did not affect the times at which they returned to trade at the posts.

Trappers who accepted the credit-outfit system were the ones most influenced by the dog teams. They began setting off each fall with larger outfits, and cut down their travel time to and from the trapping grounds. However, although they were spending more time actually trapping, and caught more fur, even they did not return more frequently to the posts.

Dogs did not change the seasonal round of life for traders at the HBC posts, either. Possibly because it had come to consider them safe in their isolation, the Hudson's Bay Company Head Office treated its posts as if they were autonomous. Therein lay another weakness which Ed Nagle would soon learn to exploit. Although the HBC traders could have extended their own winter mobility, they chose to continue isolating themselves during the winter.

Because of the way equipment and supplies for the posts were shipped north, the HBC further isolated its traders from one another. Each post's outfit was placed in its own freight scow when it arrived at Athabasca Landing. If the scow was damaged or destroyed during the downriver trip, the outfit was neither replenished nor replaced from outfits going to other posts. Rather, the trader whose outfit had been reduced was expected to make do with the trading stock he had on hand.

But even if the HBC traders had wanted to help one another, exchanging goods between posts was not a simple matter. Every trader and post factor was expected to know the needs and preferences of the Indian groups resident in his area. He ordered his trading outfit from a generalized list of goods which was sometimes supplemented with specially requested items. The Head Office provided a price, or "tariff," for each article, which was marked up for each post to include the cost of its transportation. The marked-up, or "cost landed tariff" varied according to a post's distance from Winnipeg.

Although the Head Office kept tight control of the general trading standards, execution of the fur exchange varied at each post. The Company suggested general buying tariffs, but as a particular succession of traders exercised their bargaining skills each post evolved a distinctive relationship to the general standards. Traders had maximized their profit by keeping down the amount of goods they gave in exchange for furs, and had gradually fixed the upper limit paid at their post for each kind of fur. Since they had faced no competition, the traders north of Smith's Rapids had managed to keep their buying tariffs fairly low.

There were a few checks on how far traders could depress the buying tariffs. Even with the credit-outfit system in place, trappers were not dependent on the HBC. If they did not like the exchange they got, they sometimes decided not to bother trading. Moreover, they kept one another informed as to the tariffs paid at the various posts in their immediate area — which often meant within a radius of 250 kilometres from their home territory. If one post paid appreciably higher tariffs, they would sometimes travel considerable distances to sell their furs there.

By 1891, however, the Hudson's Bay Company traders had succeeded in artificially depressing the fur prices north of Smith's Rapids. Since the credit-outfit system was bringing them larger fur harvests, and news was drifting downriver from Chipewyan of the higher prices paid for furs farther south, trappers north of the rapids were becoming generally dissatisfied.

CHAPTER 10

Through Smith's Rapids
(1891-1893)

Throughout the ride to The Landing, the last warm days of August seemed to Ed as if they might stretch deep into a glorious September. After winding down a forest-clad draw, he pulled up at Hislop's trading post. The Athabasca River flowed placidly onwards about fifty metres due north of him. South of the post, surrounded by a pole fence, vegetables ripened in a small garden plot. The government and Hudson's Bay Company had scattered their buildings to the northeast.

After unloading the outfit, the freighters turned back towards Edmonton, where Dick Secord waited to pay them. Hislop had also agreed to accept payment from Secord. He had built a sturgeon-head scow for Ed and Jack, the most serviceable of the three kinds of boats normally built at The Landing. Flatboats were cheaper, but more difficult to haul out of the water at portages; and deep-hulled Yorkboats, although seaworthy on the great northern lakes, presented real problems in the summer-depleted rivers. Sturgeon-heads combined the wide shallow draft of a flatboat with a Yorkboat's rising bow and stern, making them ideal river craft.

The new partners did not hire any rivermen to accompany them down the Athabasca, relying instead on Ed's previous experience. They would have had difficulty finding the men they needed in any case: the last riotous assemblies of Hudson's Bay Company boatmen were already gone from The Landing. Although Ed and Jack had told Frank Oliver they intended to winter at Great Slave Lake, it is unlikely that they really believed they would get that far. By the time they were loaded and ready to drift off it was simply too late in the season.

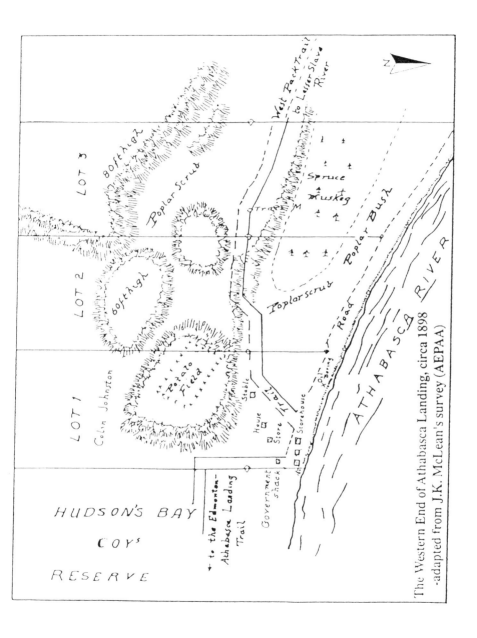

The Western End of Athabasca Landing, circa 1898 -adapted from J.K. McLean's survey (AEPAA)

Hislop and Nagle loading scows at Athabasca Landing, Jim Hislop center, leaning on box; Ed Nagle to his immediate left.

Ed knew the formidable task that lay before them. Two tons of supplies — done up in 90-pound "pieces" for carrying — were piled on the rough wooden slats lying across the bottom of their boat. The sturgeon-head's green, new-milled lumber would bounce them safely off the rocks as far as Grand Rapids. But there most of the outfit would have to be portaged.

The Athabasca flowed from west to east past The Landing, swinging northward about a kilometre east of the townsite. For approximately 265 kilometres the partners expected to drift smoothly along, guiding themselves with the long sweep oar pinned to their stern. Unfortunately, a few days after they started north the weather changed. High winds and rain repeatedly drove them off the river, and when they finally reached Grand Rapids Island, the Hudson's Bay Company refused to let them use its new tramline. From Grand Rapids Ed managed to send a letter to Dick Secord, in which he outlined the situation.

At Chipewyan, only a few of the 1887 free traders were still trading. Peter Pruden had moved south, away from Lake Athabasca, and neither Colin Fraser nor Shot were still focused on trading. In fact, Shot was devoting himself almost exclusively to river transportation — he would soon become one of the north's most famous river pilots — and

Hislop and Nagle's outfit leaving Athabasca Landing.

Fraser, too, was turning in that direction. George Elmore was the only successful one: The Hudson's Bay Company now occasionally borrowed equipment from him.

If anyone helped Ed and Jack set themselves up at Chipewyan it was probably Fraser, just as he had helped Ed and Hislop in 1887. At first, the Hudson's Bay Company took almost no notice of them. Until at least early 1892, Ed could send and receive his mail via HBC transport. As the Company was vulnerable at Chipewyan because most of its stock was already out as credit outfits, Ed's initial approach to trading was straightforward. He knew current market values for all the fur-bearing animals, and he took a dog team and shuttled small loads of trade goods between the trappers' camps. Whenever he encountered other itinerant traders, also known as trippers, he simply dared them to try outbidding him for the furs he wanted.

Jack stayed behind at Chip to waylay the trappers Ed missed. It did not take the partners long to recognize the trappers' dissatisfaction with the Hudson's Bay Company. At Christmas, many men returned to Chipewyan with just enough fur to repay their HBC debt. By that time, many of their best skins had already fallen into the hands of Nagle and Secord. In spite of his quick successes, however, Ed did not intend to merely prowl the edges of the HBC network. He was planning to outflank the Company and take control of the musk ox trade. Ever since the early 1870s, HBC traders had been receiving a few musk ox robes at the northern posts. More recently, the almost mythical beast had

At the bottom of Grand Rapids tramway, Athabasca River.

come to the attention of southerners. About the time that Ed and Jack began seriously committing themselves to the far north, Warburton Pike had appeared in Edmonton after having spent two full years near Great Slave Lake. Pike was one of the earliest of the many adventurous sportsmen who would search the Barren Lands for musk oxen. The specimens he showed and the stories he told the *Bulletin* stirred many imaginations.

Shortly after Pike had reached Great Slave Lake in 1889, the number of robes reaching Forts Rae and Resolution began to increase. By the time he came out to Edmonton, southerners already recognized the musk ox robes' extraordinary insulating qualities. They were the first successful substitute for buffalo robes, which had once kept winter travellers warm.

Sometime during the winter of 1891-92, perhaps on a scouting trip through Smith's Rapids, Ed acquired his first musk ox robe. That may also have been when he first learned about a secret northern practice. Native musk ox hunters had found a solution to one of the greatest problems northerners faced. To keep their feet warm, they were wrapping them in unborn pelts from the wombs of adult females they shot. They had discovered that these "unborn musk-ox pelts" possessed the same insulating qualities as the adults' robes, but without their bulk. North of Smith's Rapids, there was an active trade in unborn musk-ox pelts.

116

By the end of the first week in June, the partners were almost out of trading stock. So, while Jack stayed at Chipewyan, Ed hired some rivermen and tracked the fur-filled sturgeon-head upstream. On July 14, five weeks after he left Lake Athabasca, the *Bulletin* reported that he had arrived safely at Edmonton. Regarding the previous winter, he commented that despite severe weather no Indians had starved at Chipewyan; La Grippé had, however, decimated many of the more southerly posts. He also showed Oliver some globs of tar he had plucked from the banks of the Athabasca.

Colin Fraser (left) and companions.

Shortly after Jack and Ed had left Edmonton in August of 1891, Dick Secord attempted to have Colin Fraser organize a trip north for the spring of 1892. Secord had had over a third of his total assets invested in the outfit the partners had taken north, and he was experiencing tremors of unease. It is not clear whether or not he was planning to finance more free traders in the far north before Ed returned from Lake Athabasca, but he was certainly aware of the enormous risks such investment would entail.

Although his trip with Fraser came to naught, Dick had spoken with Jim Hislop during the winter. Hislop was now drinking even more heavily. Since he knew that, north of The Landing, alcohol was carefully controlled by the NWMP, Hislop agreed to go in Fraser's stead. He had two motives for returning north: to assist his friend Dick Secord and to dry himself out. When Ed reached Edmonton, Secord and Hislop were already preparing to move north. The fur Ed had with him spurred Secord to invest in more outfits.

While Ed helped grade the furs and choose three new trading outfits, he also began promoting the north country. His efforts to raffle off his musk ox robe through the *Bulletin* engaged Frank Oliver's interest. Ed started north before the raffle could come off, but Oliver's readers learned that Nagle had his sights set on Fort Good Hope, only a few miles south of the Arctic Circle.

For the winter of 1892-93, Dick Secord was not content to send his investments off unsupervised. Shortly after Ed headed north with his outfit, Secord and Hislop followed him with the other two. Shot was at The Landing when they arrived, preparing to take an oufit to Fort Smith for S.D. Mulkins. Mulkins had reached Lake Athabasca shortly after Ed had left there, and had travelled on with Colin Fraser towards Fort Smith and Fort Resolution. Shot's assistance would have been invaluable, and Nagle, Secord and Hislop probably joined forces with him for the trip to Chipewyan.

When they conferred together at Chipewyan, Ed, the Secords, Hislop and a recently retired Hudson's Bay Company trader named George Martin recognized that Mulkins must have caught the traders below Smith's Rapids at a tremendous disadvantage. He had beat the new HBC outfits down river, and had no intention of taking anything but fur back upstream. By paying high prices and catching the HBC traders unprepared, he hoped to skim off the best spring furs. The outfit Shot was taking him would last Mulkins through the winter; Shot would take the furs back to the buyers in Edmonton.

It was a clever strategy, and the free traders at Chipewyan considered it while charting out their plans for the winter of 1892-93. When their meeting was finished, Dick Secord had committed himself to returning in the spring with new outfits for the others. Jack Secord was moving to Fond Du Lac, at the east end of Lake Athabasca. Hislop remained at Fort Chipewyan, and with the last outfit, Martin and Ed were following Shot down the Slave River.

Ed and Martin probably left Chipewyan in mid-September. Since they believed that Mulkins would winter at Fort Resolution, they were not headed there. Martin intended to set up a post 67 kilometres east of Resolution, near where Cuthbert Grant had established the first trading post on Great Slave Lake. There Martin could compete for musk ox robes. After he helped Martin to get through Smith Rapids and establish himself at Slave Lake, Ed intended to carry on toward Fort Good Hope.

From the western end of Lake Athabasca, the two free traders slipped among forested islands and onto the Slave River. Drifting northward, they passed the Slave's confluence with the Peace. Approximately 8 kilometres below the Peace River's inflow, they reached the Demi Charge rapid which they passed by hugging the right bank of

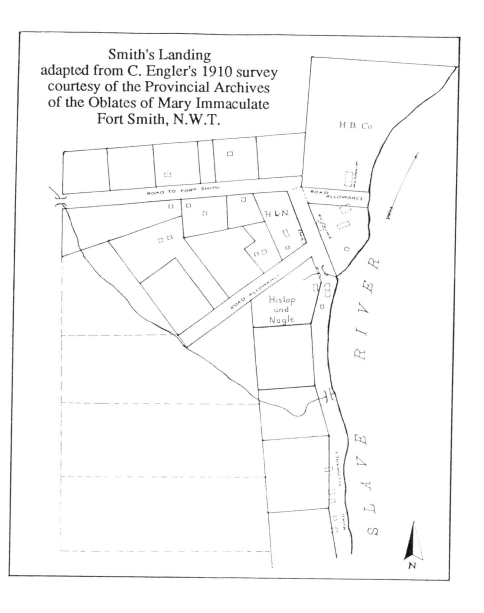

Smith's Landing
adapted from C. Engler's 1910 survey
courtesy of the Provincial Archives
of the Oblates of Mary Immaculate
Fort Smith, N.W.T.

Smith's Landing, Slave River, looking south from above the HBC warehouse.

the Slave. Below the Demi Charge they had smooth sailing as far as the head of Smith's Rapids.

When Ed first saw it, there was nothing much at Smith's Landing: the Hudson's Bay Company had only recently chopped the place out of the woods. A few log shacks littered a small clearing on the west bank of the river, vaguely associating themselves with a HBC warehouse. The warehouse huddled at the base of a long, low gneiss outcrop at the northernmost end of the clearing. It was placed there to shelter the outfits arriving with the SS *Grahame* until Red River Carts could haul them down Smith Portage, and to protect the furs from below the rapids until they could be moved south.

The rocky outcrop was part of a point that forced the river into a sharp eastward bend at the top of the rapids. Backed up behind it, the Slave swirled in a huge eddy. Above the outcrop Ed saw rising mists and spray, and beyond it he heard the dull roar of the first of the four stretches of white water that make up Smith's Rapids.

Although Martin may have known the route through the east-side islands and channels, he and Ed did not head directly toward it. As Mulkins had done earlier that summer, they pulled into Smith's Landing to hire rivermen and packers who could help them cross the

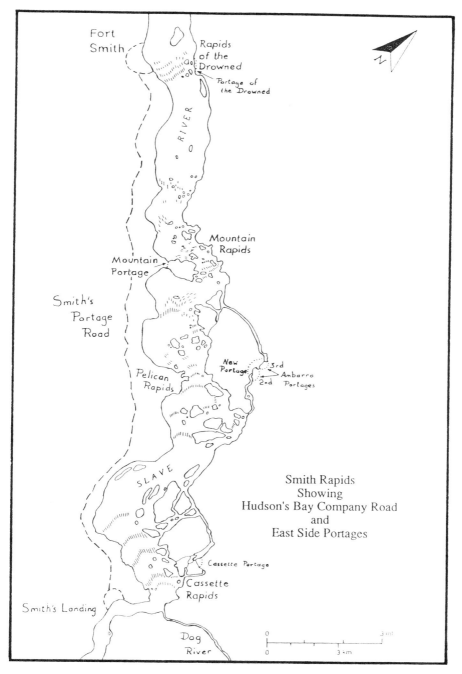

Fort Smith

Rapids of the Drowned

Portage of the Drowned

RIVER

Mountain Rapids

Mountain Portage

Smith's Portage Road

New Portage

3rd

Ambarro
2nd Portages

Pelican Rapids

SLAVE

Smith Rapids
Showing
Hudson's Bay Company Road
and
East Side Portages

Cassette Portage

Cassette Rapids

Smith's Landing

Dog River

3 mi

3 km

121

The cause of the first portage. Note the scow held on the left side of the channel in the background.

portages that lay ahead. When they eventually left Smith's Landing, they kept close to the west bank of the Slave until they were far enough above the first rapid to cross the river safely. Then they drifted down the east bank to the placid, lily-covered water at the mouth of the Dog River.

The Dog Rapid was their first short stretch of white water. A small side chute, its few riffles swept them onto the deceptively smooth water of a narrow side channel which drew them swiftly northeast for about five kilometres. Then, below a sharp westward bend their guides sculled their sturgeon heads into a small eddy on the left side of the channel and held them there. On the right side, about forty metres from where the scows wallowed, a ramp had been cut from the riverbank.

The huge impassable rapid in the main river is named Cassette Rapid for an incident that occurred in this small east-side channel. During the early years of the northwestern fur trade, a boat ferrying a HBC pay chest, or cassette, had vanished over the lip of a hidden cascade that lay just ahead. Neither the boat, its crew, nor the pay cassette had survived that catastrophic descent.

Ed and his companions were as close as they dared get to the Cassette Rapid: the left-bank eddy was the last safe place to moor and organize boats. For about five hundred meters beyond the eddy, the

122

Packing on the first portage, Slave River.

channel walls were solid ruddy gneiss, polished smooth by successive outflows of spring ice. Although the water appeared to flow directly into a large basin, a hidden boulder split the north end of the channel into a torrential cascade. The scows had to leave the water at the ramp.

On this first trip through Smith's Rapids, Ed learned the basic portage routines. Whenever more than one scow followed this route, rivermen staggered and stacked them, holding as many as possible in Cassette Portage eddy. Then they moved them one-at-a-time across to the ramp where two or three would be tied side-by-side in the water.

A cookstove and cooking gear were always the first items unloaded from any outfit. Then, while a cook prepared their meal, traders and their boatmen packed the 90-pound trade pieces 440 paces to the north end of the portage. Before the scows could be reloaded, a block-and-tackle was hooked to them and they were dragged on rollers up the ramp and over the portage.

During the Cassette Portage crossing, clouds of insects attacked Ed and his companions. Two species of mosquitoes vied for blood on his exposed flesh: the small grey ones seen throughout Canada, and larger yellow ones that live only in the north. Black flies crept beneath his clothing, and, although the horse-fly-like monsters were more danger-ous to animals than men, as sweat dripped from him the "bull-dogs"

Hauling scows over the first portage.

attacked. Fortunately, whenever he could get in the open near water, squadrons of dragon flies charged to protect him, snapping some of the galling multitude from the air and scattering the rest.

Below the basin that catches Cassette Rapid, heavily forested islands continue sheltering the channel for three more kilometres, where it returns to the main river. Once in the Slave, the guides pressed the boats close to its east bank as far as the mouth of another channel which struck off northeastward about nine kilometres below Cassette Portage. A kilometre or so below the entrance to the channel, they pulled up on the banks of a very large eddy.

Here their passage was entirely blocked by an enormous ancient log jam. Earlier in the 19th century, HBC boat brigades had made two short portages along the east bank to avoid the log jam and a short, savage chute below it. In 1892, however, Ed's party crossed what was called the New Portage, which lay on the island protecting the west side of the channel from the main river. The New Portage was longer than the others, but eliminated the need to haul the scows out of the water twice.

A stunningly beautiful cascade staggered among forested islands and tumbled over a rocky outcrop into a quiet pool at the bottom of the New Portage. A few rotting wooden posts on one side of the grassy trail marked the grave of an Indian who had died there. With their boats

Rapids at the third portage.

reloaded, the free traders bobbed along for two or three more kilometres before edging back to face the main Slave River.

On the west side of the Slave lay Mountain Portage. Of all Smith's Rapids, Mountain Rapid was the most awe inspiring. Above it the Slave swept in a mighty hairpin bend, curling around an intruding west-bank ridge. With no side channels to divert the river, almost as much water thunders over the lip of Mountain Rapid as roars over Niagara Falls. The wild grandeur of the place hushed even the most experienced rivermen. On the east side of the Slave, swallows had honeycombed the silty banks, and, framed against the backdrop of the west-side ridge, gulls nested on the rocky hummocks out in the current. Hundreds of pelicans that had colonized a mid-stream islet squawked awkwardly into the air, snapping into formation on the updrafts and spiralling skyward in a huge white silence.

Ed's boatmen sheltered themselves behind some silt-caked east-side islands. Then his guides nosed the sturgeon heads upstream, nestling briefly in the eddies behind each small rocky outcrop scattered across the main stream. About half way to the west bank the islets disappeared, and the guides ferried across into a current that increased as it swept toward the base of the ridge. After a short, wild ride they beached their scows at the bottom of a formidable ramp cut from the western riverbank.

Mountain Portage was the most formidable portage on the route Ed was following. The point it crosses is relatively narrow, but over one hundred metres high. The ridge along its crest was so sharp that the top of it had been cut down several metres, to make balancing on it less precarious. Its slopes were so steep, that there would be no stopping a breakaway scow's careen back to the river. Thankfully, this was the last time the boats came out of the water. Once again, a block-and-tackle assembly assisted the men to haul the boats onto the riverbank. This time, however, it stayed attached all the way to the top of the ridge. And the scows were carefully lowered from the ridge top down the north slope of the portage.

Packing goods down the north slope of Mountain Portage.

Below Mountain Portage the boats had to pass more than a kilometre of seven-metre standing waves that Mountain Rapid raised. Then they were ferried back to the east bank, and dropped between scattered islets to the head of another smooth-walled chute. The chute was the route's final challenge to the boatmen, and was called the Rapid of the Drowned.

In 1786, Cuthbert Grant had lost a canoe and five voyageurs in an unsuccessful attempt to run it. As leader, he had gone through first. If he thought the run was safe, he would signal with a single shot fired into the air. In fact the run terrified him, but before he could contain his exultant paddlers at the bottom, one of them had fired at a duck. From the head of the chute he had seen his other canoe overturn in the middle of the rapid. He had buried his dead comrades near the bottom of the portage trail Ed and Martin would follow.

Sturgeon heads were much larger than the voyageurs' canoes, but even they could not shoot the Rapid of the Drowned with impunity. Ed's party unloaded half his outfit at the top of the portage trail. While a guide ran the lightened scows down the chute, Ed and the others portaged the off-loaded goods past a few Indian cabins and the graves of Grant's men to the north end of the bad water.

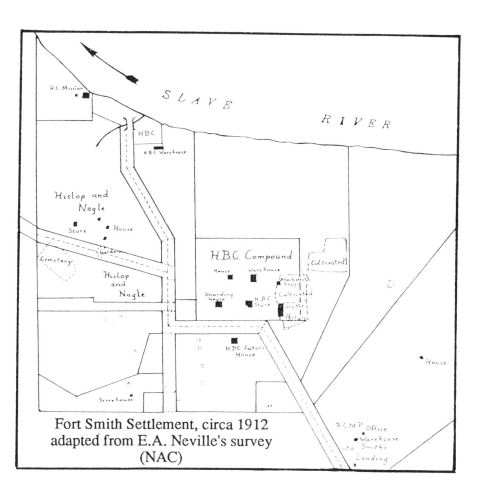

Fort Smith Settlement, circa 1912
adapted from E.A. Neville's survey
(NAC)

Because their outfit was so large, it took Ed and Martin between three and five days to make the trip through Smith's Rapids. But the Hudson's Bay Company trader at Fort Smith did not welcome them when they arrived to discharge their rivermen: Mulkins and Colin Fraser had thrown his operation into chaos earlier in the season.

Over the years, the HBC had devised a trade currency called the made beaver, or "skin," to pay trappers for their pelts. Originally, a made beaver had been the value of one prime beaver pelt, stretched and ready for market. By 1892, however, it was simply a kind of currency value worth between 25 and 50 Canadian cents. Mulkins and Fraser had driven the Fort Smith buying tariff for prime large bear from fifteen to twenty-five skins. Prime large beaver had risen from six to twelve skins, and the finest spring muskrats now brought trappers a skin for every six pelts that crossed the trader's counter.

Ed and Martin had no intention of further increasing the Fort Smith trader's anxiety and continued almost immediately on towards Great Slave Lake. By the time they had passed Le Grand Detour and the Laundry River, ice was already setting on the back channels of the Slave. When Martin was finally set up at Grant Point it was too late for Ed to proceed on towards Fort Good Hope.

Throughout that winter, Ed shuttled between Martin's post, Fort Resolution, and Fort Chipewyan. A few things became apparent to him quite quickly. Below Smith's Rapids the HBC trading system was similar to the one in place at Fort Chipewyan. By tripping to the trappers' camps he got his choice of their finest pelts, leaving them the poorer ones with which to pay off their HBC debt. Unfortunately, he also learned that tripping on winter trails wore out dog teams.

Good dogs were valuable and difficult to obtain at Great Slave Lake. Sometime during that winter Ed apparently decided that none of the ones he found were suited to his needs. He wanted dogs with deep chests, large feet, and legs long enough to handle the deep snow, and, therefore, would have to breed them himself.

By spring, he knew how disgusted the trappers southwest of Resolution had become with the trade at Great Slave Lake. Although he and Martin had combined with Mulkins to force up Fort Resolution prices (prime bears had gone from fifteen to twenty skins; beavers fetched ten skins instead of seven; martens rose from two and a half to three skins; wolverines from three to four skins; and large winter musk ox robes had climbed in value from fifteen to twenty skins), many of the Slavey Indians were now trading at Fort Vermilion. And there was interesting news from the Dogrib and Yellowknife Indians on the north

Ed Nagle tripping on the Slave River below Smith's Rapids.

shore of the lake. During the previous few years, the musk ox hunters at Fort Rae had had a very rough time. They had lost at least one man out on the Barren Lands, and several others had been badly frozen. Although men had been lost to injuries and death, the Fort Rae trader was discouraging summer hunts. Furthermore, he was cutting the credit outfits he advanced to musk ox hunters, and demanding full payment for previous advances.

Certainly, part of the Fort Rae trader's problem resulted from the fact that he was not receiving sufficient supplies. In 1891 he had been caught so short that he had finished the season owing the Indians approximately 2,091 skins; a debt he had had to pay from his 1892 outfit. To a large extent, however, his problems resulted from his insensitivity. The Rae Indians had grown so angry with him that they were bringing their musk ox robes across the lake to Resolution.

In an effort to assist his parishioners, the Roman Catholic priest at Rae was exacerbating the situation. He was supplementing the hunters' reduced credit outfits with supplies the Dominion government had issued to him. Moreover, he was forcing the Rae trader to pay twice the normal price for the furs the Indians brought him as offerings. (The HBC trader complained bitterly in his reports that the priest was trading against him.)

During that winter, Martin had decided to stop trading and take up trapping. And Mulkins intended to leave Slave Lake during the coming summer. That spring Ed visited Hislop at Chipewyan a few times to discuss the situation unfolding at Great Slave Lake. Forts Rae and Resolution were prime targets, and Ed had set his sights on Resolution.

Dick Secord arrived at Chipewyan on May 20 with the new outfits. While he bought furs and briefed Hislop on the new fur prices, Secord prepared an outfit for Fort Smith. When he and Hislop reached Smith's Landing on May 29, Ed was there waiting for them. He had somehow managed to get hold of an ox cart, in which they all travelled down the portage road to Fort Smith. His furs were the first ones carted up to Smith's Landing, whence he set off immediately to take his new outfit through the east-side portages. In four days everything was safely at Fort Smith, and Secord was on his way back toward Edmonton with Ed's winter furs.

Dick Secord's arrival panicked the HBC traders. In his reports to the head office, the Inspector of Posts called for an end to the credit-outfit system below Smith's Rapids. The HBC trader at Fort Chipewyan was more desperate, and tried out a strategy that had worked on Colin Fraser in 1890. In the hope that it would prevent him from stirring up any more trouble that summer, Secord was offered prime prices for his furs as he passed upriver. He quickly parted with them, and on June 10 started up the Athabasca with Mulkins.

To the consternation of the HBC, however, by the beginning of the third week in August, Secord was back at Chipewyan. His brother and Colin Fraser joined him for his second trip to Fort Smith. Ed Nagle and Jim Hislop met them at Smith's Landing, then started down the east-side route with a larger outfit which Secord had brought them. They deemed it sufficient to last them through the coming winter, and at Fort Smith they paid him $7,500.00 for it. Ahead of them lay Great Slave Lake.

CHAPTER 11

The Hislop and Nagle Company
(1893-1895)

Between the spring of 1893 and the late summer of 1894, a young scholar named Frank Russell kept a careful account of the events he witnessed at Great Slave Lake. Although primarily in search of musk oxen, Russell also wanted a specimen from the last free-ranging herd of North American bison. On 29 August 1893, he joined two Fort Rae Métis and a Dogrib Indian for a canoe journey south to Fort Resolution, where he intended to arrange his hunt into buffalo country. Emile, the Dogrib Indian, may only have been along for the ride, but Alexis and Vital Lafferty were on their way to meet some free traders. Paddling up an eastern channel in the Slave River Delta on September 11, they came upon Ed Nagle first.

After they left Dick Secord, Ed and Jim had floated down the Slave to Fort Resolution and engaged the Laffertys to act as interpreters and introduce them to the local Indian bands. The trappers above Smith Rapids were mostly Crees, Chipewyans and Métis who did their trading in Cree or country French. Since Nagle and Hislop had both learned Cree, and Ed (and probably Jim, too) spoke French, they had found no need for interpreters at Lake Athabasca. Conditions were different 350 kilometres down the Slave River, where the trappers were mostly Yellowknife, Slavey, and Dogrib.

In many respects the HBC traders at Great Slave Lake were still unprepared for opposition. In addition to the tight restraints the Head Office imposed on their trading practices and outfits, they were expected to fend for themselves, and they were only provided with emergency rations, flour and tea. James McKinlay, the Fort Resolution trader, was already in difficulty. During the downriver voyage, the

Fort Rae on Great Slave Lake.

transport brigade had wrecked his provisions scow in the Athabasca River. He was rationing the flour and tea he usually enjoyed, and would have to struggle just to survive through the winter.

Hislop and Nagle, on the other hand, had provisioned themselves well enough to avoid having to subsist off the land. While they awaited the Laffertys, Hislop had stayed at Resolution and Ed had explored the Slave River Delta. Four days after the interpreters arrived, Vital Lafferty, Emile, and Frank Russell accompanied Jim Hislop north across Great Slave Lake. Alexis Lafferty stayed on with Ed at Fort Resolution.

Joseph Hodgson had replaced the Fort Rae trader who had antago-nized the Dogribs. But, although his provisions scow had arrived intact, Hodgson was no better prepared to deal with Hislop than McKinlay was with Nagle. About the time Jim Hislop passed him by, Hodgson was realizing how sadly short of trading stock Fort Rae was. During the coming winter it would be all he could do merely to win back Dogrib allegiance and begin settling their still-outstanding debt.

If his post had been better stocked, Hodgson would have been the ideal trader to counter the free traders' first jabs at the Fort Rae trade. At six feet three inches tall, he was physically more imposing than anyone at Slave Lake except Hislop. But, although he towered over the gracile Dogribs, most of whom stood only between five feet six inches and five feet ten inches tall, his intellectual gifts and his love of poetry and humorous rhyme were his greatest assets.

Hodgson had been raised in Manitoba and schooled at Saint John's College in the Red River Settlement. With more than twenty years of experience trading at various HBC posts throughout the north, he responded shrewdly to the threat that Hislop represented. He wrote in

Hislop's post at Willow River, under the midnight sun.

his post journal against Company ineptitude. Then, instead of ostraciz-
ing the free trader as McKinlay was attempting to do at Fort Resolution,
he socialized with Hislop to keep abreast of his activities. In the long
run Hodgson's approach advanced the HBC effort at Fort Rae and
avoided further alienating the Dogrib trappers.

The angry Indians were almost certainly assisting Hislop to establish himself near their trapping grounds. After leaving Frank Russell at
Fort Rae, which then lay on the east side of the north arm of Great Slave
Lake approximately 25 kilometres south of the present town of Rae-
Edzo, Vital Lafferty and Emile headed north. Lafferty had a very
specific location in mind for Hislop's post: near the north end of the
Willow River, which joined Great Slave and Marian Lakes. It was a
place the Dogribs had previously suggested as the location for a HBC
post.

The north end of Willow River was almost the exact geographical
centre of Dogrib tribal territories. The hunting grounds of all four
Dogrib regional bands — the Follow-the-Shore-People, who lived in
the general area of the HBC post; the Feces Lake (Lac La Marte)
People; the Snare Lake (or Edge-of-the-Woods) People, who lived
near the Barren Lands; and the Next-to-another-Tribe People, who
lived near the Bear Lake Indians — all came together there. More
important to the Dogrib trappers, however, was the fact that a trading
post at Willow River would obviate the need for the dangerous canoe

133

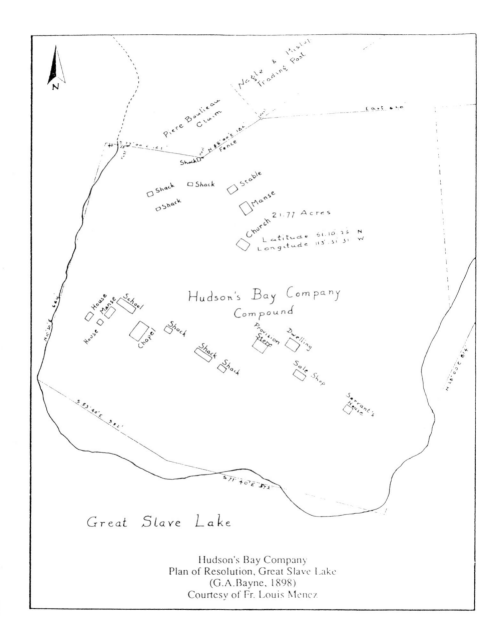

Hudson's Bay Company
Plan of Resolution, Great Slave Lake
(G.A.Bayne, 1898)
Courtesy of Fr. Louis Menez

voyage south to Fort Rae. The northerly bands had hugged the sheltered west shore when canoeing south, which meant they had to traverse Great Slave Lake's open north arm to reach the HBC post.

Despite advice from Lafferty and Emile, Jim Hislop did not locate himself at the first place he was shown. Until the river currents proved too powerful, he tried establishing himself part way down the Willow River. By the time the ice was forming on the lakes, however, he had returned to the Willow River inflow and a small, hummocky red schist peninsula jutting from the east shore of Marian Lake. Once Hislop was settled in, Emile returned to the HBC post.

During the early winter, insufficient trading stock crippled Hodgson. The three most northerly Dogrib bands paddled by Hislop's post on their way to Fort Rae, but when they learned that the HBC did not have certain items, they went to Hislop for them. Furthermore, in addition to the Lafferties, Hislop and Nagle had hired a tripper named Bouvier. Hodgson had no one to send out after Bouvier when he travelled to the trappers' camps, and by Christmas, when Russell was ready to return to Resolution for his buffalo hunt, the HBC trader was discouraged.

Ed was not as well placed on the southern shore as Hislop was at Willow River but he was well set up. He was entrenched alongside the Hudson's Bay Company post on a small plot of land belonging to a respected Métis named Beaulieu. By this point in his career he was a master trader, familiar with the current market values of the furs and all aspects of trapping and skin preparation. Like McKinlay, he was trading from a store separated from the house in which he dwelt. He kept his store unheated to discourage loitering once trading was finished and dealt with only one trapper at a time to lessen any confusions that might arise.

Although every trader did things a bit differently, they looked for the same things when they examined each lot of fur. During his initial look at them, Ed noted whether furs were "cased" — peeled whole from the animal — or "open" — ripped up the belly from the vent to the chin. If a fur arrived open when it should have been cased, he devalued it. Foxes, martens, fishers, lynx, coyotes, mink, otters, muskrats, and skunks all had to be cased. Beavers, bears, wolves, and musk ox and buffalo robes were skinned open. Wolverines could arrive cased or open, but north of Smith's Rapids they were generally open.

Ed also noted whether a cased fur was presented to him "fur side" or "pelt side" (flesh side) out. He expected some of the most valuable furs — foxes, martens, fishers, lynx, and coyotes — to arrive fur side out. If their pelt sides showed, he suspected something was wrong with the fur.

The pelt side reflected how the skin had been captured and prepared. It indicated whether the animal was trapped, speared, shot, or torn by dogs. It showed whether the skin had been badly stripped of flesh and fat, improperly dried, or left in a pile with other fresh-killed or fresh-skinned animals. When he noticed signs of abuse, Ed examined the fur side to determine whether the warmth of decomposing flesh or carcasses had produced a "fur slip" or "puller." Bad trapping practices caused pullers, which were worthless because the pelt would soon lose its fur.

As he set problematic skins aside, Ed sorted the lot for primeness. Animals taken early in the season, before they were fully prime, had dark-colored pelt sides, often with a bluish cast. Such skins were "blued," and regardless of the quality of their fur he devalued them one grade. Late in the season he looked for "springy" skins, which had veiny pelt sides that often showed blue on the legs. The sort for primeness was also an occasion for Ed to note whether or not a skin was properly stretched. If it was larger than the animal's size justified, the pelt would be thin and the fur inadequate to cover the fur side closely.

As he sorted them, Ed also sized the skins. In the Mackenzie region they were generally sized simply either large or small. Beaver skins, however, could be large, small, cub, or kit. And lynx were sized large, middling, and small. The final phase of sorting was to place a value on each fur. Then, if he bought it, Ed slipped a string through the pelt's nose and noted its size and grade both on a tag and in his books.

Ed tended to use the grades and buying tariffs set by the HBC as his benchmarks, but since Dick Secord kept him abreast of the current market values· he was able to adjust his buying prices more flexibly than the HBC traders. Four grades were established for foxes, martens, fishers, lynx, and bears. Muskrats (musquash) got five, but beavers, otters, and mink only three. And skunks, wolves, and wolverines were only graded as first and damaged. Musk ox robes were either accepted or rejected.

When he graded, Ed studied the fur, using a quick thumb stroke, from its surface down to the skin from which it sprouted. Number One fur was prime and unmarked on the pelt side, and had not been overstretched. The long outer guard hairs on the fur side were all in place and glossy, and the under-fur was thick, evenly distributed, and well coloured for the species of animal.

A Number Two fur was deficient in one of the four criteria in which the Number One had excelled. It might be slightly blued, badly stretched, have profuse or missing guard hairs, or unevenly distributed or coloured under-fur. The guard hairs were especially important for determining Number Two grades. If the under-fur was thick and "woolly" but without sufficient guard hairs to give it lustre, it was graded Number Two. In the case of otters and mink, an animal's habit of sunbathing might have crinkled (singed) the guard hairs and slightly faded the underfur.

Number Three was the lowest grade that Ed would normally accept. (He only accepted Number Fours if a trapper with a large lot resisted parting with his higher quality furs.) A "rubbed" fur — with patches rubbed bare because an animal had a small den or a case of parasites — would grade to Number Three. Very badly blued pelts became Number Threes, as did mangy skins and late season springy "shedders." And if a skin had been shot, speared, cut, or torn by dogs but still had some worth then it was graded Three or Four.

Alexis Lafferty was tripping out of Resolution for Ed, and throughout the early winter the two of them worked steadily to establish rapport with the local trappers. Early in October marten, fisher, and bear pelts came to prime. By mid-November Ed was trading foxes, coyotes, wolves, skunks, lynx, and "fall" beavers and rats. Minks, otters, and wolverines were the last pelts to "prime up." By the time trappers began arriving at Resolution for Christmas they had learned to respect the stocky, blue-eyed free trader. He paid top prices for good furs, often better than what McKinlay and the HBC offered.

As soon as groups of natives reached Resolution, they visited the HBC post for their traditional arrival gratuity: two pint measures of flour, a measure each of tea and sugar, and two plugs of tobacco per man. Then, while a general assembly questioned McKinlay about the HBC tariffs for the coming year, individual trappers stole off to Ed's to learn what he had to offer. Frank Russell arrived a week or so before Christmas. The hunter-explorer had not felt restricted by the HBC caveat against consorting with the free traders and had travelled freely to Willow River. He brought Ed up to date regarding Hislop's activities there.

Christmas was the festival the Indian families liked best. On Christmas Eve they gathered at the Roman Catholic Church for a midnight mass. The following morning they visited the HBC post for tea and treats, then moved to partake of Ed's largess. New Year's was the Métis' festival. They danced reels and Red River Jigs, drank tea, ate, sang and celebrated for two full nights and days. By about January second, however, all the bush-dwelling families were starting for home.

Russell, too, was soon gone from Resolution. After obtaining all the supplies Ed could part with, Russell started off up the Little Buffalo River but Ed was not alone long. About the third week in January, Jim Hislop arrived from Willow River.

It was partly the long periods of isolation they faced that affected traders' moods so powerfully. The big Nova Scotian was not in a pleasant frame of mind when he crossed the threshold of Ed's small cabin. His cross-eyed guide Chillouis, another of Alexis Lafferty's relatives, had proven incompetent. He had guided Hislop onto the ice between the north and south shores, then lost the trail. Hislop had spent a night freezing in the open.

Ed soon helped restore his friend's good humour. Hislop, in turn, cheered Ed. On his way past Fort Rae, he had stopped to visit Hodgson. The heaviness dragging at the Rae trader's spirit when Russell left Fort Rae had lifted when Hislop arrived. On New Year's Day a poetic fit had overwhelmed the HBC man, and he had composed a rhymed ode to the advent of the northern year:

> The day had scarcely yet begun
> When the savage native with his gun
> about the fort did wildly run,
> Intent on tea & hot cross bun.
> They took their station at the door
> Of stalwart men two score or more
> And from their guns salutes did pour
> That rivaled e'en the thunder's roar.
> Behind them, sparkling like the sand
> Of rivers in a golden land,
> The wives and maidens of the land,
> A truly bright and beauteous band.
> Then in they came, that mighty tide,
> With dauntless mien & haughty stride
> Benignant muse haste to my side
> Lest spleeny foes these lines divide__
> For how can I without thine aid
> Describe the onslaught, and the raid,

On tea & cakes by man & maid
Of indigestion not afraid .__.
The lordly eagle in his flight
The brilliant stars, those gems of night,
The sun that shines at noon so bright
Afford a scarce more wondrous sight
Than native genius when in mood
To make to disappear his food
For though untaught & somewhat rude
He knows "what's what," yea what is good.
The laugh went round and merry jest
And story with, to give it zest
A touch of scandal, through fear lest
It lose its point amongst the rest.
By *rest*, I mean, nor me nor you
If you'd been there, but just the few
You know, who cannot take the cue
Of anything not well in view ___
At length the evening shades prevail
All ushered in by northern gale
But still despite the wild winds' wail
Into the dancing hall they sail.
Those sons of Anak stout and strong,
With thews of steel, and limbs so long
And Venus daughters; passing fair,
Some crowned with dark - some golden hair
But fairest 'mongst that beauteous throng
Was dark eyed Kate who seemed among
The rest, as if, she did belong
To goddesses, who dwell in song
The fiddler played his merriest strains,
While lightly danced the youthful swains:
The ribboned lass to sit disdains
Whilst modest blush the ivory stains.
Merrily, merrily, they toe it around
With many a turn and many a bound
An eight handed reel - And the walls resound
But everything must have an end,
The stoutest breaks at last must rend,
May blessings on us all descend
And *we* our evil ways amend.

139

Jim Hislop's fur press.

Despite the enjoyment they got from one another's company, Ed and Jim were not meeting to socialize. Since they had parted in the fall, all of their communication had been by way of their trippers. Now they had to determine the success of their current strategies. They had to estimate not only how well they had done thus far, but also the value of the furs they would collect between the first of the year and the arrival of the spring supply scows. They had to plan next season's outfit, and decide how much credit they could risk with Secord.

They finished their business toward the end of January. They had probably noticed that some of Slave Lake's more reliable fisheries were failing and that the caribou appeared to be drifting farther east than they had in previous years. For the winter of 1894-95 they decided to both reoutfit and reprovision themselves.

The Willow River operation was too lucrative to leave unattended, and as Hislop's journey across the lake ice had left him unenthusiastic, Ed would travel south to Edmonton to organize the outfit. When Frank Russell returned from his unsuccessful buffalo hunt, he was anxious to return to Fort Rae to hunt musk oxen. His plans coincided with Hislop's, and on January 24 the two of them started off together toward the north shore.

Before leaving Resolution, Ed sent Bouvier off with an outfit to Fort Providence. By February 24, when he closed his post and turned his dog team south, skunks and foxes were passing their prime, and minks and otters were beginning to singe and fade.

Hislop's post in winter.

There is no way of knowing how long Ed took to travel to Edmonton, but he arrived to find that Dick Secord's status had changed. Secord no longer bought fur as a middle man for large eastern North American companies. Instead he had connected himself directly to the C.M. Lamson & Son Company of London auctioneers. Since Ed and Jim dealt their furs through Secord, their shipments would now go directly to London and their returns would be commensurate with real fur-market values.

Jack Secord was up from Lake Athabasca, so when Ed and Dick set off from The Landing early in May he accompanied them north. Ed left the Secords at Fort Chipewyan, and by mid June his three supply scows had rounded Moose-Deer Island and were bobbing in Resolution Bay. The scarlet fever epidemic that was decimating the Lake Athabasca Indians in the spring of 1894 did not affect the people at Great Slave lake. Spring trapping was good, and canoes filled with furs flocked to Fort Resolution to meet Ed. McKinlay, whose spring outfit had not yet arrived, watched in frustration as his competitors traded.

Although Hodgson had sparred all winter with Hislop, since February 10, the free trader had steadily drawn the trappers away from Fort Rae. Hodgson had tried everything he could think of, including borrowing supplies from the Roman Catholic priest and visiting Willow River twice, but had been unable to halt the attrition. The situation had become so bad at Rae, that as the winter wore on Hodgson had been unable even to assist his trappers when they began starving. By June, at the time of his second visit to Hislop's post, the HBC man was so upset that he had applied for a year's leave of absence. About his second journey to Willow River he commented:

A large number of Indians along the way but no furs made on our account, as it is a known fact that we have no tea or tobacco. Great excitement though at first; thinking our sail was of the anxiously expected boat from Resolution arriving with supplies for Mr. Hislop. I have no doubt that if a trader would come amongst us with a good stock of trading goods, he would make $5000 worth of furs within a week.

Ice prevented Ed from immediately sending Hislop's outfit across the lake, but Dick Secord reached Resolution on June 24. The water was open by the time Secord finished baling the Fort Resolution winter furs as payment for the new Hislop and Nagle outfit. A crew of Secord's men went north to Hislop, and Hodgson writhed under the humiliation of watching them pass him by. The SS *Wrigley* had stopped at Fort Rae two days earlier, but had dropped him just five bales of trade goods. When Secord's men passed by on their return to Resolution he remarked that their scow contained 22 bales of fur. It was scant comfort that very few of them were the musk ox robes the Dogribs reserved to trade for good HBC blankets. Although he had managed to collect most of the previous trader's outstanding debt, Hodgson had not impeded Hislop at Willow River.

Dick Secord did not wait for his crew to return from the north arm before he started south; the crew followed him up the Slave. When the furs eventually reached Edmonton, the *Bulletin* reported that Secord's Athabasca and Slave River investments had garnered $30,000.00.

Hislop and Nagle, however, were left with a problem at Great Slave Lake. Hislop had followed Secord's men to Fort Resolution with two bales of his most valuable furs. He and Ed had to face the fact that, if anything, their trading was proving too successful: the outfit Ed had brought to Great Slave Lake was not going to get them through the winter. Since Secord was not returning down north that fall, one of them had to return to Edmonton for more supplies.

On July 21, Ed started upriver with a scow loaded with 45 fur packs and several musk ox specimens and heads. By September 12 he had reached Edmonton. Three weeks later he was back on the Athabasca with two more loads of supplies. Shortly after he left Edmonton the *Bulletin* amended its earlier report: exclusive of the HBC trade, Edmonton's fur buyers had taken approximately $85,000.00 worth of fur in 1894. Hislop, Nagle, and Secord had gotten over half of that.

Ed was now such a highly regarded traveller that the Anglican Bishop — Bishop Young — joined him for the down-river trip. When he reached Fort

Hislop's Yorkboat at Stoney Island, Great Slave Lake.

Resolution, Ed got a sense of just how influential he was becoming at Slave Lake. Two Indians had travelled all the way from Fort Providence to trade with him. Although bad weather delayed his outfit at Smith Rapids and the Indians were gone when he arrived at Resolution, the dance he threw to celebrate his success drew them back.

At Fort Resolution, Fred Gaudet had replaced James McKinlay, who had been moved upriver to Fort Smith. Gaudet and his spinster sister were from the old HBC school. They not only spoke out personally against Ed to the trappers, they worked actively to ostracize him. But Ed remained as unconcerned about them as he had been about McKinlay. The New Year came and went, with trading as brisk as it had been the previous winter. Jim Hislop arrived on January 15, to plan the new outfit. Ed's dance had attracted new trappers in to trade in the fall, so to celebrate Hislop's arrival and irritate the Gaudets he staged another one.

After Hislop returned to Willow River in late January, he and Ed had made two major alterations to their Slave Lake operation. First they began changing their outfit to meet specific demands from their trappers. The trappers had made it absolutely clear that there were some trade goods they were not interested in. While the HBC might offer them foxtail feathers, green and powder blue capôt jackets, bridle bits,

143

spurs, stirrups, cowbells, web girthing, and flintlock guns, Hislop and Nagle could do better. The other innovation was the buying of a York Boat. Hislop had decided that crossing the open stretches of Great Slave Lake by canoe or scow was simply too dangerous.

As Ed prepared to start south again, an adventuring journalist arrived at Resolution. The journalist, G. Caspar Whitney, was another hunter seeking the far-famed musk oxen. However, whereas Frank Russell had gotten along reasonably well with all the traders and most of the natives he met, Whitney possessed an almost magical talent for antagonizing people. At Resolution Whitney demonstrated a marked affection for the Gaudets.

Whitney had already made an impact on the fraternity of free traders. He was going into the Barrens at the worst time of the year just to prove it could be done, and insisted that no Indian would bamboozle him. When he had learned that Shot was the best guide he would find, Whitney had hired him at Lac La Biche. But he refused to take any of Shot's advice, drove his dogs too hard, and accused his guide of malingering. In less than a week they had parted company.

Although the moccasin telegraph likely had much to say about Whitney, Ed would not hear the full story until he reached Edmonton. In the book Whitney subsequently wrote, he assigned Shot complete responsibility for the incident. He maligned him to such an extent that the *Bulletin* eventually printed this retort, "... Mr. Whitney is a good man, but he knows nothing of travelling by dog team to the north. Mr. Whitney kept telling him [Shot] he was going too slow and was constantly reminding Shot that he was not the 'boss' on the trip, but Shot considered that he was the boss and did not mean to travel in such a way as to wear out himself and his dogs."

Ed closed his post and turned his dogs south about February fourth. He took almost five weeks to make the trip to Edmonton. During the journey the temperature never dropped much below -36° F., and about February tenth the aurora flashed in marvelous display. Red and violet waves rustled across the stars, fading in whirls to become green-gold lancing streaks. To the *Bulletin* reporter who got the story of his trip, Ed mentioned he had enjoyed the hospitality of the Catholic nuns at Lac la Biche, and that he had travelled 5,500 miles that year, 2,300 of them by dog team.

Although he spent much of his time working with Dick Secord to modify the new outfits that spring, Ed did not fully engage his mind in the project. He was a sociable man, and Fort Resolution's isolation was

The Buffalo Club. Dog trains in front of Dick Secord's fur trading store at Edmonton.

working powerfully on him. At Secord's new fur-buying house — which the locals had dubbed The Buffalo Club — he could hear the latest northern news, have a game of cribbage or pinocle, or enjoy a horn of non-permit whiskey. But even the company of men he had known for years left him dissatisfied.

Ed was forty-one years old, reasonably successful, and tired of living alone. He found himself attracted to dark-eyed, twenty-two year old Eva Klapstein, who sewed fur garments for John McDougall. She was a calm, attractive, cheerful girl who placed great faith in her ability to read tea leaves. Her father and brothers approved of Ed, so he courted her throughout the month and a half he stayed at Edmonton he courted her.

By the end of April, however, the ice was breaking on the Athabasca River and Dick Secord had sent the forty-ton Hislop and Nagle outfit to Athabasca Landing. Ed could no longer delay his return north. His downriver trip was notable mostly for the efficiency with which it was accomplished. From Grand Rapids to Fort McMurray, fires had stripped the riverbanks and hillsides and part of the Grand Rapids Island tram had been destroyed, so Ed and his men had to portage the outfit down the free traders' trail. At Fort McMurray he paused briefly to install George Slater and "Billy" Clark in a new Hislop and Nagle Company post. Below McMurray, his five scows hoisted sails to make better time to Chipewyan.

A brief encounter on the river resolved some of Ed's unanswered questions about Whitney. The Buffalo Club had rumbled with speculation about the New York City journalist. Few people had believed he would be successful, but as Ed sailed down the Athabasca below McMurray he came upon a white man sitting smoking meditatively on the riverbank. When he got within hailing distance, Ed shouted,

"Hello, are you Whitney?"

"Yes," was the reply from the riverbank.

"They are getting worried about you at Edmonton. They are organizing a search party."

Whitney's response was sanguine: "I hope to get there before they are started."

With just time for one more exchange before they moved beyond voice range, Ed asked, "Were you successful?"

"Yes," the journalist replied.

Between Forts McMurray and Chipewyan Ed stopped just once, at a large pool of natural black tar that had seeped from the riverbank. There he sealed and caulked his boats. Nearer to Athabasca Landing a government drilling rig had been searching for petroleum. In Ed's opinion, they were working 150 miles too far upstream.

H.B. Round and Campbell Young were among the men who were accompanying Ed north. Round was an especially good man. He had spent more than twenty years with the HBC, but after fourteen years trading at Fort Dunvegan on the Peace River, the Company had summarily dismissed him. He was a master trader and fluent speaker of Cree with an implacable anger toward his former employers. He was taking over Ed's Fort Chipewyan operation.

When Ed and his crew reached Resolution, Campbell Young took over that post and Ed prepared the furs for shipment south. He had no intention of doing any trading in 1895. By the end of July Hislop's outfit was at Willow River, and Ed had almost tracked the Hislop and Nagle furs upstream as far as Fort Smith. He stopped at Chipewyan to collect Jack Secord, Round and the furs they had accumulated. Dick Secord awaited them at The Landing, and when the furs reached Edmonton Ed considered his summer's work completed. Dick Secord would be responsible for shipping them to London.

Poor Dick Secord was under a bit of pressure that fall: for years his wife had urged him to take the temperance pledge. Her persistence was starting to grate on his nerves and alter his attitude towards his old friends. As he broke up and graded the Hislop and Nagle fur packs, Secord jotted angry comments in his journal. On September 12, he believed he had a pretty good idea where Ed had gone. On the fifteenth he noted curtly, "Nagle slept in the office last night - drunk." And by September 17 he could barely contain his irritation, "Nagle did not turn up today, at all, or yesterday, drunk." But on September 20, Secord was surprised and honestly pleased to note, "E. Nagle was married last night at the Catholic Church to a German girl."

Eva Klapstein was not German, however, but Polish. Shortly after Ed arrived from the north, she had accepted his proposal of marriage. Father Lacombe had returned to Edmonton from the east a few days earlier, and had agreed to perform the wedding ceremony at Saint Joachim Church. As Eva was Protestant, he had required that she promise to raise her children as Catholics; when she acceded to that condition, he arranged a Special Dispensation of the Faith from Bishop Grandin at Saint Albert. The rain that fell on September 19 did nothing to dampen Ed's double celebration: on the day he turned 42-years-old, Eva Klapstein had become his wife.

News of the wedding did not become common knowledge until September 23, when the *Bulletin* published an official notice of the nuptials. By then Ed and Eva were already on their way to Athabasca Landing. They had stopped to visit Secord before they left. Besides the silver cup and cutlery he offered as wedding gifts, he had special news for the couple. According to his calculations, the furs Ed had brought south were worth more than $20,000. Hislop and Nagle were well on their way to becoming the most important free trading partnership north of Athabasca Landing.

CHAPTER 12

A New North, Eccentrics and Gold
(1895-1898)

Ed had ignored the Gaudets' petty attempts to ostracize him, and he refused to even consider letting them harass Eva. Father Lacombe had married Frank Vickery and Alice Noseda at the same time as he had married the Nagles. Vickery had acted as one of Ed's witnesses, and he and his new wife accompanied Ed and Eva down river to winter with them at Fort Resolution. Eva would have friends of her own when she reached her new home.

Ed and Eva Nagle setting off from Athabasca Landing , on their honeymoon.

Although the rain that fell on the day of the weddings continued pelting down as the couples made their way along the Athabasca Landing Trail, the clouds parted and the sun shone once they reached The Landing. Since the Hislop and Nagle outfit had gone north in the spring, Ed chose not to travel in a large freight scow. Instead, the newlyweds and a new Hislop and Nagle book-keeper named Stagg, embarked in a smaller boat.

The young brides did not expect silk sheets or velvet-papered rooms for their honeymoons, but it is unlikely that they were fully prepared for the rigors that lay ahead of them on the river. Storms lashed the small boat as it drifted down the Athabasca. At Grand Rapids, the party crossed to the north end of the island then settled to await a river guide by the name of Jacob McKay. Below Grand Rapids the journey would become one of the most demanding Ed ever undertook.

Since the boat had not been large enough to carry all the supplies the group needed, Ed was hunting as he floated down river. Towards the end of one long day, someone spotted a moose on the riverbank. Although Eva was in the boat when Ed shot it, rather than pausing to put her ashore, he and McKay rowed hard to get the animal before it was swept away. And as they strained to drag the carcass aboard, they overturned the boat. Leaving McKay to worry about the boat and the meat, Ed snagged Eva before she drifted off downstream, then dried her off before a roaring fire.

But when, after the unexpected revelation of Stagg's epilepsy, ice began closing off the river, Ed was almost prepared to return to Edmonton. Fortunately, at the moment he felt most concern for his wife, Eva's strength of character carried them onward. With calmness and humour she converted their near disasters into a kind of adventure outing. She and Alice Vickery organized a comfortable camp near the Ambara Channel, where the wedding party could pause until the ice set firmly enough for Ed to send to Chipewyan for dog teams. And while they waited at Chipewyan for teams to take them on to Fort Resolution, she persuaded Ed to teach her how to trap. The silver fox she triumphantly claimed as a prize helped shield her from the -30° to -40° degree temperatures that assailed the party during the final leg of its journey.

Speaking for the Hudson's Bay Company, the Gaudets insisted that Ed and Eva Nagle had no right to be at Great Slave Lake. The HBC factor and his sister considered themselves members of a landed elite. Although Eva was a kindly and sociable young woman, as soon as she and Ed arrived at Fort Resolution, Miss Gaudet began snubbing her. Had the Vickerys not wintered at Resolution, Eva would not have been entirely isolated but she would have felt very uncomfortable.

Fortunately, she soon discovered that in addition to Alice Vickery she had another friend at Resolution. The Reverend Father Dupré was a convivial "old country Frenchman" who habitually imported several pounds of raisins expressly for making wine to offer guests. The Roman Catholic priest was at least as influential as the Hudson's Bay Company trader, and he welcomed the newlyweds to his parish. By the end of the Christmas and New Year celebrations Eva was comfortably settled. She had realized that the Hislop and Nagle Company was reckoned a force at Great Slave Lake.

When Jim Hislop arrived from Willow River in January, he quickly understood why Ed would not return to Edmonton that winter: the newlyweds were no prepared to separate again. During 1896 Hislop and Nagle planned to expand down the Mackenzie River. Campbell Young, who had overseen Resolution while Ed was away fetching Eva, was sent off to examine Bouvier's operation at Fort Providence. Boniface Lafferty was trading for the partners at Liard River, and when Young finished at Providence they planned to have him move below Lafferty to Fort Norman. After Hislop headed south, Ed concentrated on the Fort Resolution trade. But by the end of February Eva was pregnant, and he was also devoting a great deal of attention to her.

In Edmonton, Hislop worked hard to enlarge his company's scope and was able to negotiate a new agreement with Dick Secord. As of April 1896, Secord allowed Hislop and Nagle to pay flat rates for their outfits: at 25% advance on his costs for dry goods and clothing, and 20% for groceries and hardware. When Secord became a full partner in John McDougall's operation in the late fall of 1896, Hislop and Nagle would gain direct access to the supplies they needed. In return for the interest he had previously received on his Hislop and Nagle accounts, Secord accepted a five per cent commission on all the company furs that his London contact managed to sell for the partners.

Despite his agreement with Secord, soon after reaching Edmonton Hislop had grounds for suspecting that the future might not unfold as smoothly as he and Ed were hoping. The Dominion seemed determined to actively govern the far north. On January 1, 1896 new hunting regulations had gone into effect. The regulations, called "The Unorganized Territories Game Preservation Act," restricted access to virtually all of the animals and birds important to the fur trade.

It seems strange that none of the people most affected by the Game Act were consulted prior to its enactment. Although only the Act's three-year moratorium on hunting wood buffalo would immediately alter their lives, neither the free traders, the Hudson's Bay Company employees, nor the northern natives were aware of the pending restrictions. When Hislop first learned of the new Game Act, he had absolutely no idea how aggressively the government intended to enforce it.

He did not, however, allow it to upend the plans he and Ed had already set in place. The outfit he gathered together was the largest they had yet invested in. And as soon as he and Secord finished negotiating, he hired men to set up and support the new Hislop and Nagle posts. By April 30 the ice had broken in the Athabasca River, and by the second week in May Hislop had collected the tracking outfit Ed had left with Colin Johnson at The Landing and was on his way down river.

The Game Act was just one indication of the radical changes the western north was facing. The region was no longer isolated. New generations of people, organizations, and laws were beginning to disrupt the influence previously enjoyed by the Hudson's Bay Company and the Roman Catholic Church.

The Hislop and Nagle Company was no longer the only free trading company below Smith's Rapids. There was, in fact, such a deluge of traders in 1896 that conditions resembled the 1887 rush to Fort Chipewyan. The HBC was returning Joe Hodgson to the north, to take charge of Peel's River and block free traders from the Mackenzie River Delta. W. "Bill" Connor, who had scouted with Ed during the 1885 rebellion, had put Frank McLeod in a post at Fort Smith. Colin Fraser had established posts at Smith's Landing and Fort Smith. "Billy" Clark had left Fort McMurray — and Hislop and Nagle — to strike out for Hay River with Harry Anthony and outfits for Armstrong and Company and an Anglican minister named Marsh.

Moreover, the traders were not the only ones whose influence was extending. Reverend Thomas Jabez Marsh, the Anglican at Hay River, was one of two men Bishop Young had sent north to battle the Roman Catholics for souls. Of the two, though the Reverend Spendlove settled at Resolution and would eventually move on down the Mackenzie, it was with Marsh that Ed would form a lasting friendship.

T.J. Marsh was an ex-pugilist, a heavyweight prize fighter who put himself and his skills in the service of the Slavey Indians at Hay River in ways that often astonished them. When he first arrived at the mouth of the Hay River in 1893, the Slaveys still lived in teepees. A Catholic priest tried to persuade his first congregation, which consisted of twenty men and boys and three women, to say they did not want an Anglican there. But Marsh stayed, and a small village of log cabins soon sprang up around his mission house.

Marsh was one of those pioneers who did so much for an area that their most valuable contributions are often overlooked. Certainly, Hay River owes him an unacknowledged debt. Those new cabins represented the influence he was exerting on the Hay River Slaveys, but when Marsh noticed a correlation between them and a rising incidence of tuberculosis he persuaded his flock to return to their tents.

It was not an easy task. In some instances he had to resort to drastic tactics to get his point across. The father of one tubercular young woman trenchantly ignored Marsh's arguments, and refused to move his family out into the cold. When debate failed him, the minister set a harder line. He bodily threw the man and his family out and nailed the doors and windows of their cabin shut. Understandably, the usually pleasant and agreeable Slaveys reacted furiously. But, although they threatened to shoot him, Marsh stood firm. The incident resolved itself that spring, when the young woman returned to Saint Peter's Mission cured of her tuberculosis. Under Marsh's ministry, Hay River remained largely free of a disease that devastated other northern communities.

Of the new men Hislop had hired, Jack Russell would have the most impact on both the Hislop and Nagle Company and the Great Slave Lake region. He was an enormous, fearless, brawling riverman; a capable scow-builder, bushman, and trapper. More importantly for Hislop and Nagle, he was the first man with whom they were willing to entrust responsibility for their fur shipment to Edmonton.

In August, Father Dupré baptized the Nagle's first child, Eva Geraldine. When Jack Russell returned from Edmonton in the fall of 1896, the news he brought with him helped Ed appreciate how well fixed they were. McDougall and Secord had incorporated their partnership, and McDougall was now mayor of Edmonton. With his political clout, and Secord's strong ties to London, and little indication that The Game Act would be a problem, the Hislop and Nagle Company's prospects looked pretty good.

Things had, in fact, gone so well for Ed that he may have missed news heralding more drastic changes for the western north. It was said that an old-timer named Siwash George Carmack had made a big gold strike somewhere on the Yukon River. The Edmonton *Bulletin* had

Hislop and Nagle Company trader, and trappers.

reported that William Ogilvie — the Dominion Land Surveyor working near where Carmack had made his strike — predicted that the
richest claims would show on the Canadian side of the Alaska-Canada
frontier.

It would not have been surprising if Ed had missed the news. What
with the new baby and the Hislop and Nagle Company his hands were
pretty full. The Fort Norman operation was not panning out, but a post
he and Hislop had established east of Resolution at Stoney Island was
doing quite well. Fortunately, the network of Hislop and Nagle trippers
held firm, and Campbell Young set off with George Martin to trap for
the winter. Plentiful caribou and trout would help defray the costs of
feeding the new Hislop and Nagle employees.

Shortly after Christmas, Ed got a brief lift when an English musk
ox hunter and explorer named D.T. Hanbury arrived from the Barren
Lands. Hanbury mentioned that the caribou were numerous at the east
end of Great Slave Lake, which meant the Indians at Fond du Lac were
not starving. And he had no intention of letting the Game Act interfere
with his plans. After re-outfitting himself, the Englishman set off to
hunt the buffalo that ranged west of Fort Smith.

However, North West Mounted Police Inspector Arthur Murray
Jarvis constituted the first proof that the Dominion would no longer

tolerate attitudes like Hanbury's. The policeman reached Fort Resolution on February 13, 1897, just as Ed was about to push south towards Edmonton. Jarvis' affable, even-tempered personality disguised his penetrating character-judgements. His instructions were "to look into various matters such as the prevalence of destructive fires, traffic in liquor, and the allegedly wholesale setting out of poison." His mission was to explain the Game Act, and to block the continuing escalation of the unborn musk ox trade.

The government had chosen a man of political skill to lead this first northern police patrol. Jarvis had stopped at most of the settlements between Edmonton and Resolution, and had cautioned against the fires set to burn off moose range. He believed that the permit system sufficiently controlled liquor traffic, but had noted potential trouble spots and fined a few trouble makers. Poison was the most challenging problem he dealt with.

Since at least 1893, when Frank Russell had commented that nearly every trading post clerk set a few poisoned baits each winter, "which usually succeeded in killing the favorite dog of the post," Indian trappers had complained about strychnine. Many were terrified that they might eat a poisoned carcass. By sentencing and fining the few trappers he caught setting poison, Jarvis made an enormously favourable impression on the northern Indians.

However, he did not succeed nearly as well in attaining his other goals. After witnessing starvation at Chipewyan, he recognized the dilemma facing the native hunters. Although he warned the Indians not to hunt buffalo, for the edification of his superiors he noted, "The Hudson's Bay Company and Mr. Colin Fraser, before my arrival had advanced a certain amount of assistance to these starving people, some of whom died during my stay at Chipewyan. I also gave a small amount of relief."

Conditions were better at Smith's Landing and Fort Smith, which brought some levity to his reports. Protecting the buffalo was an important aspect of the Game Act and he persisted in trying to explain that, but it was plain how briefly his visit would affect the northerners. "These people had never heard of a Game Law," he reported of the natives at Smith's Landing, "and were much surprised on hearing of it. A party who had prepared their outfit for a buffalo hunt, ... cheerfully desisted and postponed their hunt, ... during my stay in the country."

But for white hunters like Hanbury, Jarvis took a firmer stance. Although he was certain that the Englishman would not even pause, he threatened him with a $200.00 fine if he continued chasing the buffalo.

Hislop and Nagle dog trains on their way to Edmonton, circa 1898.

By the time he reached Resolution, Jarvis had honed his arguments to slice away dissension. He explained to Ed and the other traders that open seasons coincided with the times specific pelts came prime, and closed seasons protected animals during their breeding periods.

Jarvis was much impressed by the handsomeness of the richly brown, tightly-curled unborn musk ox fur he saw. Although Resolution was not a big producer that winter — only 18 unborn pelts came in — he felt that more had probably reached Fort Rae, Willow River, and the posts along the Mackenzie. It was clear to him that restricting the established and active Barren Lands hunts would be very difficult. He could only warn the hunters of the dangers of overhunting, and suggest to the government that resident northern game wardens be appointed to monitor the buffalo and musk ox populations.

Ed knew he would have to change some of his policies, particularly with regard to outfitting hunters for the Barrens, but the Game Act did not displease him. It seemed designed to protect the fur trade. In fact, for two primary reasons he considered it a good thing: it indicated that the government could affect HBC activities, and Jarvis' appearance at Resolution got Eva believing that she and her family were not beyond the reach of civilization.

That winter Ed set off for Edmonton with the Hislop and Nagle Company banners flying. He had put together a dog train to rival the ones that dragged Hudson's Bay Company factors throughout the

Ed Nagle's cariole at the end of Jasper Avenue, 1898; left to right: Duffle (trail breaker), Jacobs, Lafferty, Ed Nagle in cariole.

north. Embroidered tapis — dog blankets — covered the backs of his hand-picked dogs; coloured plumes and bells adorned their harnesses. His cariole's distinctive embellishments gave notice that the Hislop and Nagle Company was on the move.

Earlier in his career, Ed had to either tramp behind his cariole or break trail in front of it, like most other northern travellers. Now his employees ran ahead of him. Hislop and Nagle Company prestige demanded that he sit swathed in a capôt and musk ox robe inside his cariole, strapped in like an Indian baby on a carrying board. The ride was not always pleasant — the wraps left only his arms and hands free, and almost nothing absorbed the shocks when his toboggan rattled over ice — but it emphasized his accomplishments.

From Fort Resolution, the dog trail struck west to the mouth of the Little Buffalo River, then south for 85 kilometres to a short portage to the Slave River. That route lopped more than 150 kilometres off the big river's twisting course. Above Smith's Landing Ed kept to the main river channels, stopping before he reached each settlement along the way. While his dogs rested, his forerunner and driver changed into their best clothes. Then, when everything was ready, the outfit charged into town with its bells jingling and plumes flying.

When Ed reached Edmonton, the town was humming excitedly. The rumours of gold in the Yukon River had become tales of miners raking fortunes off the ground. Secord was careful to immunize Ed against the fever: The Hudson's Bay Company was shipping hundreds of tons of supplies down north; fur prices had declined at the January sale in London; no one knew how many of the people who awaited breakup at The Landing were really going to the gold fields. It would take acumen and careful management for Hislop and Nagle to maintain the fur territories they had claimed.

About the time that the *Bulletin* formally proclaimed the Yukon a modern Eldorado, Ed Nagle and Jack Russell led another Hislop and Nagle crew north from Athabasca Landing. The water had risen very high that spring, floating away a section of the Grand Rapids tramline. Despite a delay at the rapids, and stops at McMurray and Chipewyan, by early June Ed was at his Fort Smith staging centre. By mid-June he had reached Fort Resolution, and Hislop's new outfit was on its way to Willow River.

Furs had already reached Resolution from the Hislop and Nagle posts at Fort Norman (where Campbell Young had returned in the spring), Fort Liard, Willow River, and Stoney Island. By the time Ed got them baled and ready to ship, however, he was uncomfortable about returning south. Very few of the 300 people at The Landing had been headed for the Klondike, and strange characters were passing through Resolution. Although Jack Russell, Campbell Young, and H.B. Round all probably told him that they intended striking out for the Yukon, Ed prevailed upon Russell to take the fur shipment south again. By mid-September, Dick Secord was grading what was reportedly the largest lot of Hislop and Nagle furs ever to reach Edmonton.

The *Bulletin* did not actively promote Edmonton as a back door to the Klondike until the second week in August. But by the time Russell's crew reached the bottom of the Grand Rapids, almost 130 gold seekers were strung out along the north-flowing rivers, the grotesque downstream petroglyphs had already been witness to the first fatality Grand Rapids had known in years.

The Patterson Klondike party had innocently drifted its scow into the impassable western river channel. Shouts and warning shots had failed to awaken Patterson, who had lain sleeping on the bow of his vessel, and when the scow struck a rock he had vanished overboard. Although the rivermen on Grand Rapids Island managed to rescue the rest of the group, Patterson's body was not found until the spring of 1898. Some Indians discovered it "completely enclosed in a transparent coffin of ice." Fortunately, the Patterson tragedy was an exception. Most of the first Klondikers were experienced northern travellers. Many of them actually reached the Yukon, and several from Edmonton stopped at Fort Resolution.

Each of Ed's visitors brought him news. Among other things, he learned that his Fort McMurray post had proven extremely successful: the HBC was closing its post and moving its McMurray horse teams to Fort Smith to handle the rush of Klondike-bound freight anticipated for 1898. He also probably learned that Frank McLeod was headed for the gold fields, and that Bill Connor would take charge of Fort Smith. The inrush of men and information culminated, in late August, in an encounter with a true eccentric.

Since January of 1897, Dick Secord had been receiving letters from Charles Jesse "Buffalo" Jones about a proposal to mount an expedition to capture live musk-ox calves as breeding stock. As Jones himself put it later, "My mission was to bring out from the Arctic regions musk-oxen alive, if possible; also silver-grey fox, marten, and other valuable fur-bearing animals, to propagate on an island in the Pacific Ocean." The notion was absurd and wonderful: remarkable enough for Secord to mention it to his friends.

Buffalo Jones was better qualified to undertake the scheme than anyone suspected. As a young man he had left Illinois and moved out onto America's buffalo plains. Between the 1860s and about 1880 he had hunted buffalo professionally, and the carnage he caused and witnessed worked powerfully on his Quaker conscience. By 1886, after settling in Kansas, he had ridden into the Texas Panhandle and roped himself a few buffalo calves. Two years later he had a herd of fifty animals. Colonel Sam Bedson had bought the Winnipeg calves and moved them to Stoney Mountain, Manitoba, and in 1888, when Jones learned that Bedson wanted to sell, he had travelled north and bought the animals. When the eighty pure-bred and thirteen cross-bred Canadian animals reached Kansas, Jones' herd was more than one 150 strong. He had maintained it by selling buffalo and a hardy cross-breed that he called "cattalo" to whomever could afford them.

Buffalo Jones had become one of America's foremost buffalo ranchers. When financial hardship eventually forced him to sell his herd to Michael Pablo in Montana, he had searched out another animal husbandry scheme. On learning that musk oxen were nearing extinction, he had decided to preserve them.

Even in buffalo country, however, Jones was considered a yarner. He claimed to have entered the Oklahoma Land Rush and won himself a town. He asserted that in 1882, while stopped in Mesillia, New Mexico, he had guarded Billy the Kid; to which a contemporary replied that it must have been his easiest duty, because Pat Garret had shot the Kid in 1881. Jones had set off from Perry, Oklahoma on June 12, 1897, stopping at Edmonton just long enough to speak to Secord, publicize his plan in the *Bulletin*, and buy himself an inflatable rubber life-preserver before moving on to The Landing.

While building a sturgeon head on the banks of the Athabasca, Jones had tried to hire himself a guide. Unfortunately, his assertive tee-totalling did not endear him to the rivermen. One man briefly considered travelling with him, but backed out when a convenient excuse presented itself. But the prospect of making the journey north alone didn't deter Jones. In his memoirs, he maintains that his time at The Landing was not wasted. He believed he had gained a working knowledge of northern Indian languages, and secure in the belief that Athabasca meant 'God forsaken,' he had donned his rubber life-jacket and pushed off on his own.

He surfaced briefly on July 19, when Edmontonians learned he was hung up on a rock in Grand Rapids. Rivermen dragged him to safety and he continued onward, but paranoia had begun to cloud his thinking. The ridicule he had borne at The Landing and Grand Rapids had soured him towards northerners. By the time Dr. McKay, the HBC man at Chipewyan, informed him that the Game Act would prevent him from hunting musk oxen with dogs, Jones was convinced he was the victim of a conspiracy. He believed the Company's most influential men were plotting to abort his mission, and insisted:

> A letter had also been sent ahead of me to the high priests and big chiefs, bearing the commands I have referred to [to block him from capturing any musk ox calves]. I tried hard to get a photograph of the letter, but the Hudson [sic] Bay Company's interpreter at Fort Resolution, who had it in his charge, declared he had lost it, which I knew to be a subterfuge to prevent me from photographing it. The document was one mass of hieroglyphics and characters, readable only by the natives.

Happily for him, during the downriver journey he had managed to find a companion for his Barren Lands trip. Suspicious of HBC motives and infuriated by the thought that they might be turned from their goal, they turned to Ed for help when they reached Resolution.

Although he may have doubted Jones' capacity to attain his objectives, Ed helped him and his partner build themselves a new boat. He agreed to protect their extra supplies until they could return for them in the spring. In Buffalo Jones' opinion, Ed was "a gentleman in the strictest meaning of the term," and Eva was "the only white lady in that region."

The encounter was so remarkable that Ed would later reminisce in a letter about:

... Buffalo Jones, the noted cowboy and great hunter of buffalo on the American plains long ago. He went south to Africa with eight or ten cowboys and lassoed all the wild animals that Teddy Roosevelt was shooting. Jones brought them out alive, Tigers, Lions, Giraffes, Hippopotamuses and many other kinds, too many to mention. He was the best man with a rope that I ever saw. He would catch an Indian dog by the leg on the run.

Jones' visit helped alleviate some of the anxiety that was mounting in Eva. She was pregnant again, and Alice Vickery had returned south in the spring. Fortunately, before she really had to contemplate spending a frigid winter in the grip of Miss Gaudet's prohibitions, one of the last Klondike-bound groups settled to winter at Resolution. The Klondikers were an enthusiastic and imaginative lot. The woman with them, Mrs. A.C. Craig, was bright and active, and quickly shattered the icy wall Miss Gaudet sought to raise between Eva and a larger world.

The Klondikers worked a definite change on Fort Resolution. Although they had some interest in the fur trade, dogs, snowshoes, caribou, and mail packets that served as the normal stuff of winter conversations, gold stood foremost in their minds. They had discovered how vast the north was, and were speculating. Had anyone ever prospected the shores of Great Slave Lake? By Christmas, rumours of a local gold strike had them buzzing like wasps around meat.

Word came west from Hay River that a hunter had stumbled across three white men camped more than 165 kilometres south of Saint Peter's Mission. When he had asked what they were doing, they told him they had stopped trapping in order to work a gold claim. It was so rich that each pan showed gold worth $150.

Ed knew that rich mineral deposits lay somewhere nearby: since the introduction of muzzle-loading rifles, local Indians had been mining lead for rifle balls. But when the rumour-mongers reached Resolution at New Year, they claimed frustration had driven them to spin their golden yarn. Instead of settling near Saint Peter's Mission and trading there, Billy Clark and Harry Anthony had moved inland to trap. They were unsuccessful, and when Ed's tripper arrived at Hay River at Christmas they were not there to compete with him for the Slavey furs.

Although their story had no basis in fact, Clark and Anthony refused to accept full responsibility for the tale the Klondikers had heard. They had claimed they were getting $75.00 in each pan, not $150.

Anthony had decided to search for real gold, and Billy Clark was breaking their partnership. There was a lot of bluster and bullshit in Clark but he was a good riverman, so Ed hired him again for Hislop and Nagle's spring boat brigade.

Hislop was refusing to travel south, and this was the second winter in a row that Ed would have to leave Eva alone. But preparations for the trip were complicated: Eva was pregnant and, since T. J. Marsh's wife was a nurse, Ed persuaded the Marshes to see her through her delivery, and to care for her until his return.

The Hislop and Nagle Company plans for the coming year were so involved that while Ed was talking to the Marshes at Hay River, Bouvier travelled there to confer with him. As he and Hislop told Police Inspector Routledge when the second northern police patrol arrived at Fort Resolution, they felt they had to improve their Smith's Rapids operation. They had owned property at Fort Smith since 1893, and because the Hudson's Bay Company was not preventing them from using its Smith Portage road, so they intended to operate a team of horses from there.

Ed's start south was further delayed by one of the two Willow River Métis who were accompanying him to Edmonton. Bob Erasmus was a special man in whom Ed believed he had found a replacement for Jack Russell. He was the son of Peter Erasmus, the famous Métis interpreter who had conducted the negotiations for many of the Plains Indian treaties, and had already worked a year or two as the tripper and interpreter at Willow River. He was intelligent and trustworthy, and Ed was teaching him how the Hislop and Nagle operation worked.

Julian Camsell, the Hudson's Bay Company's Chief Factor for the Mackenzie District, was at Hay River when Ed finally entrusted Eva and Geraldine to Mrs. Marsh. Camsell's attitudes were more akin to Joe Hodgeson's than the Gaudets'. The Hislop and Nagle Company was hitting his district hard. He decided that the best way to learn about the free traders lay in socializing with them. It was with mutual respect and to their mutual benefit that Camsell and Nagle agreed to travel together as far south as Fort Chipewyan. When the party set off from Hay River on February 18, the weather was holding near -50° Fahrenheit.

Ed did not reach Edmonton until mid March, but during his trip he encountered more parties of Klondikers. At The Landing, nestled almost in the shadow of the *SS Athabasca*, an enormous encampment

Building the Sparrow at Athabasca Landing.

of them had gathered. Two portable sawmills were milling timber stripped from the surrounding hillsides. At least one boat-yard produced vessels for the gold seekers, and at another place a sixty-five foot, pre-fabricated steamboat called the *Sparrow* was rising above her ways. In order to control the mob of frenetic gold-seekers the HBC had placed a gate on its section of the Athabasca Landing Trail, blocking and infuriating the freighters working between The Landing and Edmonton.

Almost as soon as Ed arrived at Edmonton, a Grand Rapids improvement committee sought him out. They felt it was imperative that a good channel be cleared on the east side of Grand Rapids Island. The government had refused to fund the project, but together with the Klondikers the committee had raised enough capital. Ed agreed that if the committee compensated the Hislop and Nagle Company for the inconvenience, it could hire Billy Clark to blast away the east-channel boulders.

Edmonton was as fervid as Athabasca Landing. The *Bulletin*'s publicity campaign was attracting all kinds of hopefuls toward the backdoor routes to the Klondike. Every imaginable kind of vehicle was being harnessed to their needs; every vacant lot in town was covered with tents; every pack-horse, ox, and dog was spoken for.

Ed had not anticipated having any difficulty buying a team of horses. Nor was a shortage of horses his only problem. McDougall and Secord were moving into a newly constructed brick store, so his outfit lay scattered between their old and new stores. Furthermore, his cousin Charlie Nagle had appeared from Arnprior, Ontario. Charlie was an absolute greenhorn, but Ed felt obliged to treat him royally.

By mid May, Ed had managed to get his outfit and two teams of horses to The Landing, where his scows awaited him. The place was even more chaotic that it had been when he arrived in March. A tent city had popped into existence: between six and seven hundred men had gathered into suburbs named Fifth Avenue, East and West Chicago, and Bohemian Row. Billy Clark had stopped on his way back to Edmonton to inform them that he had successfully completed his work at Grand Rapids. So more than forty strange river-craft awaited an opportunity to chase the spring ice down river.

The most impressive vessels at Athabasca Landing were the three steamers. Of them, the *Sparrow* was the finest. A Scot named G.T. Leitch had freighted her in from Minnesota, and intended operating her on the waterways below Fort Smith. She had a steel frame covered with an oak and elm hull and superstructure, with 60-horsepower Scotch marine engines driving each of her twin propellers. Leitch had already published the rates he intended to charge for passengers and freight.

Ed's crew was not the first one away from The Landing, and by the time they reached Grand Rapids it had become plain that Hay River gold was not Clark's only yarn. The ex-Hislop and Nagle man was now considered the most reliable guide for the rapids, and commanded good wages for his services. Even river pilots who had run Grand Rapids since the early 1880s were baffled by the changes he had made in the eastern channel. When Leitch and the 65-foot *Sparrow* arrived at the head of Grand Rapids, they awaited the return of the only man who could pilot boats down.

Klondikers were lined up to use the tramway, for which the HBC was charging $5 a ton. After a glance at the seven rocks Clark had battered, Ed pulled for the old portage trail. This spring he was chasing Bill Connor down north: the Fort Smith trader had bought a 50-foot stern-wheeler named the *Enterprise* and already had her down Grand Rapids. He intended taking her through the east side portages at Smith Rapids and sailing her on Great Slave Lake and the Mackenzie River. If he got to Slave Lake first, he would outflank the Hislop and Nagle Company.

At McMurray Ed stopped to pick up his horses, which he had sent overland from Grand Rapids. By July 4 he was at Smith's Landing, where he learned of Connor's success with the *Enterprise*. She was only ten feet longer than the boats the rivermen were used to handling; Connor had pulled out her boilers and machinery and sent them down the Smith Portage Road. The experienced Métis rivermen he hired then had little trouble with her flat-bottomed hull.

Although Klondikers were already bottling up the east-side portages, Ed's sixteen-man river crew was experienced enough to get his outfit smoothly by them. He put his horses to work as soon as he reached Smith's Landing, but competition for the Klondikers' freight was fierce. In addition to the teams from McMurray, the HBC had brought another fourteen animals down river, Colin Fraser had two yokes of oxen and a team and wagon working the portage road, and the Alaska Mining and Transportation Company had teams of its own.

Only the HBC had decent stables for their animals, however. Ed paused in his downriver run long enough to buy a lot behind the one he already owned in Fort Smith, and arrange feed for his horses. He put men to work building a small stable in the compound he and Hislop had perched on the lip of the precipice overlooking the Rapid of the Drowned. Then he set off down the road from his post to the river.

CHAPTER 13

Gold at Great Slave Lake
(1898 - 1899)

From Fort Resolution, Hislop's outfit went across the lake and Bob Erasmus set off in a small sailboat Ed had bought from some Klondikers to retrieve Eva and the children. Ed could not restrain himself for long, however, and soon set off in a canoe to meet his family. On April 10, Eva had delivered a son, whom T.J. Marsh had baptized Edmund Harry Nagle.

When she and Ed finally reunited and returned to Resolution, she was overwhelmed by the scenes that greeted her. Boats of every style and shape bobbed in Resolution Bay. Hundreds of Yukon-bound prospectors were camped near the Hislop and Nagle and Hudson's Bay Company posts. Some musicians had even formed a band that played for every approaching vessel, so she and little Teddy arrived to a coronet fanfare.

Buffalo Jones was one of the crowd at Fort Resolution. He had captured his musk ox calves, only to have someone slit their throats before he could get them out of the Barrens. Although he was quite depressed, he was finding some solace at Resolution. Everyone, especially Ed and Eva, fed him very well, and the music lifted his spirits. To enrich his grubstake, Ed paid him for a cabin he had built at the east end of Great Slave Lake. By July 17, Jones had joined the stream of hopefuls headed toward the Klondike.

Fort Resolution, however, faced a new swarm of travellers. Folks in Edmonton had heard Billy Clark's rumours of gold, and speculators were arriving to winter at Great Slave Lake. Although mention of Clark generated skepticism in Ed, it was impossible for him to ignore

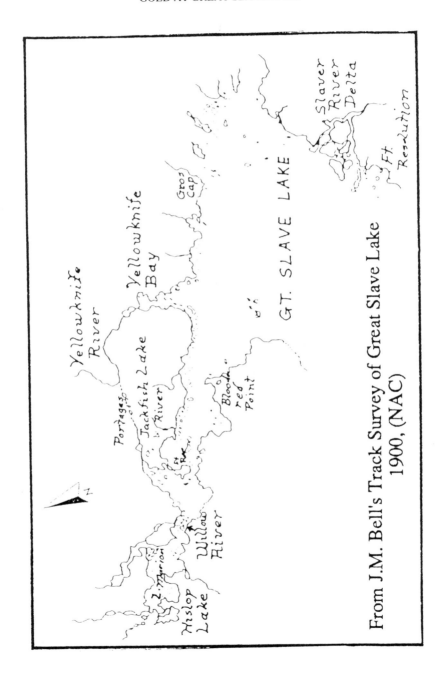

From J.M. Bell's Track Survey of Great Slave Lake 1900, (NAC)

Hislop and Nagle post at Fort Resolution, Ed Nagle near the right window in the background.

these enthusiastic new arrivals. His correspondence had already appeared in the *Bulletin*, and now he began acting as that newspaper's Great Slave Lake reporter. Late in the summer of 1898 his first few comments on the new arrivals appeared in the *Bulletin*:

> There are quite a number of parties who have made up their minds to winter here (at Resolution). We may have a big mining camp here next year, as people are finding gold and silver-bearing quartz on every island.
> The miners are not troubling the Indians as much as I expected.

Although Ed only alluded to it in passing, the interaction between the prospectors and the Indians was of real concern to him. His interest remained, of course, fixed on the fur trade. He had a healthy distrust of the behavior of people in crowds, and he recognized that misunderstandings between natives and prospectors might destroy attitudes of trust that Hislop and Nagle had worked hard to establish. By the late summer of 1898 he was wondering if a treaty might not benefit the Indians north of Edmonton.

In spite of his qualms regarding Resolution's new settlers, Ed had plenty of cause for celebration. Bob Erasmus had proven a capable surrogate for Jack Russell. When entrusted with the fall fur shipment, he got it safely to Edmonton. With the Hislop and Nagle Company network intact and flourishing Ed could invest more time in his family, and his new son Teddy was his pride and joy.

On the north arm of Great Slave Lake, however, Jim Hislop was not so satisfied with life. Notwithstanding his popularity among the trappers and boatmen, and the intellectual stimulation he got from tormenting the Hudson's Bay trader at Fort Rae, he longed for a close companion. During his years at Willow River, Hislop had fathered a few children for whom he cared and provided, but he wanted a wife who would share at least some of his interests.

James Hislop in the Nagle home at Fort Resolution.

Fortunately, he mentioned his loneliness to Father Dupré, and the priest had the Catholic Nuns at the Fort Resolution introduce him to a girl studying at the Mission School. Nancy Redech was a stunningly beautiful Slavey Indian girl fluent in Slavey, Chipewyan, Cree, Dogrib, and French. Her father, a hunter named Lamaliece who had moved from Hay River to Fort Rae, had recently died. On September 21, she married Hislop at Willow River, and the Hislop and Nagle Company celebrated his good fortune by hosting a dance there in November.

At Resolution the new prospectors were not as well behaved as the 1897-98 Klondikers had been. Gold fever had gripped them. As winter set in, they repeatedly twisted Ed's attention away from his family. But despite the aggravation they were causing him and the Indians, their wild optimism intrigued him. He charged his next *Bulletin* report with detail and speculation:

We have several parties of miners wintering here: The O'Brien [and] the Willard, of Chicago; the Minstrel Boys; Livermore and Baker; [the] Bolton boys, and what is left of the Holt party. They claim to have found some very rich quartz and are satisfied to

168

remain here. I am of the opinion that next summer will prove this lake to be better than the Klondike. There were plenty of good specimens brought in by the Indians, and they claim that where they found them there is mountains of it.

[However,] we are greatly in need of a government assayer. We have local ones, but they are tongue-tied for some reason. In one instance an Indian brought in a piece of quartz. They made the test. Told Mr. man it was no good, or comparatively so. [Then] they learned where he found it, hired a white guide and located in the neighborhood of 30 claims [at the place], and left Mr. man in the cold. You know the nature of the red man. Once scalded he is always afraid, [even] of cold water. I hold quite a few specimens of theirs, awaiting some competent man.

Shortly after my arrival here last spring a party pulled out to cross the lake. Shortly before, there had been trouble in the party: One of them was a woman. Three days after their departure they returned, one man less in the party. The story I got and the one my man got did not correspond. This disagreement of accounts of the affair aroused some suspicion of foul play. A few days afterwards the party went on. Everybody else crossed the lake in safety.

I saw it mentioned in some paper that when the [treaty] commissioners are at Fort Smith next summer to make a treaty with the Indians there, they wish to meet the Indians of Great Slave Lake. [In order to meet them] the Providence and Fort Rae Indians would have to cross the lake to Resolution and then go up [the Slave River to Fort Smith].

[It is worth noting that our gardens have been very good this summer.] The Roman Catholic Mission had over one hundred bushels of potatoes. The Hudson's Bay Company is about the same. I had not quite so many potatoes, but in place had fine carrots, cabbage, cauliflowers, onions, beets, etc., but no melons or peaches. Many of the half breeds had small gardens also. Our milkman sold milk at 25 cents a cupful. Trout sold at $1.00 each.

Our fall fishing has not been very good. The lake low, and very high winds being the cause.

Our first snow came on the last of September. [The] first ice on October 1st. I had my dogs out for a drive to-day, the first of the season.

But events at Slave Lake were unfolding more quickly than Ed could record them. His letter did not reach Edmonton until about

December 15, and even as Edmontonians read it and wondered about the Treaty Commission that would head north on 24 May 1899, the Bulletin began publishing a series of reports that would affect four successive generations of northerners.

Ed's letter probably travelled south with Leon Bureau, who was one of the Resolution prospectors. When he arrived at Edmonton, the *Bulletin* naturally reported his comments too. Bureau repeated that the fishing was bad, but added that immense herds of passing caribou had provided meat enough to offset the food shortage. His most noteworthy information, however, concerned the samples of quartz he had with him. They were studded with minerals, and he was off to Paris to have them assayed. If the results were good he would return to Resolution in the spring.

W.J. McLean pounded into town hard on Bureau's heels, and the ghostly and triumphant voices of Samuel Hearne and the already-historic Klondikers rang through his observations on the prospects at Great Slave Lake. He had been at Slave Lake since March, and had taken samples from sixteen different locations. Swearing that Great Slave Lake ore would yield between $5,800.00 and $5,900.00 a ton, McLean struck off to secure Canadian incorporation for his Yukon Valley Prospecting and Mining Company.

McLean's samples had destroyed all restraint and reason among the prospectors at Fort Resolution. The balance that had suspended traditional native culture in relation to specific southern values swung wildly. Just seven years earlier, the only whites that Indian trappers had encountered were either priests or Hudson's Bay Company traders. Now they suffered a plague of madmen searching for gleaming stones near the lakeshore. In an effort to attain some perspective on the lunacy, trappers kept to their usual trading routines, but they soon found cause to question the sobriety even of Ed and the other traders.

Ed was only partially attentive to his Christmas trading. Billy Clark's Hay River gold story no longer seemed so far-fetched, tied as it was to a galena deposit near the Little Buffalo River. Although McLean had been vague about his locations at the east end of Great Slave Lake, Ed felt they had to be close to the water. He believed that the people familiar with that area could probably find them, and he began asking his trappers to bring in the shiny rocks they found. By January first most people at Resolution were fixated on mining, and Ed's personal letters and subsequent *Bulletin* reports vividly record the tumult that ensued.

What a change the discovery of rich gold mines will make in a country. Of course you read of [the] Klondike and hear people talk, but until you are one of a party rushing to where gold was found you do not realize the fever of it. Gold, too, that pays so many thousands [of dollars] to the ton that we fear to quote the figures lest we should be disbelieved. Imagine yourself at Resolution and hear[ing] news of such a find. It was in the month of January, 45 and 50 below zero [Fahrenheit], and a gale [was] blowing.

We were only a few, comparatively speaking, but you ought to have seen the rush when one party on the 2nd of January disappeared. They were soon followed by his lordship [the Roman Catholic Bishop], who came upon them before daylight. Before I left and was ready to return, another party arrived; well this was nothing, it [the Pine Point galena deposit] being but a short way from here [Fort Resolution]. The next move [to the northeast shore of Great Slave Lake] was ten days to go and return. Fish had to be taken from here for the round trip, which meant 250 lbs. of provisions for three or four men, so you can see there was very little riding, such was the excitement. People who could hardly be induced to go 200 yards from home, cheerfully started on this long journey and reached their destination and returned with frozen faces.

I don't think the Klondike would ever be more excited. Why people were simply crazy, and outfit after outfit started out getting their provisions and running the great risk of getting lost and freezing to death. Several parties have returned from down the lake and gone out without a guide or even an idea of the country.

The cabin that Ed had bought from Buffalo Jones now proved very useful. With extensive experience as a winter traveller and a cabin at the east end of Slave Lake, he was better prepared than most prospectors, but even for him the journey east was a memorable one.

I went as far as the Hoar Frost River ...; camped on Christy Bay one night, stayed on King Beaulieu's point five days, then went to Hoar Frost River. Right across from there I owned a cabin that I had bought from Buffalo Jones, ...
... and ..., dry wood was not too plentiful ...

The old-timers at Great Slave Lake had struggled and worked together for years. If the ore deposits were valuable, they fully intended to control them. Since some of them had businesses to care for and none of them was prepared to raise working capital on his own, they put aside their previous personal differences and banded together. James McKinlay had retired from the Hudson's Bay Company, so he acted on behalf of Ed and the others.

> The next step after this was to form a party composed of all the influential people in this part of the country, for the purpose of developing the claims. We had a meeting and formed a party, calling it the McKinlay Barren Ground Prospecting and Development Company, with Dr. Hallwright, Chas. Holt, and Jas. McKinlay as the board of managers, and J.S. Camsell, chief factor of this district in the Hudson's Bay Company, as our president. We are not afraid to talk as we are sure we have the mine. We saw the mine, melted the rock, and Dr. Hallwright has samples of the gold.

When Hislop reached Fort Resolution for the annual winter meeting, he was immediately conscripted by the McKinlay party. By the time NWMP Inspector Routledge arrived with the winter police patrol in February, the McKinlay group was well organized. Routledge immediately began selling mining licences on the government's behalf. And to keep track of the prospectors he transferred Corporal John Trotter north from Fort Smith, where he had been guarding the buffalo, to Fort Resolution. After Routledge visited the Pine Point galena mine and the Hoar Frost River claims, Ed gave him a set of samples to take out and have assayed.

Ed's fragmentary reports to Edmonton in the *Bulletin* had raised tremendous interest, so when Hislop and Charles Griffin arrived from Resolution in March the *Bulletin* demanded information. Griffin obligingly mentioned having visited the Pine Point silver claims and examining the fifteen-foot shaft that had been sunk there. Then Dr. Hallwright arrived - having killed a team of dogs to get the McKinlay Party samples south - and headed east to raise money in Ottawa and England. When Bill Connor brought gold-bearing slate from Fort Smith, and McLean returned as the sole designated agent for the Yukon Valley Prospecting and Mining Company of Chicago, the *Bulletin* saw the north country as boundlessly rich.

As an official representative of the Department of Mines in Ottawa, Dr. Robert Bell's eventual arrival at Edmonton lent credibility to every report and opinion that the *Bulletin* had presented. The samples of Pine Point galena that the Department of Mines had assayed had showed 38.86 ounces of pure silver to the ton of galena. Dr. Bell was on his way north to examine the ore deposits.

Despite their interest in the Slave Lake rush, during the spring of 1899, Hislop and Nagle remained sober with regard to their fur business. In August of 1898, Billy Clark had hung the *Sparrow* up on the rocks at the head of Grand Rapids. In the flood of news about Klondikers and gold rushes, the partners had learned that Dick Secord had quietly bought her from George Leitch for $2,000; at their winter conference they had decided to refloat her and sail her below Smith's Rapids. On behalf of the Hislop and Nagle Company, Hislop paid Secord $2,800.00 for the little steamer when he reached Edmonton.

Before returning north Hislop hired Jack Kelly on as steamboat engineer, and by May 24 they were away from The Landing. But it was getting increasingly difficult to freight supplies down north. At about the same time that Clark had grounded the *Sparrow*, the Hudson's Bay Company had leased the whole of Grand Rapids Island. In previous years they had attempted only to prevent traders from using their tramline. Now they were trying to close off the island. Hislop portaged his outfit down the free traders trail.

Although the *Sparrow* rested on the rocks in the boiling center of the east side channel, no holes were punched in her bottom. With the Athabasca River in full flood it was a relatively simple, if somewhat delicate, operation to offload her cargo and redirect her downstream.

As soon as the ice was off the Slave River, Ed started upstream to meet his partner. Leitch's original plan had been to slip rollers under the *Sparrow*, and use her steam capstan to winch her down the Smith Portage road. Hislop and Nagle had Connor's precedent to follow. When they met at Smith's Landing, the partners stripped the little boat of her boilers and mechanisms. And while her hardware travelled down the Smith Portage road, her hull went over the east side portages. The Klondikers had cut the riverbanks down to water level at each of the take-out places, and they had clipped several metres off the top of the Mountain Portage and placed a Spanish Windlass there. The *Sparrow* was deeper hulled than Connor's boat, but it took the traders and their boatmen only seven days to get her to Fort Smith.

Ed had scouted the Slave River Delta for a suitable place to moor the steamboat. For the past few years he had used the farthest western channel of the Slave as a bypass route for his trade scows, and the locals were calling it Nagle Channel. It was deep and narrow, with fine stands of timber lining its banks and a low spot where the steamer could be dragged from the water. Hislop and Nagle were having Kelly lengthen the little boat, and after a short sail on Slave Lake they hauled her out in Nagle Snye and started a crew of five men felling logs and whip-sawing boards for the work.

While the *Sparrow*'s boilers had rolled down the Smith Portage road, however, Ed and Jim had had a shock. The Hudson's Bay Company had applied to the government for a lease on the road, intending to monopolize Smith Rapids the same way it was controlling Grand Rapids Island. To establish its right to the road, it was already installing a telephone line connecting Smith's Landing to Fort Smith. As soon as Hislop's outfit got to Willow River and his furs were back at Resolution, the partners started back up the Slave intending to survey a portage road and apply for a government lease of their own.

Once again, Bob Erasmus was put in charge of the fall shipment. After Secord estimated the value of the Hislop and Nagle furs at between $40,000 and $45,000, Edmonton looked toward the Slave Lake ore deposits. The fur traders had worked long and hard to build their businesses, but gold and silver would make quicker fortunes.

When Robert Bell had reached Slave Lake on July 20th, the McKinlay Barren Ground Party was the only really organized group there. A group of discouraged Klondikers had sold J.S. Camsell the steam launch *Ethel*, and Fred Gaudet had purchased the *Argo*, so McKinlay's group had two available boats. The *Ethel* was put at Bell's disposal. And within two months the government geologist had shattered the dream of quick fortunes at Great Slave.

After his examination of the ore deposits, Bell stated unequivocally that there were no precious metals at any of the sites he had visited. He did not rule out the possibility that there might be gold somewhere on Great Slave Lake, but he cautioned that the chances were slim. Furthermore, although the Pine Point galena was of very high quality, he maintained that the costs of mining and transporting it would be prohibitive. Leaving his nephew behind to examine the region between Great Bear and Great Slave Lakes, the government representative returned to Ottawa.

CHAPTER 14

The New Order
1899 - 1902

After Robert Bell's comments, Great Slave Lake's old timers turned back to the businesses they had worked to develop. The government did not grant Hislop and Nagle a lease for the Smith Portage road they had surveyed, but it did not allow the Hudson's Bay Company to monopolize the existing road either. While Bell made his way south, Ed and Jim returned to Fort Resolution, where Kelly had their new steamer up on ways. By the time Hislop was ready to start north from Nagle Snye, she had been renamed the *Eva Nagle*.

Although the Slave Lake boom had busted, James Mackintosh Bell remained with the Gaudets and helped buoy Fort Resolution's collapsing social roster. Bell was a thin, affable young man, only 23-years-old. This stay in the north would be both his first extended sojourn from home, and the first test of his geological career. While his uncle examined the mineral deposits, he had mapped the north arm of Great Slave Lake. The region surrounding Great Bear Lake, which he had been assigned to explore during the summer of 1900, was neither mapped nor extensively explored.

Young Bell was excited by the adventure that lay ahead of him, but he was also homesick and apprehensive. He had grown up at Almonte, and when he learned that Ed's family had originally settled there he sought out the free trader. Soon even Fred Gaudet's prohibitions could not keep him away from the Nagles. Over the course of the winter, Ed quelled some of Mackintosh Bell's despondency and developed an affectionate and abiding friendship with him.

The S.S. Eva Nagle *at Nagle Snye.*

Throughout that winter, Ed remained the *Bulletin*'s Great Slave Lake correspondent. On the strength of the gold rush he had urged the government to institute a regular northern mail service. Now he began carefully tailoring his Bulletin reports. David Hanbury was a "hard looking pelican" when he returned to Resolution. He had lost his canoe and outfit in the Lockhart River on his way out of the Barrens, and Ed re-outfitted him and helped him on his way. But his accident did not merit mention in the *Bulletin*. Nor did the proof of Buffalo Jones' prescience: The Duke of Bedford paid $2,500 for a pair of live musk ox calves and James McKinlay turned from gold mining to musk ox wrangling. Instead of rambling on about adventures in the wilderness, Ed concentrated on the sense of community developing among the settlers established at the lake.

That fall and winter was a busy time for the Hislop and Nagle Company. Bob Erasmus had trouble during his return north from Edmonton. Ice on the Slave River forced him to leave an outfit at Fort Smith, and carry on to Fort Resolution. As soon as the snow was deep enough for dog trains, Ed sent him back to Smith. When Erasmus returned to Resolution, the Hislop and Nagle Company started him out again for Edmonton to organize the new company outfits.

Kelly was adding an extension-insert and passenger cabins to the *SS Eva Nagle*, so Ed turned his own attention toward breeding the dogs he wanted. He needed large animals - weighing between 60 and 70 kilograms - with the stamina of Indian dogs but legs long enough to handle deep snow. He had obtained a big Russian Wolfhound named Bones from a passing Klondiker, and began mating him with some Eskimo Huskies from the Mackenzie River Delta. Within a few years his Mackenzie Valley Huskies would be famous throughout the north.

By the time Mackintosh Bell was ready to start for Great Bear Lake in the spring of 1900, Fort Resolution was awash with news of the approaching Slave Lake Treaty Commissions. Anticipation was running so high that Bell could persuade only two men to join his Bear Lake expedition: a riverman of bad reputation named Louis Tremblay, and an overweight, but breezy and good-natured ex-Klondiker named Charlie Bunn. Ed sent his young friend and his companions off with as much warmth and optimism as their circumstances warranted. Fortunately, near the west end of Slave Lake, Bell improved his chances for success by recruiting Charles Camsell - son of Ed's old adversary, Julian Camsell - and a riverman by the name of Johnny Sanderson.

In 1899, two Government Commissioners had moved towards Fort Resolution: one whose concern was the Indians, and another concerned for the Métis. Neither had actually reached Resolution, but the Indian Commissioner had attained most of his other objectives. By overstepping his authority and implying that hunters who signed his treaty document would not be bound by the Game Act, he had managed to persuade most of the Indians he met to sign the government treaty.

The Half Breed Commissioner had not been as effective. Fearing a repeat of the fiasco that had disenfranchised the prairie Métis, the government had placed limits on its offer to the northern half breeds. Land pirates had stripped the plains Métis of their scrip lands. So, although the Commissioner offered every northern half breed - man, woman, and child - scrip entitling them to 240 acres of land, title to the land was not transferrable.

Unfortunately, the prairie Métis who were now settled in the north had cried out vigorously against all government conditions, and another band of real estate speculators - one of whom was Dick Secord - had followed the Commission north. Due partly to the cash that Secord and his companions waved at them, the northern Métis had refused to accept non-transferrable land scrip. Since the Commissioner's primary objective was to settle with them, after consulting with the resident northern priests and traders, he agreed to make the scrip transferrable. As a result, by the fall of 1899, Dick Secord and other white investors owned most of the scrip lands between Edmonton and Fort Smith, by the fall of 1899.

In the spring of 1900, both the Indian and Half Breed Commissioners were on their way to Great Slave Lake to finish the tasks they had begun the previous summer. Their July arrival at Fort Resolution had an astonishing and irrevocable effect on that post's routines. Disregarding their usual practice of gathering only at local posts for Christmas and New Year, Indians appeared at Fort Resolution from all regions of Slave Lake. The Slaveys came east from Hay River; the Dogribs and Yellowknives came south from the north shore; and the Chipewyans came from as far away as Fort Smith and the east end of Slave Lake.

As a result of all this springtime activity, Ed and Jim anticipated poorer fur returns than normal. However, since they knew that the Indian Commissioner would make cash payments of $32 to each chief, $22 to each headman, and $12 to each band member who adhered to the treaty, they planned to collect as much of the cash as they could. Moreover, since cash annuities would continue into the future - repeated each year that the Indians recognized their commitment to the treaty - the Hislop and Nagle Company instituted special treaty-time discounts on their trade goods.

That spring's Fort Resolution treaty gathering was a time for Ed to perfect a dictum he would later commend to his sons: "avoid politics and religion and get your business done." Avoiding politics was easy enough. After observing the prospectors' search for mineral deposits at Slave Lake, he honestly believed a treaty would help protect the Indians. But when T.J. Marsh arrived at the gathering, Ed's friendship with the Anglican placed him squarely in the midst of a religious conflict.

The Commissioners' arrival augured an end to the old Hudson's Bay Company-Roman Catholic power cabal. Marsh was one of the men who recognized that. In defense of his Slaveys, he proclaimed they required protection from Catholic predation. The Catholic priest at Fort Resolution, on the other hand, maintained that faithful Catholics must continue shunning all Anglicans. The rivals distrusted one another and, upon encountering the host that had gathered to meet the Treaty Commissioner, could not resist casting nets on behalf of their faiths. Entries from their respective journals reveal their deep mutual antagonism, and describe aspects of the social waters through which Ed and Jim were navigating.

Regarding the Catholic presence at the treaty gathering, T.J. Marsh noted:

> About midnight of [July] the 24th the Commissioner arrived at Resolution, and at 1:00 P.M. of the 25th the Treaty was read to the Indians and signed by them, and then payment was made forthwith. The R.C. priest made himself very conspicuous before the Indians and seemed to succeed in making himself very popular with the Commissioner, A.J. Macrae, somewhat to the cost of absolute justice and fairness, although in the end I think the impression was that Englishmen are universally Protestants, which was encouraging to us, and inclined the Indians to listen more readily to us.

However, from the Catholic priest's perspective:

> Mr. Marsh (Anglican minister) showed to the government officials all the Indians gathered around him as being Protestants, and boasted about having civilized them. The officials, being themselves Protestants, were quite happy to meet at last a minister who seemed to have succeeded in his work. He received everything he asked for on behalf of the Indians. This government help is a new obstacle for us.

Ed worked carefully to preserve the integrity of the Hislop and Nagle Company in the eyes of both clerics.

Secord and his associates did not follow the Half Breed Commission to Fort Resolution in 1900. Yet, although their business might have profited from it, there is little evidence to suggest that either Hislop or Nagle seriously exploited the opportunity for scrip speculation.

There were, however, two land titles with which the Ed and Jim were very concerned. Ed had only been able to establish his Fort Resolution post by settling on Pierre Beaulieu's land. When Beaulieu "took scrip," Ed made a determined and successful effort to purchase the plot of land on which the Resolution post sat. Because there was no Hudson's Bay Company post nearby, Hislop was not as vulnerable at Willow River. Nevertheless, to ensure that no claim would be made

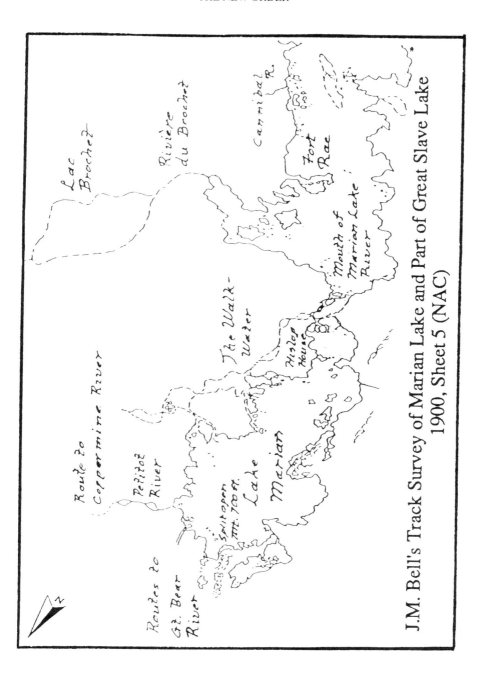

J.M. Bell's Track Survey of Marian Lake and Part of Great Slave Lake 1900, Sheet 5 (NAC)

on the Willow River post, Nancy Hislop took scrip and signed it over to her husband.

For many reasons, the summer of 1900 was an extraordinarily pleasant one for Ed. On June 19 Eva had given birth to the Nagles' second son, Sarsfield Barry, whom the Catholic priest had immediately baptized. And after the long winter of work, the *SS Eva Nagle* had proven so seaworthy that Ed sailed her up the Mackenzie River as far as Fort Good Hope. The fur harvest was better than he and Hislop had expected, too, and through the long days of August Ed spent many hours lounging with his children in the sun on the front porch of his Fort Resolution home, planning how to invest his company's treaty cash.

In mid-September, however, apparent tragedy shattered his general sense of well-being. When the remnants of Mackintosh Bell's party straggled into Hislop's Post, the news sped across the lake: Charlie Bunn had vanished on the Barren Lands and was presumed dead. The stories varied, but he had disappeared so completely that northerners were suspicious. His body had not been found. Mackintosh Bell was distraught.

Ed did not get the full story until Bell arrived from Hislop's Post. Bell's group had been on the eastern shore of Great Bear Lake when Bell decided to look at the Coppermine River. Sensibly, the group left a cache at the mouth of the Dease River before starting northward. But they began feeling uneasy almost as soon as they left Great Bear Lake.

They had hunted as they moved across the Barrens, and then made another cache about fifty kilometres inland. But Johnny Sanderson became so frightened by signs of Eskimo encampments that he deserted, taking the only rifle they had with them. Although menaced by a polar bear, Bell and Camsell decided to carry on towards their objective. They sent Bunn and Tremblay back to Great Bear Lake, and that was the last they saw of Bunn. When Bell and the rest of the party finally returned to Great Bear Lake, neither Bunn, Tremblay, nor Sanderson were there. Both Tremblay and Sanderson eventually found their way back to the Dease River cache, but Bunn never did.

According to Tremblay, the American's feet had bothered him and he had stumbled on the Barrens. Tremblay told Bell that Bunn had sent him ahead to build a fire. However, when Tremblay and Camsell went back through the fog to search for the American, Bunn was nowhere to be found. After an extensive but fruitless search, Bell had concluded that a longer delay would trap the whole party in the

The Hudson's Bay Company's Fort Resolution post.

north for the winter. Concern for his other men had forced an awful decision on him. Leaving behind a canoe, a rifle and some ammunition for Bunn, Bell had led the others south.

When James Mackintosh Bell reached Fort Resolution, he was suffering from a recurrent nightmare in which he saw Bunn wandering lost on the Barrens until he starved. Bell did not stay long on the south shore of Great Slave Lake. Although there was nothing Ed or his other friends could do to alleviate Bell's anguish, he was especially grateful for the support Ed gave him, and when he returned to eastern Canada they began a correspondence that ended only when Ed died.

By the fall of 1900, Hislop and Nagle had determined that the best way to invest their new capital was to revamp their summer transport operation. Kelly was retained as their steamboat engineer. When the *Eva* was up on her winter ways in Nagle Snye, he would move south to Fort McMurray to build a new steamer to run between the Athabasca River rapids and Smith's Landing. Hislop and Nagle also arranged to have Shot organize their northern freight in 1901. For $450.00 per scow, the Métis river guide was contracted to deliver their outfits as far as Fort Smith.

The Hudson's Bay Company had attained its early preeminence partly because of its wealthy stockholders, government influence and the fact that its traders were the only men in the field, but also because it helped the trappers when times were hard. After the Northwest Territories was transferred to Canada, however, the Company began abrogating the responsibility it had once assumed. Concentrating exclusively on business, the HBC traders lost some of the respect that had previously been accorded them. Recognizing this, Hislop and

The Eva, *towing scows north from Fort Smith.*

Nagle had made every effort to act compassionately in their own business.

By 1900, their success was about equally dependent upon business acumen and social commitment. Unhampered by the extreme distances separating the HBC posts from their sources of supply, Hislop and Nagle consistently provided exactly the trade goods the trappers requested. They also helped the hunters make the transition from muzzle-loaders to modern repeating rifles, and each fall organized large caribou hunts. In addition to the game required to support the company operation, caribou and fish were killed and preserved as emergency supplies. Trappers and their families had learned that if the game vanished they could rely on help from the Hislop and Nagle Company.

Ed and Jim had also worked hard to increase their company's prestige. Their new steamers did not hurt their image. Nor did the fact that they now had eleven trading posts - at Forts Smith, Resolution, Providence, Liard, Nelson, Simpson, Wrigley, Norman, Good Hope, and McPherson, and at Willow River, - and could afford to pay Shot to freight their outfits down north. With posts to the Arctic and trippers working the south shore of Slave Lake from Hay River east to Fort Reliance, within the Mackenzie watershed they had become as highly regarded as the HBC.

Midway through the winter of 1900-01, Charlie Bunn unexpectedly appeared at Fort Resolution. As Bunn told it, he had gotten on badly with Tremblay throughout the expedition. When he had slipped and sprained his ankle crossing a stream on the way back to Bear Lake, Tremblay had not bothered to help him. The riverman had called back that he would go a little farther then build a fire, but had left Bunn alone on the Barrens. Although hampered by his injured ankle, Bunn had made a desperate attempt to reach the Dease River cache when he realized he had been deserted. Bell's party was already gone by the time he got there, but after eight days of wandering without food or shelter he had miraculously stumbled upon an encampment of Dogrib hunters. The Indians had cared for him and taken him out to Fort Norman.

It would have been characteristic of Ed to have immediately written the news to Mackintosh Bell. During the summer of 1901, a different sort of visitor entered the North. When the SS *Eva* reached Fort Smith, C.W. Mathers was travelling with Shot. Mathers was a pioneer photographer who had been in Edmonton since 1891, and had already taken several photos of Ed. Now he was embarked on the first photojournalistic expedition into the Mackenzie Region. He had travelled with Bill Connor from The Landing, receiving a short tow from Colin Fraser across the western end of Lake Athabasca, and had joined Shot for the trip through Smith's Rapids. At Fort Smith he persuaded Ed to tow him north to Great Slave Lake behind the *Eva*, so he could attend the Fort Resolution treaty gathering.

Mathers' photographs show clearly how successful Hislop and Nagle had become. In the fall of 1901, Shot freighted $65,000 worth of their pelts south to Secord and during the winter of 1901-02, Ed began shifting his business tactics. He turned more responsibility over to Bob Erasmus and the other men he and Hislop had hired and trained. The advertisements he placed in the *Bulletin* helped him put pressure on the Dominion government. He demanded a northern mail service, and applied for and got an appointment as a Justice of the Peace for the Northwest Territories. By the spring of 1902 he was an integral part of the government's northern administration, empowered to enforce the Game Act and minor aspects of the law.

CHAPTER 15

The Retreat to Edmonton
(1902 - 1905)

In July of 1902, shortly after the Treaty party made its third visit to Fort Resolution, Ed and Eva became frightened for their children's health. As Ed had ferried the commissioners to Hay River, he had underscored the need for a northern mail service. As many other old-timers appear to have done at that time, he probably also emphasized how necessary a medical officer was for the region. He had already returned to Fort Resolution when word reached him that the government party would continue on to the Mackenzie outflow. Fort Providence needed the services of its doctor.

Increased traffic on the Mackenzie River had brought new threats to the western north. A measles virus menacing Fort Providence had originated among some whalers who had wintered near the Mackenzie Delta. It had spread south in the wake of the trade boats plying between the Beaufort Sea and Great Slave Lake. By the time the Treaty Commission was prepared to leave the north, the measles had reached Fort Smith, where seven people were reportedly dead.

There is little indication that Ed and Eva had thoughts of leaving their Fort Resolution home before the epidemic. Their newest child, a girl named Tess, was baptized by Fort Resolution's priest in August. And, although they were planning to educate their six-year-old daughter Gerry, they had likely intended to register her in the new school rising at St. Joseph's Mission. But by mid-winter, they felt that leaving Great Slave Lake was the only way to protect their children's lives.

The Eva *arrives at Fort Resolution; Ed Nagle stands between two of his men, near the stove on the scow.*

Throughout the early winter, the *Bulletin* published no reports on the epidemic. After an accident on the Athabasca nearly killed him, Bill Connor commented only on the whalers and how necessary he believed a mail service was. And when Captain Mills of the HBC steamer *Wrigley* arrived in Edmonton with his wife and children, he mentioned only that he had not been south for ten years. In fact, until January there is apparently only one *Bulletin* reference to measles: when the epidemic began to abate at Fort Chipewyan.

The winter of 1902-03 was, however, the first in years that the people of Edmonton received no news from Ed. The silence was curiously ominous, as if conditions at Great Slave Lake left him little time to spare. At Fort Resolution, the Nagles were indeed anxious and under siege. In January, an anonymous, journal-like two-part letter to the *Bulletin* catalogued the catastrophes at Great Slave Lake:

A word or two from Great Slave Lake and the far north. Our people have been very sad and downhearted this past summer [sic], so many having died from the measles. Fort Smith had seventeen deaths, Resolution thirty-one, Yellowknife — just a small band of Dogrib Indians — twenty-seven deaths. They are

187

only the ones who have come in since treaty. The other bands have not been heard from, except by those Dogribs who saw the others on their way out to the hunting grounds. There were twelve children from their party had died.

This is the first time in thirty years that these Indians have failed to come to the fort for their little supplies. We are looking for very bad news from that quarter. The greater part of them will have succumbed to the dreaded measles. When anything like that gets among them they are perfectly helpless, and will not hunt, fish or do anything but lie around their camps. Hay River was also visited by the measles and there was [sic] thirteen deaths in that small band of but a few souls, and a great many were still sick, both in the mission and in the woods. Of course, a great many more will have died.

Baptiste Bouvier, of Providence, in charge of a post for Hislop and Nagle, lost his youngest child. His whole family was down [with the measles] at one time. The little child lived but a few minutes after his father's arrival. The steamer was held over there for one day in order to assist at the funeral, which took place the following day at 3:30 p.m. There was a very large number of friends and relatives attended, as he is a very popular personage in that place.

I also felt for the poor sisters. Just fancy six of them tending about fifty Indian children. They looked very tired and almost done up. In spite of all their kind and attentive nursing several of their patients died. There was also a great many deaths outside the convent in the little village, and amongst the Indians in the woods. At Fort Simpson, fortunately, but few died. At Fort Wrigley several deaths occurred. It is a very unfortunate place. Just two years ago, a great many died from la grippé. At Fort Norman but four died. At the time of our reaching there, no deaths had been regarded as in.

Good Hope was not so fortunate. Several were then sick and a great many deaths had taken place. Both daughters of Mr. Gaudet, officer in charge of the Hudson's Bay Company trading post at that place, were ill with the measles, but I am happy to say that they have thoroughly recovered and are none the worse from their illness...

Unloading the Hislop and Nagle outfit at Fort Resolution, Great Slave Lake.

The correspondent tried including some regular news in his report:

> The Roman Catholic mission have put up a very nice little sawmill on a site 2 miles from Resolution, and have been able to saw five hundred logs. They are now building a large building to be finished by spring, as they are expecting six sisters who are coming to open up a [larger] school for the Indians. They intend putting up a large convent next summer.
>
> Hislop and Nagle have built a new warehouse, twenty by thirty.
>
> Fishing was very good last fall, the catch being about forty thousand. Hislop and Nagle [got] 8,000 lbs., [the] R.C. 8,000, [the] R.C. mission 8,000, [and] Folk & Swiggart 7,000. The rest are in the possession of several half-breeds.
>
> Mr. Nagle, of Hislop and Nagle, brought down a horse, the first of the horse kind so far north.
>
> J.E. Kelly is putting a new engine in the steamer *Eva Nagle*, and will also put in a new engine and boiler in Hislop & Nagle's new steamer *Alfa*, which will ply between Smith Landing and McMurray to tow scows down and bring back their furs in the fall.

Mr. Harrison, an English gentleman, and one of the Oblat[e] fathers arrived here on the 28th of October. The father is to remain here in order to learn the Indian language. Mr. Harrison intends going to hunt musk ox and caribou sometime during this coming winter.

But the overall tone was overwhelmingly bleak. During winter's onset the omens had been bad:

Winter set in very strangely. It commenced with a very heavy fall of snow in September. Then came rain, which lasted several days, and then it snowed every day for two weeks. At present our snow is deeper than it was last winter, being 21 inches in the woods and no cold weather as yet. Fur will be very scarce this winter. [The] Indians seem to say that there are but few signs.

As winter progressed, the people of Resolution struggled desperately to overcome successive catastrophes.

Since writing the above, we have had a very sad accident. A house belonging to the Church of England mission was burned to the ground on the night of December 18th. The wife of Jas. McKinlay and [her] three children, [and] Willie Brown's wife, sister, and one child were in the house at the time the fire broke out.

Mrs. Brown was the first one to awaken and realize their danger. She, being unable to reach the door, had presence of mind enough to break open one of the windows and throw Mrs. McKinlay's children and her own little girl out on the snow, passing out her sister as well. She then went to Mrs. McKinlay's room and wakened her, informing her that the house was in flames, and then rushed out herself.

Mrs. McKinlay, of course, was not aware of the open window and immediately made for the door. Not being able to find the door, and being overcome by the flames and suffocated by the smoke she fell in the midst of the burning flames. She remained but a short time until she recovered her breath, made for the door a second time, [and] finally found the latch and got outside.

Her clothes were all on fire. To extinguish them she threw herself in the snow. Her sister-in-law, thinking she was dead, ran away to the first house for shelter, as she was freezing because everyone escaped only in their night dresses with no shoes. Mrs. McKinlay finally came to herself and rushed to Mr. Nagle's house for shelter.

Mr. Nagle never saw such a sight. Her hands were cooked, her arms as well and her face, head, chest and back. She arrived at Mr. Nagle's house before any fires were made, it being 6:00 a.m., and Mrs. Nagle — with the assistance of Mr. Hilker — bandaged her burned parts as quickly as possible. Later Miss Gaudet, sister of F.C. Gaudet, H.B. Co. officer in charge here, has been dressing her burns.

Poor unfortunate people, they simply lost all they had. Hislop and Nagle, Swiggart, F.C. Gaudet and C. Hilker replenished their larder, dressed the children in new clothes, supplied cooking utensils and found them a new and comfortable shelter. [However,] It is very doubtful as to Mrs. McKinlay's recovery. Again we cry out for a medical man. We are at our wits' end how to act under fire of that kind.

Mr. McKinlay was away at the time of the fire, having started the day before with W. Brown for a two-week's absence to set their traps and hunt moose. Mr. Nagle immediately started two men and a dog team after them, overtaking them 25 miles out at 3:00 p.m. Mr. McKinlay and Mr. Brown returned immediately, arriving at Mr. Nagle's, where Mrs. McKinlay was, at 2:00 a.m. the following morning. He (McKinlay) felt very bad on hearing the sad news, of course, [as] he was not aware of his wife being burned. Mr. Nagle had forbidden his men to say any more [than that an accident had happened], as he was afraid Mr. McKinlay would not reach the side of his suffering wife [in time].

I have just received letters from Fort Rae giving statements regarding a number of deaths: [there] being 48 Indians [dead], with three bands not heard from. Hislop and Nagle's interpreter, Vitalle Laffertie [sic], lost his wife and baby by the measles, [she] being a great loss as she leaves six children [motherless].

A letter from the sister superior, [at] Providence, mentions twelve deaths [there], all [of them] school children in the small town, and 36 Indians [dead] in the woods.

Mrs. McKinlay is getting very weak.

When Jim Hislop arrived from Willow River for the winter meeting, he learned of the Nagles' intent to flee south. Since the children were too small to immediately travel by dog train, Hislop allowed

The Nagle family leaving Fort Resolution in 1904; left to right: Ted Nagle, Ed Nagle, Sarsfield Nagle, Eva Nagle holding Tess, Geraldine Nagle, and Jim Hislop.

himself to be persuaded to undertake the mid-winter buying trip to Edmonton.

Ed did not allow concern for his children and wife to divert him far from business. He and Hislop decided to buy a steamboat that Bill Connor had built the previous summer at Fort Smith. Ed had already applied to write the examinations for the government's Masters and Mates Competency Certificate; the partners decided that he should stay at Fort Resolution until after the exams. Then, they agreed, he would take over responsibility for the outfitting and freighting operations from Edmonton.

Eva Nagle's whole married life had been spent at Fort Resolution. For eight years she had built a home for her family, filling it with everything required for comfort in the wilderness. In Edmonton they would not even have a house of their own. She knew the struggle her four small children faced, and she prepared them for it by helping them pack their favourite possessions.

Since Hislop would take responsibility for all the northern posts once Ed was gone, he made a brief trip to Nova Scotia to visit his family before returning north. By July 4, 1903 he was back at Great Slave Lake. His outfit went quickly to Willow River and he returned to help sort and bale the company furs. Ed easily passed the government exams, and a short time later the partners bought the *SS Cariboo* from Connor.

Just before the Nagles started south, Ed had an interesting encounter in his role as Justice of the Peace. The NWMP was dispatching a permanent detachment to the high arctic. When it arrived at Fort Resolution, Ed received its officer-in-charge. Frank Fitzgerald was a steady, soldierly young man. Although he had enlisted in the police in 1888 and had served in the Klondike, this was his first permanent posting since his return from the South African Boer War. Ed and Eva enjoyed a short, pleasant visit with him. And when he left he promised to report to them on the conditions in the Mackenzie Delta.

The journey south was fraught with complications. During the first leg, Ed captained the *SS Eva* to Fort Smith. Recalling her own first northern adventure, Eva was hovering protectively at baby Tess's side. Gerry and Teddy were old enough to help her as best they could, but Sarsfield was unstoppably set on his terrible twos. Because his attention was diverted to the fur shipment, Ed could do little to resolve his worries about his family. His old friend Jack Russell, who had returned from the Klondike, was helping Shot with the furs, so as a special favour Ed asked them both to watch over Eva and the children.

From Fort Smith, it took teams of oxen two full days to lumber up the Smith Portage Road to Smith's Landing. The first night the Nagles slept at the Half Way House, away from the mosquitoes and bulldog flies. The following night they camped in a Hislop and Nagle building at the landing. Thence they took the new steamer *Alpha* as far as Fort McMurray, where they started tracking up the Athabasca River.

When tracking got underway, however, Eva's assistants were occasionally forced to ignore their charges. On the Athabasca, Sarsfield focused alertly on the work at each portage. He watched the rivermen lay poles and planks from the scows to the riverbank, and slide the fur packs and supplies ashore. Near the bottom of Grand Rapids, Shot discovered him edging gingerly shoreward along a plank. Fortunately, the river-guide plucked him from this potential tumble toward the river. Thenceforth the guardians were more watchful.

When the family reached Edmonton, John and Louvisa McDougall gave them a temporary home. Since the last time Ed had been south, Dick Secord had taken a seat on the Northwest Territorial Assembly. McDougall, too, had moved beyond frontier commerce toward the realm of national politics: in March of 1903 he had travelled to Ottawa to lobby for the northern postal service. From him, Ed probably learned that the mail service would begin in the spring of 1904, and that he would be appointed Fort Resolution's postmaster. He also learned that Wilfred Laurier's Liberals were planning to establish two new western provinces — Saskatchewan and Alberta.

Ed's move south could not have been better timed. Quite coincidentally, he had arrived in Edmonton when McDougall and Secord were in the midst of a major re-organization. The partners intended to continue linking the Hislop and Nagle Company to the fur market, but would no longer personally coordinate the operation. McDougall was passing his company shares to his son, so, with Secord committed to political life, one of the first things Ed had to do was repack the furs and send them off to London. Then he and McDougall set about restructuring the liaison between the two companies.

Life was not all work, though. Edmonton's social currents quickly swept the Nagles in. The children met Eva's parents, and she gloried in her freedom from the Gaudets. Ed joined the Edmonton Old Timers Club. After they placed Gerry in school, Ed and Eva set about planning a new home for themselves. They chose a lot that lay west of the old Hudson's Bay Company fort, between Jasper Avenue and the lip of the North Saskatchewan valley. It was carefully buffered from First Street and the Old Town area, where Nelly Webb and her professional colleagues still practiced.

During the spring of 1904, Ed put his outfits together after McDougall had received the annual wire from London detailing the results of the January and March sales. By that time he had placed the steamers *Eva* and *Cariboo* on the government's Rat Portage (Kenora) registry. Before he started north with his trade goods, contractors were building the new house.

Both Ed and Eva decided to return to Fort Resolution that spring, and intended to stay through the winter of 1904-05. Eva wanted the time to pack and move all their possessions, and Ed intended to establish the government post office at Fort Resolution, and choose the trader who would replace him. Although they left Gerry in a boarding school, they took the rest of their children with them.

At Fort Resolution, a letter from Frank Fitzgerald awaited them — Ed could appreciate the effort the policeman had made to keep his promise. The letter had come up the Mackenzie from Fort McPherson by dog team during the winter, and hinted of loneliness and cabin fever. Although Fitzgerald did not say much about the whalers, the northern detachment's presence had apparently affected them.

Dear Mr. Nagle,

Though I cannot give you any news, I thought that I would write you these few lines that I promised you. It is no use telling you anything about this place, you know what kind of a place a northern post is like, with only a H.B. Co. store in it. Jacquat comes over now and then. I think he is doing pretty well. The Indians over there [at Arctic Red River?] all seem to like him. I think he is going to get the best of Campbell, the H.B. man this winter. All the boys wish so anyway. Well I have been down to Herschell Island twice and seen the world renowned Huskies.

I went down by whale boat this summer. [We] stayed there three weeks, and took Mr. Whittacker's steamer to come back in. Well, we wrecked it on the coast, she went to pieces, not a stick left. We had a peach of a time getting back.

I went down again in November with dogs, and stayed nearly three weeks again.

The island is a fine place to have a good time, the girls are all that can be expected. If I could stay there most of the time I would not mind staying there a couple of years, but this God forsaken hole is hell. I am going to leave here early in March for Dawson, if it is possible to get a guide. You can guess what a time I will put in in that place if I ever get there.

You might drop a line any chance. I will always be pleased to hear from you. Remember me to all I know up there and kindest regards to Mrs. Nagle.

I remain
Yours sincerely,
F.J. Fitzgerald.

There was pressure on Ed to start work immediately. Hislop had not supervised the company's Fort Resolution trader during the winter, so the stores and furs were in disarray. Moreover, the *Eva* was still on her ways at the steamboat camp in Nagle Snye. She had to be in the water and up the Slave by the time Shot got the outfit scows to Fort Smith. The Indians would soon be arriving to meet the Treaty Commission.

It took five days to repair and launch the *Eva*, during which time Ed heard the disastrous story of his partner's winter. In October,

Hislop had taken the *SS Cariboo* across Slave Lake to Willow River. On the way back to Nagle Snye he had put her aground on Les îsles du Large, at the entrance to Great Slave Lake's eastern arm. Before he could refloat her, she had frozen in, and drifted with the pack ice until it set fast. He was still working to free her.

Ed managed to beat the Hudson's Bay Company boat to Fort Smith, so the Treaty Commission joined the scows in tow behind the *Eva*. Since the Hislop and Nagle outfit and the Commission reached Resolution at the same time, and the Hudson's Bay Company supplies had not yet arrived, business was brisk during the treaty gathering.

Unfortunately, there were kinks in the fur operation. Changes in the Game Act now prohibited traders from exporting pelts graded lower than #3, and the musk ox trade was in catastrophic disarray. The unborn musk ox trade had almost stopped, but efforts to save the animals from extinction had boomeranged. European menageries were now paying high prices for calves, so Scandinavian whalers and sealers had changed their professions. Throughout the winter they had rampaged over the musk ox grounds, slaughtering the adult breeding stock to take away their calves.

Despite his success at the treaty gathering, frustration and calamity tracked the rest of Ed's summer. Wind trapped the *Eva* in Resolution Bay for two days. There were ten scows filled with supplies for the Mackenzie posts, but Hislop could not free the *Cariboo* in time to help Ed sort the outfits. Then, as the *Eva* started west, one of her crewmen slipped overboard. After two fruitless days of searching, Ed posted a reward for the body and towed the Treaty party onward to Hay River. At Fort Norman he faced another tragedy. In September of 1904, his Fort Norman trader, a man named Patton, killed himself with a shotgun. Ed learned the details from George Ball, who had gone north in January as Patton's replacement.

By the time Ed got back to Fort Resolution, he was desperately tired and in need of support from his partner. Fortunately, Hislop awaited him with the good news that the ice had not damaged the *Cariboo*. And as they sorted and re-baled the fur they realized how incredibly successful the season had been. Added to a shipment that George McGlaughlin had taken south for them in the spring, this was by far the largest lot of furs they had ever collected.

Taking advantage of Ed's rising spirits, Hislop put a proposition to the Nagles. Nancy Hislop had not conceived any children of her own, and she was lonely. Teddy was six-years-old. Hislop would

Part of Hislop and Nagle's fur in one corner of the Buffalo Club fur warehouse.

travel south that winter to organize the outfit, but he wanted the boy to spend the winter with Nancy. Since Teddy wouldn't be going to school that winter, Ed and Eva agreed to send him off to adventure at Willow River.

At Fort Resolution, the winter was interesting but unthreatening. Trading was excellent. A few small fires broke out, but were easily controlled. As usual, the native families came in for Christmas and New Year. Eva and the children enjoyed their visits, and became quite excited when the wolves grew bold. Various packs killed several adult moose near the mouth of the Little Buffalo River, and pulled down a large bull buffalo near Fort Resolution. The Indians grew leery of camping out, but no one was attacked.

For Ed, the arrival of the first mail packet was a highlight. The government mail service was not much different from what the Hudson's Bay Company and the free traders already provided for themselves; it still took a packet from February to July to complete the 6,170-kilometre round trip from Edmonton to Fort McPherson; there were still severe limitations on the size and weight of the items that could be sent. But never again would mail be controlled by the HBC. Two regular packets now went as far as Fort Resolution, and instead of the previous four-dog trains, the government had put six Mackenzie River Huskies in front of each of its sleds.

197

That spring, Charlie Hilker became Ed's replacement at Resolution. By the time the *Eva* steamed to Fort Smith to meet the new outfits and the Treaty Commission, Ed already knew the fur returns would be high. When the first Hislop and Nagle shipment went south, he and Hislop estimated it was worth $80,000.00. By the time all the returns were in from the Mackenzie they upped the figure to $125,000.

The disarray of his trading business at Fort Resolution had irritated Ed when he arrived the previous spring. But by August of 1905, he and Eva were anxious to get back to Edmonton and he was again preparing to entrust his post to Hislop. Teddy had returned from Willow River as wild as the wind. Hislop's Post was on an island, which the boy had not been able to leave. He had, however, run loose with the native boys, and the Dogrib hunters had armed him and taught him to hunt. Since returning to Fort Resolution he had become so frustrated by the restrictions his parents imposed on him that he had shot to pieces the military duck coat Ed had worn during the Northwest Rebellion. Sarsfield, too, was always in trouble. He wandered Fort Resolution curiously, oblivious to its dangers. During the early summer Eva had dragged him from the midst of a pack of attacking dogs. They had not identified the pack leader until a few weeks later, when Charlie Hilker kicked one of the Mackenzie River studs off Teddy and shot it.

Ed and Eva started towards their new Edmonton home in mid August. The trip was uneventful. They got a burst of excitement between Athabasca Landing and Edmonton, where the people were celebrating riotously: Alberta had just become a province. By mid September, they had Gerry with them, and the Nagle family were settled in their new house.

CHAPTER 16

Shattered Allegiance
(1905 - 1913)

Ed was glad to be resettled in Edmonton. At 52 years of age, he no longer wanted Fort Resolution's worries. He wanted his family safe, near medical facilities and schools. Furthermore, he and Hislop needed an Edmonton representative. The H & N-embroidered flag now fluttered above fourteen permanent posts which lay scattered below Smith's Landing as far north as the Mackenzie River Delta, and up the Liard River northwest to Fort Nelson. Trippers and travelling outfits ranged the south shore of Great Slave Lake. A special outfit accompanied the Treaty Commission to each of its stops south of Smith's Rapids, and the *Eva* frequently towed the commissioners' scows from Fort Smith to the more northerly gatherings.

Hislop and Nagle's freighting operation, for which Ed was personally responsible, was particularly well conceived. Freighters on contract moved outfits between Edmonton and Athabasca Landing, a regular crew of boat builders put new scows on the Athabasca each year and three steamers — each one with its own engineer and crew — plied the waterways between the Athabasca rapids and the Beaufort Sea. With warehouses at Athabasca and Smith's Landings, Fort Smith, and the Steamboat Camp on Nagle Snye, and teams at Smith's Portage, freight was protected at each stage on the route between Edmonton and the Arctic. At the Steamboat Camp the *Eva* and *Cariboo* came out of the water each winter, machine and blacksmith shops maintained company equipment and produced its metalwork, and a sawmill cut lumber.

The Cariboo at Nagle Snye steamboat camp; Ed Nagle on the upper deck.

Even after Ed resettled in Edmonton, the *Bulletin* continued printing his opinions and comments. Few people had travelled the Mackenzie watershed more regularly or extensively than he had. By late 1905 he was so well known and respected that an errant and aspiring English adventurer named Lord Dundonald sought a personal interview with him.

That December, storm clouds on the international scene also darkened the Hislop and Nagle horizon. A wire Dick Secord received augured a disastrous market for the coming year. It forecast sharp declines in fur prices. Russia, normally a big player in the fur trade, was embroiled in a frontier war. There were disturbances on the Franco-German border, and a European war seemed imminent.

Despite the predictions, Ed steamed irrepressibly onward with his plans, and by spring he had cause for optimism. First came a report that the overall market was maintaining its stability. Then Brendin, Cornwall, and Roberts, who were trading at Lesser Slave Lake, sold out to a French firm called the Revillon Freres. Things could not be too bad in Europe if the French were buying Canadian companies. When Secord's spring wires arrived from London, they actually showed a general rise in fur prices.

That spring, however, Ed found it extraordinarily difficult to start north. For the first time in many years he was moving away from home, not toward it. He had one of the largest outfits he had ever put together: 150 tons of supplies in 16 scows. When he finally got away from Edmonton, low water in the Athabasca held him up until May 25. Although the journey down the Mackenzie and back went smoothly, when he reached Arctic Red River he was saddened to learn that another of his traders had died. Isolation had claimed another victim.

Some interesting people caught his attention during the summer. Elihu Stewart, the Dominion Superintendent of Forestry, was on his way to the Yukon via the Mackenzie. And a young anthropologist named Viljalmur Stefansson was heading off to prove he could live like the Eskimos. But after 1906, successive spring trips grew increasingly difficult for him to make.

That summer, efforts at Great Slave Lake were complicated by a rumour that the Hudson's Bay Company planned to change its Mackenzie District operation. The Company had stripped every stick of burnable timber from the hillsides within eight kilometres of Rae Point. Since Hislop was skimming off its Dogrib trade anyway, it was relocating Fort Rae to an island at the north end of Willow River, near Hislop's Post. The move would cluster the opposition and the Oblate missionaries at Hislop's backdoor.

Hislop had not moved to Fort Resolution to oversee the northern posts, as Ed had expected him to. He was, therefore, in an ideal position to counter the HBC intrusion, which was underway when Ed reached Great Slave Lake in 1907. Rather than evade confrontation, Hislop was delighting in the opportunity to fur-

The Nagle family, 1905; left to right: Ed, Baby Tess, Eva, Geraldine foreground Sarsfield and Ted.

ther flummox the HBC. He had strengthened his alliance with the Catholic priests by surveying a site for their new church.

Unfortunately, Ed had some bad news for his partner. McDougall and Secord had decided to sell their retail, wholesale, and outfitting operations. Dick Secord would continue shipping Hislop and Nagle furs to London, but the partners had to find themselves a new outfitter. On receiving this news, Hislop dove morosely into his permit liquor.

Hislop's response upset Ed. He had the Treaty Commission in tow, and he carried on down the Mackenzie for the Hislop and Nagle furs. But, although he returned south with 121 fur bales worth between $110,000 and $125,000, by the time he got to Edmonton he was prepared to sell his share of the Hislop and Nagle Company.

The spring of 1908 found Ed again floating north, this time intent on talking business with Hislop. Fortunately, a cast of fascinating characters helped divert him from the drudgery of the journey and the confrontation with Hislop that lay ahead. The groups going north with Ed did not travel together until Smith's Rapids, but as they crossed paths at the short rapids and portages on the Athabasca, each one's story came out.

Anthropologist Viljalmur Stefansson was the willful, whip-thin son of Icelandic parents. Born in Arnes, Manitoba and educated in Iowa, North Dakota, and at Harvard University, he was northbound on his second Arctic expedition. The American Museum of Natural History was paying him to prove that there were Eskimos living in the areas that the Dominion had marked "uninhabited" on its maps. He was keeping a close record of his journey, and a zoologist named R.M. Anderson was along to enlarge the expedition's scope.

Of the other travellers Ed met, only a hard-bitten ex-schoolmarm from Rhode Island, named Agnes Deans Cameron, was contemplating writing a book. She travelled with the Hudson's Bay Company though, so she and Ed met only in passing. The anthropologist has stuck in the minds of northern old-timers; the schoolmarm has not. But two of the other parties on the river were on their way to becoming the stuff of northern legend.

After his wife's accident, James McKinlay had left the north. Now he was drifting back, guiding a heavy-set Englishman named Cosmo Melvill toward Great Bear Lake. With McKinlay as guide, the Melvill party was confident and capable. Ed enjoyed their company, and saw nothing strange about their plan to winter at Bear Lake. They did, however, have one odd character with them. McKinlay and Melvill had consulted Joe Hodgson in Edmonton and, on his recommendation, hired a weedy little blue-eyed eccentric named John Hornby to accompany them to the Barrens.

Although Hornby was only about five-feet-tall, he was vigorously active on the portages and appeared to Ed to be a rugged traveller. It would take years of lonely isolation and starvation, and the horror-filled Great War's trenches to bring on the pathological self-assurance that would kill the little man. When Ed met him, Hornby was simply another eccentric on his way north. Not until Ed's son Ted was fully grown would Hornby persuade two boys to join him on the slow journey to death that has assured their place in northern lore.

The other group that snared Ed's attention was embarked on a somber errand. In 1904, William McLeod had been at Fort Liard and heard about gold in the Nahanni River valley. The following spring he had come out of the Nahanni with several ounces of coarse gold, and that fall he took his brother Frank and man named Robert Weir back to his claims. Charles McLeod was leading a search for his brothers. They had left a map to their destination with the Catholic priest at Fort Simpson, then vanished.

Ed reached Smith's Landing before the other groups, and sent one scow and some supplies over the portage road by wagon. His response to the situation he found at Fort Smith only makes sense as an indication of his underlying conviction that the Hislop and Nagle Company must soon be sold. Smith had seen a disastrous winter. The precipitous eastern side of the townsite had slipped into the Slave River. Many of the Hudson's Bay Company's oldest buildings had been dragged down by the mud, its riverside docking facilities were battered, and its warehouse had burned to the ground. The mud slide had not damaged the Hislop and Nagle post, but because of it the NWMP were checking outfits at Mountain Portage rather than Smith.

Ed immediately sent a crew to Fort Resolution for the *Eva*, while he himself returned to Smith's Landing. He would accompany his outfit down the east side route. Before starting toward the Dog Rapid with Melvill and another man, he checked each of his fifteen scows carefully. The only change since he had last crossed the east-bank portages was at the New Portage. Rivermen had stopped using the island and returned to the two shorter mainland portages. After the Mounties checked his permits and outfits, Ed moved on to Fort Smith and laid off his portage crews. Then he sold his horses, oxen, wagons, and a hay rake to a man named Johnny Bellcourt, and shut down the Hislop and Nagle overland transport operation at Smith's Rapids.

Melvill, Stefansson, and McLeod had all carried on below Fort Smith ahead of Ed. Until they reached the Slave River Delta they had gotten along pretty well, but northwesterly winds were holding them up in the delta. When the *Eva* steamed by on her way to Resolution, Ed offered them all a tow down the Mackenzie.

Although he did not regret having extended the offer, his new companions soon caused him some irritation. Stefansson was an aggressive nonconformist. He and Anderson were installing barometers and thermometers at various locations for the government to help institute systematic meteorological studies. At Hay River they held the *Eva* up for a while, but the lost time was not as irritating to Ed as the anthropologist's willfulness. Stefansson had wanted to consult T.J. Marsh, but the missionary and his wife had left Saint Peter's Mission the previous summer. Against Ed's advice he bought the mission's derelict whaleboat, which he joined to the string of vessels trailing behind the *Eva*.

At Fort Providence, McLeod split off to start his quest. The mystery of the Headless Valley has survived in several conflicting accounts, and has been the subject of debate since it first began to emerge. Although Ed never saw McLeod again, he followed his story with interest.

Did Charles McLeod know about the map to his brother's claims? Perhaps not. Certainly, when he started up the Liard it stayed behind with the priest at Simpson. At the Nahanni deboucher, McLeod left the Liard. After picking his way among the meandering channels called The Splits he rested at the hotsprings of the Tropical valley, which Klondikers had discovered in 1897. And as he passed through the First Canyon he may have paused at the foot of the high cliff on the east bank to fish for the brook trout darting through the clear cold waters of an underground river that surfaces there. From the entrance to the Flat River - or Dead Man's - valley, however, he pushed resolutely through the Second Splits and a canyon called The Gate.

About 150 kilometres from the Liard, McLeod made the discovery he had dreaded. Scattered around a temporary camp nestled in a thick clump of spruce trees, were the partial remains of two men. The tufts of hair he found resembled his brother Willy's, and some of his brothers' possessions lay near the bones. Two questions sprang to his mind: Why were there only two corpses? And where were their skulls? He buried the remains where he found them, blazing nearby trees to mark the site of the graves.

In light of his subsequent actions it is clear that McLeod did not believe that Nahanni Indians had murdered his brothers, contrary to what he told the police. But the police response to the reported murder is not as easily explained. Did Nahanni Indians actually discover a third partial skeleton on the banks of the Liard? Did Sergeant Nitchie Thorne lead a patrol to the Nahanni the following winter and find the skulls, and because it was too difficult to exhume the bodies, bring the heads out on the front of his cariolle for identification? Did the

Fort Good Hope, with the Hislop and Nagle Post on the left.

Catholics insist that news of Thorne's desecration of the remains be suppressed? Various sources report all this.

McLeod, however, was pursuing his own investigation. In spite of what he told the police, he believed that Robert Weir had murdered his brothers. Weir had not reappeared on the Liard so McLeod headed to the Yukon, where he learned that a man fitting Weir's description had traded a small sack of gold for supplies. He tracked the man to the west coast, then followed him across Canada as far as Saskatchewan. But when the fugitive discovered he was being followed, he vanished. Shortly afterward McLeod disappeared too, and nothing more was heard about either man.

Charlie McLeod's story lay in the future, however, and Ed had more immediate problems to contend with. The *Eva* churned down the Mackenzie to Fort Wrigley, where Ed closed the Hislop and Nagle post and picked up Bob Erasmus. At Fort Norman, Melvill's party broke away to track up the Bear River to Great Bear Lake. Ed could not give Stefansson time to install his weather station, so Anderson stayed behind to complete the work and study the local fauna until the HBC boat arrived. Beyond the towering Ramparts, which squeeze the Mackenzie between Norman and Fort Good Hope, Ed unexpectedly encountered a scow crawling slowly upstream. His brother Jim was tracking toward Good Hope.

James Nagle shared Jim Hislop's addiction to alcohol, but compounded his problem with fervent Catholicism. To combat his demon he had persuaded Ed to isolate him at Arctic Red River, but the strategy had not proven entirely successful. He had already escaped, at least once, for a monumental binge in the south for which he had tried to atone by joining a monastic community. Eventually, he had asked to be reinstated at Red River, and Ed was relieved to learn the reason he was heading upstream. He had traded so heavily during the winter that his shelves were bare. He was on his way to Good Hope for spring trading stock.

Ed breezed by Good Hope, and replaced Jim's outfit from the scows behind the *Eva*. He was on his way to permanently close Fort McPherson, so he did not stay long at Arctic Red River. McPherson had never been a particularly productive post; now that Jim was drawing Eskimos to Red River, there was little reason to keep it open. It was, however, the location Stefansson chose as the start for his trip into Eskimo country.

By the time Ed returned to Great Slave Lake another free trader was also trimming back his operation. Swiggart had fallen on hard times, and sold his company to a trader named Strauss, who was closing Swiggart's Fort Providence post and streamlining the Fort Resolution operation.

Until they knew the results of the McDougall and Secord sale, Ed and Hislop were stymied. It is frustrating that no documents survive to record the summer meeting between them. Both men were strong willed and it is possible to infer from later records the extent of the tension that was developing between them.

As Ed moved south through Smith's Landing, the Smith's Rapids area was mourning the tragic loss of two of its Catholic priests. Shortly after Ed passed down in the spring, a resident priest had taken a newly arrived brother for a canoe trip above Cassette Rapid. In the main riffles, where the currents converged, the new man had panicked. People on the riverbank watched the canoe capsize and saw an arm raised in supplication to the sky. The bodies were never found.

By 1909, Ed's frame of mind had improved. The government was increasing the number of its northern mail packets to five, with two that went all the way to the Mackenzie Delta. Furthermore, the Revillon Freres had agreed to replace McDougall and Secord as Hislop and Nagle's outfitter. Best of all, Dick Secord was prepared to transfer all of McDougall and Secord's northern transportation contracts over to Hislop and Nagle. Instead of having to sell, it appeared as if he and Hislop could strengthen their position.

Unfortunately, anticipating a break with his partner, Hislop had not left a trader in charge of Fort Resolution. When Ed arrived there, he again found his old home in a state of filthy chaos. Moreover, Hislop was not there to meet him. In light of Ed's subsequent journals and letters, he appears to have suspected that Hislop had no intention of fulfilling his administrative responsibilities. At the end of the summer, after some debate, the partners put Joseph Burke temporarily in charge as the Resolution trader.

That fall, Ed left Slave Lake frustrated at the impasse between Hislop and him. He did not doubt the importance of the Willow River trade, but Hislop was not taking responsibility for anything else. There was no indication that he was concerned about the overall state of the company. The cap on Ed's summer came when he reached Athabasca Landing. While his furs awaited shipment to Edmonton, someone stole 29 prime silver-fox pelts. Despite the insurance on

James Hislop, co-founder with Ed Nagle of the Northern Transportation Company.

the furs, the robbery angered Ed. The Mounties recovered 18 of them within ten days, but the eleven that went missing were worth between $2,000 and $3,000.

It would be unfair to maintain that Hislop alone was affected by the uncertainties the partners faced, but his refusal to adapt to their changing situation preyed on Ed more than anything else. Hislop's midwinter appearance in Edmonton finally snapped Ed's patience. When he did not stay long enough to help with the outfits, Ed started north in the spring of 1910, determined to finally sell the Hislop and Nagle Company.

Fort Resolution posed the first problem to deal with. Joseph Burke had done a reasonable job of trading, but Ed had left Eva's brother Mike Klapstein and an engineer named Angus Clifford in charge of the Steamboat Camp. Although Burke had tried to mediate between them, Angus Clifford had been viciously quarrelsome throughout the winter. Ed set a hard line to straighten things out, then sailed the *Eva* up to Fort Smith to meet his outfit scows.

Frank Oliver and Joe Hodgson were with him on the river that spring; old friends, tied to memories of better times. Visits with them considerably improved Ed's state of mind. Hodgson was starting on an adventure that he had wanted to undertake for some time. Great Bear Lake was calling him. He was his witty, poetical old self, and the freedom he felt added an edge to the friendly insults he directed at Ed. Oliver, on the other hand, was travelling on business. As Canada's Minister of the Interior, he was taking his first extended look at the country he had worked so hard as a newspaperman to promote. He travelled on the *Eva* from Fort Smith to Fort Resolution, and took the opportunity to have Ed outline the development of Resolution.

Tragically, the amusing sojourn with Oliver and Hodgson came to an abrupt end. Ed was very fond of Eva's brother, and to get Mike away from Angus Clifford he invited him along on the Mackenzie River trip. A short way below Fort Providence, Mike slipped from one of the scows behind the Eva and sank out of sight. When he did not rise to the surface, Ed was forced to post a reward for Mike's body and continue on down north.

Each stop on the upriver trip from Arctic Red River found Ed anxious for news of his borther-in-law. But when the *SS Mackenzie River* passed the *Eva*, Captain Mills could tell him nothing. And when Ed met Joe Hodgson again, eighty-five kilometres below Fort Simpson, Mike's body had still not been found. Not until Ed's furs were all up the Smith Portage Road, did Captain Mills reach Fort Smith with Mike's body. Some Indians had discovered it on the bank of the Mackenzie, and Ed buried him in a grave surrounded by a white picket fence on a knoll overlooking the Slave.

On the basis of discussions they had had in Edmonton the previous winter and in Resolution at the end of that summer, Ed and Hislop agreed to dissolve their partnership. J.K. Cornwall, who had sold out his Peace River trading operation to the Revillon Freres in 1905, now wanted to get back in the fur trade and two long-time Hislop and Nagle associates - Campbell Young and George Slater - wanted to go into business for themselves. The three men were banding together to buy out Ed and Jim.

During his trip back to Edmonton, Ed must have wondered why things continued to go so wrong that summer. At Fort McMurray he let a few passengers travel with him as far as The Landing, and at the Cascade Rapid, one of them disappeared. After an extensive search, he was forced to conclude that the man, a Dominion Land Surveyor named Selby, had fallen in the river and drowned.

Fortunately, some satisfaction awaited him at Athabasca Landing, however. A trial was underway when he arrived: early in June, the Mounties had captured Charles Lawson with eight of the eleven stolen silver fox pelts. Lawson was plainly aware of their value, and seemed both extraordinarily degenerate and slightly insane. He was on trial for theft, but the perverse little man claimed that a bitch he owned had led him to the pelts. A bizarre twist was that because of a reward he had bestowed on the animal, he was also on trial for public bestiality. Lawson was sentenced to six months in jail for possession of the silver foxes.

At Edmonton, Ed did not delay the arrangements for the sale. Soon after his furs were shipped off to London, he opened his negotiations with Cornwall, Slater, and Young. Dick Secord agreed to finance the deal, and by March 1, 1911 its initial aspects were covered with notes worth $30,000.00. By May 4, all of Edmonton knew that Hislop and Nagle were selling the company. Although the *Bulletin* didn't comment on the details of the transaction, it announced that the Northern Trading Company was the buyer.

During the trip down north in 1911, Ed felt strangely ambivalent: after more than twenty-six years of struggling with it, he was finally leaving the north country. Although his journal resonates with some of the same fascination that had carried him west in 1874, he is clearly apprehensive. He did not know quite what to expect when he arrives at Slave Lake. Hislop had wintered at Fort Resolution, and antagonized Burke and his wife. Their letters to Ed had chronicled Hislop's emotional oscillations - on one he had been reported as dying. After conferring with Burke on the Athabasca River, Ed sent him upstream to meet the owners of the Northern Trading Company then continued on to meet with Hislop. A series of journal entries records the partners' last northern exchange.

May 31, Wednesday Steamboat Camp
     Up at 6:30 a.m.; breakfast and to work. Unloaded boat[s], that is post (2) and transport. [At] 2 p.m. [I] started for Resolution with F. Lafferty, T. McDonald and Joe Hope, arriving there at 4:30 p.m. [I] Found Mr. Hislop looking well for a man that was reported dying. A good deal of it is *humbug*. He was quite ready to start in at his permit, and did, I am sorry to say. Then came the pleasant end to my visit. [He] talked nothing but rot and *rubbish*. He kept on the move all night, taking drinks between *times*. After a big struggle I fell asleep, out of which I heard nothing until the R.C. Mission bell at 5 a.m. called the flock to morning Mass. My bed was better than I have at home.

June 1st, 1911, Thursday Resolution

At 6 a.m., after a good smoke in bed, [I] arose. Made my ablution .... [I] found Mr. Hislop up and awaiting my coming down, taking appetizers during the meantime, and from that moment I was made very uncomfortable. My nerves were very much tried listening to his sad tales of woe and how he had put Burke and his fair lady to rights. I cannot express my feelings all through this ordeal. [He] kicked during breakfast about my not bringing down more whiskey. At 9 a.m., with the help of God and my rustling, I got off for camp. I arrived there at 12 a.m. Puttered and sent a canoe to the mission camp for tools.

June 2, Friday Steamboat Camp

At 7:30 a.m. [I] sent Branch and R. Jensen to the R.C. Mission Steamboat to see if they could get some fittings to enable us to put in the second engine. [They] returned with nothing. [I am] compelled now to use the one engine. Too bad. Joe Burke was over for the mail bags. Old Jacob and his wife have arrived and are camped here. The boys finished setting [the] jack screws to raise the boat up. Weather cloudy and mosquitoes very bad. [I] learned from J.E. Burke that Hislop was having a good time and is very sick. Too bad, is it not? [The] mosquitoes are simply hell. [I] was obliged to get up during the night, and fixed my mosquito bar.

June 3, Saturday

7 a.m. All hands at work. [I] sent two men for sand. R. Jensen went to Resolution. [At] 7 p.m. His Lordship, Bishop Breynat, called on me on his way to the Fort at Resolution. [At] 10 p.m. Johnny Sanderson and Pierre arrived with a letter from J.E. Burke, requesting me to give them his permits of whiskey, and [saying] that Hislop was very sick, having no more of his booze, having drank it all. I am sure they had a lively time last night. As Jensen did not return as he said he would, [I] came to the conclusion that we can not fix [the] second engine. [It] rained quite a bit during the night.

June 4, Sunday Steamboat Camp

Up very late. Breakfasted at 9:30 a.m. While [I was] shaving, Mr. Connibear arrived from the Mission Steamboat Camp. Having invited him to dine, we talked on different subjects. [I] had him examine the boat and the two engines, and he claims they can be put in O.K. Branch felt cheap, as he had given it up. [At] 3 p.m. he (Connibear) departed. It rained some after dinner. [I] am alone in my tent trying to read, but cannot. [I] am thinking of home and dear ones. I fancy what they are doing on Sunday, but I console myself by thinking that it is my last trip. Rudolf Jensen arrived from Resolution with a black and blue eye. [I] don't know anything about it.

June 5, Monday Steamboat Camp

[It] rained during the night, but cleared up towards morning. [I am] waiting on the boys to come over from [the] fort and jack [the] boat up a foot. [At] 10:30 a.m. Joe Burke and Mr. Hislop arrived with four men. [We] raised the boat up before dinner. Hislop was stupid drunk, not [a] falling but a crying one. He was playing poodle with R. Jensen to get a drink out of him. Then he came to me, so I gave him a drink. Then he got a bottle from R. Jensen. When leaving he was simply disgusting: crying in talking with me, telling me how we would continue as we are and we would throw [it] all into one pot and after he would help two sisters he had, he would give a share to my children. What rot, the *son-of-a-bitch*. I would not be a partner of his again, the drunken sod and double-faced son-of-a-bitch. [At] 3 p.m. Hislop and Burke left for the post with [a] scow and six men.

June 6, Tuesday Steamboat Camp

[It] rained during the night, then turned very cold. [The] Ice in [the] basin [is] 1/2 inch [thick], but it is a fine morning. I let Fred Lafferty and Tommy go to the fort to help clean up Hislop's place and put up a fence. Joe Hope and Jacob [are] fixing [the] grade for launching. Branch and Jensen are at work on [the] engine. I'll bet any man that J. Hislop is good and sick, but I cannot cry. No news from the siege of drink except that they had a dance .... [The] Ground [is] frozen. Very slow work. [We] will finish tomorrow. [It is] a beautiful evening. [It is] 10:30, [and the] sun [is] up still. Mosquitoes bad. During the night they were very quiet. It was cold.

In spite of his anger Ed had to come to a working agreement with Hislop, but he knew it was useless trying to talk business while liquor was still available. He therefore devoted himself to preparing the *Eva* for the downriver trip. Hislop had been gone five full days before Ed returned to Resolution.

June 10, Saturday

[At] 6 a.m. [we] started to get up steam. At 9:30 a.m., all [was] ready. We started downstream to the mouth of [the] river.

Tied up. [I] had an early lunch: myself and two men who were to go over to Resolution with me. [At] 11:30 a.m. we started, arriving there at three. [I] called on [the] sisters, [the] priest, Mr. and Mrs. Harding, and last but not least Dr. Rymer. When [I was] through [I] had a business talk with Hislop and a general look around. [At] 5:30 p.m. [I] started again for the steamer and started for up river. At [the] Steamboat Camp [we] stopped and took on more wood, and other things. [At] 10 p.m. [we] started for Smith. The wood being green, [we] went very slowly ....

Campbell Young and George Slater awaited Ed at Fort Smith with the summer trading outfit — Young wanted to join him for a final talk with Hislop. Once the *Eva* had travelled to Arctic Red River and back, the Hislop and Nagle posts would be in the hands of the Northern Trading Company.

June 17, Saturday Steamboat Camp
    [At] 2 a.m. [we] arrived at [the] Steamboat Camp. We tied up four scows at a clear place below Willow Point. A nice place to sort the outfits. [I] took [the] Resolution and Rae outfits to store at [the] Steamboat Camp. Unloaded same, and was finished by noon. After dinner, C. Young and myself started for Resolution with two canoes and three men. We went to Mr. Hislop's house. We talked over all our business. He seemed to think the deal very satisfactory. We spent a pleasant evening, but of course there are no mosquitoes. My first sleep was of one hour, and was all right. My friends (the mosquitoes) had not to catch my bed. But from 1 a.m. until they heard some talking below, they never let me sleep.

When both Hislop and Campbell Young were satisfied with the arrangements for the sale, Ed sailed the *Eva* northward. It took him slightly more than three weeks to visit all his posts, introduce his traders to Young and Slater, and return to Resolution with the Hislop and Nagle furs. And when Hislop arrived from Willow River, the two of them started south together.
    If the surviving documents account for all the monies that changed hands during the sale, then Cornwall, Slater, and Young transferred $53,000.00 to Dick Secord to pay for Hislop and Nagle's assets. At least $30,000.00 was available to Jim and Ed as soon as they reached

Edmonton in early September. The men who had sustained themselves for so long against the Hudson's Bay Company in the Mackenzie Region parted company without regret or sentiment.

CHAPTER 17

Rock Forest West
(1912 - 1929)

Once Jim Hislop had received his share of the money, he travelled east to visit his relatives in Nova Scotia and New York City. Within a few months, Ed also headed east. He travelled with Dick Secord as far as Woodstock, Ontario. Beyond Ontario, he carried on alone to visit his boyhood homes in Saint Hyacinthe and Rock Forest. By Christmas he was back with his family in Edmonton.

The eastward journey helped bleed off the frustration and anger Ed felt towards his ex-partner: when Hislop returned from New York City, the two men reconciled. Hislop was on his way back to his wife at Fort Resolution. His appearance shocked Ed. Throughout his trip east he had been drinking heavily. His constitution was in ruins

JAMES HISLOP, an old-timer who was overtaken by death while on his way to his home at Fort Resolution. Hislop was 63 years of age and came to Edmonton in 1881, when he was employed by the Hudson's Bay company. He was a partner of the firm of Hislop & Nagel

Jim Hislop's Edmonton Bulletin obituary notice.

214

and he bore little resemblance to the giant who had started north in 1887. Ed agreed to act as executor of his will, and generously lent his old partner a 16-gauge Greener shotgun for the northern trip.

When the news reached Edmonton that Hislop had died on May 29, 1912 of liver failure and exposure near the Lac La Biché River, it did not surprise Ed. Unfortunately, he was too deeply embroiled in his own affairs to immediately travel north to help Nancy Hislop settle the will, and by the time he and Teddy reached Resolution in 1913, she too was dead and everything had gone to Bishop Breynat and the Catholic Church.

The Hislops' deaths sliced the last knots binding Ed to Great Slave Lake. Never again would cold spring mornings find him surrounded by trade goods on the north-flowing rivers. Never again would he risk the kind of winter journey that killed Frank Fitzgerald during the winter of 1910-11 on the trail from Fort McPherson to the Yukon. But Jim Hislop's death also released sentiments Ed had strained to control. To the end of his days he would remain weirdly attracted to the north. Joe Hodgson's extraordinary farewell letter to him is just one testament of the affection and esteem that Ed's friendliness and generosity had earned him. It sings a vivid paean to the fascinating and rigorous lives the old-timers shared.

> To my friend and fellow voyageur, Mr. Nagle:
> While passing my friends in review
> I thought my dear Nagle of you,
> So took up my pen
> And my Muse just then
> Said we'll write him a letter — we two.
> A lady divine, and a man past his prime
> With a curious penchant for writing in rhyme!
> A strange combination — you'll say my dear sir —
> But Lord! 'Tis more pleasant than trading for fur.
> And surely where such a fair charmer doth lead
> The path, though most arduous, seldom we heed.
> Six days after saying good bye on the beach
> A harbour at Norman we safely did reach,
> And there I fell in with a jolly old friend,
> And tasted some whiskey of very fine blend.
> You only get such from a Hudson's Bay Store,
> And having once tasted, you'll sure say encore.
> This is not an ad for the old Hudson's Bay,

But merely a passing remark on the way.
I stayed at this place somewhat more than a week
Then set out again my fortune to seek.
Here Hornby and Melvill joined forces with me,
Which brotherly help was a saving to me.
Six days after that, without hitch or a break,
We reached the old fort on the shores of the lake,
Where dwelt in rude huts of the natives three score,
The elders I'd known in the good days of yore.
Shook hands with them all, yea even the babies,
But, not being a trader I kissed not the ladies.
(As all do allow, there are tricks in all trades.
In **some** it's a duty to kiss e'en old maids.)
But there! I will stop. Your mind I won't harass.
Besides, 'tis unkind one's friends to embarrass.
Here then we did tarry a day, and a week,
Just feasting our dogs till they grew fat and sleek.
The waters were teeming with various fish.
The herring was one — a delicious dish —
But nothing compared to the many-hued trout,
Which once having tasted you can't do without.
The natives round here, though devout in their prayers,
Indulge much in dances to drive away cares....
Now it happened that in this party of mine
A lad on the fiddle made music divine,
With soul stirring strains the night air seemed replete,
Heart moving, pulse throbbing, seductive and sweet.
His services therefore were much in demand,
Each Maid would have willingly given her hand
To have kept in the village such an acquisition,
In fact they did almost draw up a petition.
Excuse he did make for untimely desertion,
He had to get back to his home at McPherson...
But I do digress; so back to my theme,
No more will I bolt like a runaway team.
Of our trip o'er the lake it is no use to tell,
For nothing of interest to us befell.
We ran up the Dease on September the third,
Our boat skimming over the waves like a bird.
Three miles up the river we now went ashore;
All happy and glad that our wanderings were o'er.

That eve as we each in our tents did recline,
I, for one not the least, for the South did repine.
The forest trees round with our axes we fell,
To put up a shanty in which we could dwell
When winter came on; with a chimney quite wide,
Windows three has the house and a door on one side....
Soon after this, say the fifteenth of September,
I think that's the date, if I rightly remember,
While out on a hunt to the east of this place
Perchance some strange Huskies we met face to face.
From the mouth of the Coppermine, there were some,
From around Coronation Gulf others had come,
And there was another outlandish band
Hailing from far off Victoria Land.
It seems that each summer they follow the deer,
Tho of contact with Indians they always steer clear.
Their spears and their arrows with copper were tipped,
From horn spoons and stone kettles water they sipped.
Their needles of copper, their knives of the same
For making their arrows or cutting up game.
At first sight of us they did seem much afraid,
But by peace signs we soon their feelings allayed.
With presents of needles we pleased all the wives,
And made the men happy with shining steel knives.
Our rifles they seemed to behold with great awe,
No doubt 'twas the first of the kind that they saw....
At all times the caribeaux graze at their wills,
Through muskeg and forest and on the bare hills.
We killed a great many, and made cachés strong
In which we did place them; but it was not long
Ere the wolves and the wolverines gnawed through the wood,
Their howls making hideous the whole neighbourhood.
We killed quite a few; but their number is legion.
They're the curse and the bane of the Northern region.
To tell you the truth they devoured forty-five,
This gives you some idea how they do thrive....
Misfortune pursuing did add to our care
Another marauder, in the shape of a bear.
Dimensions extreme — the size of a cow —
Forbidding in aspect and loving a row.

217

Tremendous his head, and the measurements clear
Extended twelve inches from ear to ear,
Eyes gleaming like rubies, and distaining flight,
Roaring a challenge, and burning to fight.
At first touch of bullet he uttered a roar
Which woke all the echoes along the lake shore.
Then onwards toward [me] on the muskeg he tore,
His glistening white fangs incrimsoned with gore,
But courage and strength are no match against lead,
And close to my feet he rolled over dead.
It was a close shave — some would vote it quite fine —
But to go through again I would rather decline....
Few foxes are here, and scarcer are marten,
We got very few our spirits to hearten.
Conspicuous by absence the far-famed muskox,
For now they are more rare than the silver fox.
Some few years ago they were numerous here,
In numbers almost like the migrating deer.
The far-reaching rifle has sounded their knell
And their bones alone show where once they did dwell.
Well friend, don't expect a long letter from me,
For if you reflect, you plainly will see,
A man so remote from civilization
Has no news for pen, nor yet for narration.
Of hardships; there's none except isolation,
Our health, though, is good — a great consolation —
Perhaps 'tis because there's no doctor around,
Or maybe because constitutions are sound,
Or truth in that proverb which fits the forlorn,
"God tempers the wind to the lamb that is shorn."
I see my Muse preening her wings to depart.
I can't say her nay, though most sad grows my heart.
Without her nor wit, nor pen of a writer
Have I — No I'll just make an end to this letter.
                                        — Joseph Hodgson

In addition to the $15,000.00 Dick Secord had arranged to have waiting for him when he reached Edmonton in 1911, Ed expected at least a further $5,000.00. When he returned from Quebec he began investing heavily in real estate. Fortunately, it later turned out, he did not restrict his investments to Edmonton. In addition to having a

Hislop and Nagle Estate surveyed at Athabasca Landing, he anticipated the eventual completion of the Alberta Great Waters Railroad
and bought lots in Fort McMurray.

Despite the home he owned in Edmonton, Ed did not plan to
continue living there. He had never intended settling in Edmonton in
1882, and by 1912 it was too large a city for him. So the early summer
of 1912 found him in Victoria, British Columbia, buying land on Foul
Bay. But Victoria was not really the place for him, either. On his way
back to Edmonton he stopped briefly at Penticton, where he found the
new home he was seeking in the warm Okanagan Valley.

There were no buildings on the property he bought south of
Penticton, but it had luxuriant orchards and sweet water flowed in a
nearby creek. He called it Rock Forest By the following spring,
contractors had started building a large stone house for him. But
before he and Eva could move to the Okanagan, an unexpected snag
tugged at them. Their children were apprehensive. They had already
moved twice from Fort Resolution, and Edmonton had been their
home for nine years.

Ed was offering his children the same kind of opportunity his
father had offered him: the chance to establish a sanctuary for themselves. And they were as reluctant to leave Edmonton as he had been
to leave Saint Hyacinthe. Nonetheless, since they were younger than
he had been when Gerrard moved to the Magog River, Ed had less
difficulty persuading them. As soon as he and Teddy returned from
the trip north to settle the Hislop Estate, the Nagles started for
Penticton.

Within a year of settling at Rock Forest, Ed and Eva had a new
daughter, Louise. Ed was now 62 years old and his family was rising
up around him. But just when he most needed stability and security
for them, J.K Cornwall and the Northern Traders Company failed
him. The Canadian Northern Railroad's financial problems had overturned Edmonton's property values in 1913, but Ed had remained
unconcerned. The fur trade was still strong, and his attorney, J.E.
Wallbridge, had assured him that the Northern Traders' debt was
good. By early 1915, however, Ed knew that Cornwall and the others
had concentrated on the transportation network at the expense of the
fur trading side of their business. And when things had looked bleakest
for them, J.K. Cornwall had joined the armed forces.

Ed struggled to make ends meet throughout the latter part of the
First World War. A drop in fruit prices crippled Rock Forest, and in
1916 he returned alone to Edmonton to work as a fur buyer. His new

Ed Nagle in his Penticton, B.C. orchard.

employers sent him west through the Yellowhead Pass, to Prince George, B.C. and beyond, but he missed his family and disliked the continual travelling. When his bosses shifted from questioning his ability to grade and buy fur to doubting his honesty, Ed had had enough. He stopped in Edmonton just long enough to straighten out their books, then returned to Rock Forest. Trapping, not trading, would supplement the income from his orchards.

Despite that incident with the fur-buyers, Ed's reputation for integrity and capability remained intact. As the economy rebounded from the war, his past accomplishments brought him to the attention of the Imperial Oil Company. He was surviving mainly by slowly selling off his investments when, in 1920, Imperial Oil decided to curry favour with the northern old-timers. It proposed to employ surplus German Junker aircraft as a link to its oil deposits at Norman Wells on the Mackenzie. But Imperial Oil also wanted a river-based system in place to support the airplanes and Ed was offered the job of organizing it.

He was 67 years old, and, despite his financial predicament, he turned down the oil company's offer. He had no use for aircraft, and no intention of ever returning north. While he had worked out of Edmonton, Campbell Young had assured him again that the Northern Traders' debt was good. Before too long, however, the Northern Traders Company was auctioned off as a tax sale. The new management renewed Young's promise, but neither Ed nor Dick Secord was ever paid in full.

The joy of watching his children grow up and the long, hot Okanagan summers, when the smell of pines mingled in his orchards, were the compensation Ed received for his trials. In spite of the humiliation he often felt at not having more to offer them, his children blossomed at Rock Forest. They were confident and gregarious, and one summer afternoon in 1915 Teddy and Sarsfield brought him a new friend. The tales the Nagle boys had told J.J. Warren's sons had intrigued the balding little corporate lawyer. He wanted to meet this buffalo-hunting fur trader for himself.

Unlike Ed, Warren had not retired to Penticton. He was there supervising work on the Kettle Valley Railroad, of which he was president. But he was also president of the Consolidated Mining and Smelting Company, and he was curious about the north's untapped potentials. Over the years that followed he and Ed pored over Ed's collection of reports and maps. Ed reminisced and they discussed the ore deposits he felt most strongly about. Eventually, in return for his indulgence and hospitality, Warren arranged work for Ed's sons: Sarsfield on the railroad, and Teddy with the Consolidated Mining and Smelting Company.

By 1924 Gerry, Teddy, Sarsfield, and Tess were all having to help bear Rock Forest's financial burdens. Ed's orchards just could not support his family, and he was beginning to feel the weight of his seventy-five years. In 1925, shortly after Ed's brother Garrett died, J.J. Warren's son was married in Penticton. Because he was in mourning Ed did not attend the wedding, but afterwards J.J. Warren came out for a last visit to Rock Forest. On Warren's advice, the Consolidated Mining and Smelting Company was sending a geologi-

The Nagles at Geoff Warren's wedding reception; left to right: "Doc" Netherton, Sarsfield, Ed, Ted.

cal exploration team north in 1926. He wanted Ted Nagle to be a member of it.

The gesture pleased Ed. To him it meant that the Nagles could have another shot at the north. By March of 1926, when Teddy finally learned that he would be part of the C.M.&S. team, Ed had his counsel prepared. The only gifts he could offer were introductions to all his old northern friends, but his reputation would help open the north country for his son.

From the spring of 1926 onwards, Ed's life unfolded on two distinctly different fronts. Each day he struggled to maintain Rock Forest, where Eva, Sarsfield, and his daughters were his joy. He worked to provide what he could for them, and in the evenings he retreated into his den. But it was in the person of his eldest son that his lifelong adventure was carrying on. Ed had forced the north to accept him. Now Ted strode across the north country with Jack Russell and Bob Erasmus, competing against J.K. Cornwall for its riches.

Ted's constant stream of letters whirled Ed into the modern north. His mind was fired by the tales of overland treks, conflagrations, and flights in impossibly fragile aircraft over regions as unmapped and little travelled as when he had crossed them. He responded with cautions, advice and congratulations. And every fall that his son returned safely, a prodigious bout of celebratory drinking alarmed Eva and the other children. There was a part of Ed Nagle that was not confined to an orchard in the Okanagan valley. In the person of his son, he paddled the north's rivers and crossed its skies.

During the spring and early summer of 1929, however, Ed felt unwell and depressed. A cold made his wind so scant he was unable to carry water from the well to the barn at Rock Forest without resting once or twice along the way. And his rheumatism was bad again. But his own health was not what depressed him. Ted had not visited home in more than two years, and anxiety was wearing hard on Ed.

When good news came, it arrived in a rush. Ted was working with James Mackintosh Bell at Pine Point, and had flown to Yellowknife Bay. He had rediscovered the Lost Bruce Mine, about which he was excitedly optimistic. He might soon go as far north as Great Bear Lake, and that fall he expected to break his two-year absence from Rock Forest. With happiness and relief Ed shared each letter with Eva, and began plans for a hunt to celebrate his son's return. On the evening of August 11, 1929, he retired again to the sanctuary of his den. And there, surrounded by the trophies of his life, his heart stopped beating.

*   *   *

During his lifetime, Ed Nagle celebrated Canada's birth and helped repel her first invaders. He traversed the country from Quebec to the Pacific Ocean, and voyaged on her rivers north to the Beaufort Sea. He worked to smash the HBC domination of the Mackenzie region, only to watch as the economic importance of the northern fur trade gave way to mineral exploitation. In Manitoba and the Northwest Territories, he had witnessed the collapse of native lifeways and the advent of the modern era. Through it all, Ed's foresight, tenacity, compassion and generosity earned him a position in the pantheon of extraordinary Canadian pioneers.

Though historians would sometimes uncover tantalizing references to the free traders who had embarrassed the HBC, Ed's name slipped from general awareness after his death. Adventure in the north too often became associated with names like "Peace River Jim" Cornwall, or tragedies like the ones suffered by Frank Fitzgerald, John Hornby and the McLeod brothers. But Ed's reputation remained intact in the country he had made his own. On the rivers and in the bush camps, where people continue to endure the mundane frustrations and drudgeries of northern life, Ed Nagle and Jim Hislop are linked to notable accomplishments. The oldest riverman can still recall the *Sparrow's* astonishing journey through Smith's Rapids. And until the 1960s, trappers valued Mackenzie River Huskies more highly than any other sled dogs. Although Jim Cornwall ran the fur business into the ground, he could not destroy the network Ed had established. In its present incarnation as the Inuit-controlled Northern Transportation Company, the Hislop and Nagle Company remains alive on the rivers today.

PHOTO CREDITS

NOTES

For reasons of space, the following endnotes have been dramatically reduced from the originals. Names mentioned in the individual entries refer to works or informants cited in the bibliography. Scholars and research-oriented readers concerned with specific aspects of the textual material can examine a copy of the original annotated manuscript at the Alberta Historical Resources Foundation library in Calgary, Alberta; or may write to the author—c/o Lone Pine Publishing—to have their questions answered.

Notes to Chapter 1

p.13 *when Gerrard Joseph Nagle...newborn son.* All of the Saint Hyacinthe parish records kept prior to 1854 were destroyed in a fire that razed the Saint Hyacinthe cathedral. However, an extract from the Registre des Actes des Baptemes, Mariages set Sepultres, faits et celebres en l'eglise paroissials Notre-Dame-du-Rosaire de St. Hyacinthe (Reg. 1854, Fol. 218, No. S-102) indicates that Margaret Stevenson-Nagle died on 27 August 1854. Although there is no official record of Ed Nagle's birth, it is safe to assume that he was born in 1853. (Documentation courtesy of Mrs. Frances Kimpton, Nagle family historian.)

p.13 *...preparing to inherit Rathcormack* Frances Kimpton has only recently managed to established Rathcormack as the Nagle family's Irish estate.

p.13 *A small group ... they were proposing.* See Peter L. and Monica Maltby, "A New Look at the Peter Robinson Emigration of 1823." *Ontario History*, Vol. 55, #1, March 1965; and Jean S. McGill, *A Pioneer History of the County of Lanark* (Bewdney: Clay Publishing Co., 1977).

p.14 *In return for passage ... colony of Upper Canada.* According to the age guidelines laid down for the program, settlers could be no older than 45 and no younger than 18. Garrett was 55-years-old when the joined the Robinson Settlers, and so should not have been eligible. He certainly moved to Ramsay, however, and a message that Robinson sent his superiors in 1825 (National Archives of Canada (NAC)/Peter Robinson Papers— on microfilm — B885, p.188) suggests that he was so pleased with the effects Garrett had had on the settlers of

1823 that five older settlers would accompany the 1825 group.

p.14 *There Gerrard had taken...islands in them.* See McGill, *op. cit.*, p.90; and NAC/ UCSP/RG.1, E.3, Vol. 41A, p.91 (read Gerrard Nagle for all mentions of Gerald Nagle). Gerrard's homestead lay at the west end of the bridge to the modern town of Blakney, above Norway Pine Falls.

p.15 *Their daughter Mary was born in Michigan City, Indiana.* A search of the Ypsilanti archives has failed to uncover the location of Michael Dominic's property.

Notes to Chapter 2

p.19 *twin towers rise above a new cathedral.* See Ch.1, fn.1. Construction on the new cathedral started in 1855.

p.19 *the huge grey-stone seminary school. Ibid.* At that time the Saint Hyacinthe Seminary was one of the finest Catholic colleges in Canada, and a great center for the order known as the Oblates of Mary Immaculate.

p.20 *His father's reaction...ruined him financially.* Although neither Gerrard nor Ed Nagle ever noted a specific date for the fire, with the assistance of M. Lucien Lefrancois I have been able to date it quite accurately.

p.20 *By the time Brookes was sentenced in 1860.* The last letters mentioning Brookes in the ANQ collection are dated 1860.

p.21 *sufficiently prosperous ...on Rue Cascade.* Most of the land at the east and west ends of Rue Cascade belonged to the Dessaulles family.

p.21 *Sarsfield...study law in Montreal.* In a letter dated 27 January 1860. Gerrard Nagle mentions some problems that his son Sarsfield is having. Soon after that, Sarsfield moved to Montreal.

ENDNOTES

p.21 *...a proclamation from Pope Pius IX.* This was the *Syllabus Errorum,* which condemned Liberalism, Socialism, and Rationalism.

p.24 *Their spokesman, a Métis named Louis Riel.* Interestingly enough, Riel is a French variation of Reilley. Louis Riel was of Irish-Indian extraction, and the presence of the shamrock on the Métis Provisional Government flag suggests that in 1869 Riel may have exploited a connection with the Fenians to a greater extent than is assumed. For a fascinating account of the French-Métis view of the historical events leading up to the Red River incident see Leandre Bergeron (pp.161 ff).

p.24 *And they made...southern neighbours.* The best account of the development of the home guard and their intelligence network is presented in *The Fenian Raids, 1866-1870, Missiquoi County* (Sherbrooke: Missiquoi County Historical Society, 1967).

p.25 *Captain Romuald Saint Jacques - a business associate of Senator Dessaulles.* Together Dessaulles and Saint Jacques created La Compagnie Manufacturiere de Saint-Hyacinthe.

p.25 *Ed had still not seen a skirmish.* The Saint Hyacinthe Infantry Company was demobilized at Saint-Jean-Sur-Richelieu.

p.26 *claim ...first military defense of the Dominion of Canada.* Ed Nagle received his Queen's Service Medal at Edmonton in 1899. It is part of the Nagle Collection, at the Glenbow Museum in Calgary.

Notes to Chapter 3

p.27 *Since 1859, Gerrard ...southeast of Saint Hyacinthe.* In a pencilled note to himself (QQA/E-21, Art. 806-26, loc. 5A00-000A, 1859 #16980), Gerrard's supervisor comments that Gerrard seems particularly interested in some land near the Magog River.

p.27 *Ed quit college to begin training as a millwright* Since I have not been able to locate records of Ed Nagle's college registration, I am unable to say exactly when he left school to take up training as a millwright.

p.28 *"Toronto to Prince Arthur's ...own provisions."* This reference is quoted from J.W. Stranger, "Dawson Route," *Western People* (a supplement to *The Western Producer*), 3 May 1984, p.15.

p.29 *convinced his elder brother Garrett* Garrett was the elder brother closest in age to Ed.

p.29 *Ed began the first of many journals* All of the journal entries that follow are from NFP/ENJ, 1874. When quoting I have taken great care only to punctuate and provide some transitions for ease of reading. In no way have I changed any of Ed's constructions, or altered the tone of his writing.

p.29 *including the Provincial Parliament Buildings* Part of Ed's fascination with the Provincial Parliament Buildings at Toronto, which were located on Front Street at that time, had to do with the fact that identical buildings in Lower Canada had been destroyed by a mob in 1849.

p.30 *SS International of the Beaty* This may be the Beatty Line.

p.34 *U.S. intrusion called the Northwest Angle* The citizens of British North American had already noticed a tendency for U.S. frontiers to drift north. Whether the curving reach of the Northwest Angle was due to Pond's incompetence as a surveyor, or a willful swing north is still a question debated by historians.

p.34 *Dawson's Route crossed the Northwest Angle* The finest single resouce available on the Dawson Route is a map in the collection of the Provincial Archives of Manitoba (MWPA); MWPA, D22, 1132 "Red River Route Map Shewing Land, Roads, and Navigable Sections between Thunder Bay, Lake Superior and Fort Gary [*sic*], Red River Settlement," (Traced by W. Eustace Maxwell, February 1875, Indian Branch No. 2790).

p.34 *C.P. Snow was sent* It is not clear whether Snow went to the Red River Settlement as an official government employee, or as the unofficial appointee of the soon-to-be-designated Governor General, William McDougall.

p.34 *The 1869 Red River Uprising...direct response to Snow's actions.* For a fine description of the part the surveyors played in bringing about the the 1869 Red River Uprising see D.W. Thompson, *Men and Meridians* (pp. 7ff).

p.35 *made our bed tender-foot fashion* In making their bed "tender-foot fashion," Ed and Garrett had laid their blankets directly on the ground, without putting a groundsheet or cushion of boughs beneath them or a cover of any kind over them.

p.37 *they were not...of the Dawson Route in 1874.* A partial search of the secondary sources suggests that during the six years that the Dawson Route was used only about 2500 emigrants actually followed it. In 1870 Col. Wolsely led 1200 troops, 400 voyageurs, and hundreds of workers across it as he improved it on his way to the Red River Settlement (Stranger, *op. cit.,* p.15). In 1871 the Dawson Route was completed and put into use (*Ibid.*). Between 1872 and 1873 more than 1000 emigrants crossed it (see J.G. MacGregor, *Edmonton Trader* (ET), p.6). Also in 1873, three Divisions of the Royal North West Mounted Police crossed the Dawson Route and improved it (*Ibid.*, p.17). In 1874, 300 emigrants travelled it to Manitoba (Stranger, *op. cit.*). In 1875, 2700 travellers - 800 of whom were emigrants -

crossed Dawson's Trail, and in 1876 it was officially abandoned by the government of Canada (*Ibid.*).

p.37 *After 1872...runs between Duluth and Moorehead.* See J. Macoun, p.580.

p.38 *we started for Broken Head* There is no telling why Ed confused Broken Head with Moorehead. The Moorehead Historical Society can find no record of the city ever being known by that name.

p.40 *The tall-grass prairie...reached the Buffalo River.* By travelling southwest from Duluth along Interstate 35, then turning west on Highway 210, and west-northwest on Highway 10, one can still follow the route of the Northern Pacific Railroad. Buffalo River State Park, located between Hawley and Glyndon on Highway 10, preserves a portion of the tall-grass prairie Ed and Garrett saw.

p.43 *Talk about coyotes!...pulled out again.* This is the last entry in Ed's 1874 journal.

Notes to Chapter 4

p.44 *"two streaks of rust across the wilderness."* This quote is from Bruce Hutchison's The Unfinished Country (Toronto: Douglas and McIntyre, 1985), p.224.

p.44 *About October 1,...Dakota Territories.* The dates I have used to fix the buffalo hunts are from MWPA, MG.9, A76, "Introduction to John Norquay's Account of the Buffalo Hunt," and "Buffalo Hunting, by John Norquay."

p.45 The Immigrant Sheds were also known as Immigration Hall.

p.48 *shaganappi* Shaganappi is thin strips of untanned buffalo hide.

p.48 *"scrub oak,...and squeals."* MacGregor, ET, p.30.

p.48 *"Like men of honor...it was too late."* This is from M.A. MacLeod's translation of "The Ballad of Seven Oaks" (also known as The Ballad of Frog Plain) which may be found in her paper, "The Bard of the Plains" (*Beaver*, Spring 1956). Used with the permission of *Beaver*.

p.49 *No surviving document mentions it*, Unfortunately, I was refused access to the J.A. McDougall papers, so I was never able to definitely establish that McDougall and Nagle met in Winnipeg.

p.53 *...masters of the plains* See MacGregor, FL, pp.46 ff. for a description of the Battle of Grand Couteau, which is considered to have been the decisive battle in the Métis-Sioux conflict.

p.53 *...only when approached.* Palliser mentions the strength of Métis belief in this ubiquitous folktale. Dr. James Hector found that the sound issued from a species of small frog.

p.54 *...not yet available* The Henry 44-40 Flat lever action repeating rifle was never sold in Canada.

p.54 *...from the hunting grounds.* See Dary (pp.66-67); for another reference to the Sioux herding the buffalo see MacGregor, ET, p.110: letter from Louvisa McDougall, 7 July 1879.

Notes to Chapter 5

p.58 *...Dawson Route's muskegs.* See Tuttle, p.402, and J. Macoun, pp.594-95. (Macoun is quoting Hind's pamphlet entitled *Navigation of Hudson's Bay*.) Despite the dates of these two works (Tuttle and Macoun), there is little doubt that Winnipeggers and other Red River settlers advocated the Hudson's Bay Route quite early on in the railroad debates.

p.59 *...on February 24.* I have not found any definite proof that this was, in fact, done.

p.59 *...paid them off* I have not been able to locate Martin's field books for this expedition. They do not appear to be in the collections of MWPA, but may be among the records of the Department of Indian Affairs at NAC.

p.60 *pemmican* These are 90-lb. sacks of pemmican.

p.61 *...far behind them* Otter's farm appears to have been located in Township 22, Range 14.

p.61 *...on the buffalo hunts.* There is no record of Ed ever having learned to play the fiddle in Quebec, so it is possible that he got his first lessons while on the buffalo hunts.

p.62 *...Northwest Territories.* See Macoun (p.570). Ed would undoubtedly have been amused by the eulogy that Lord Dufferin delivered re. the Dawson Route during one of his Winnipeg speeches.

p.63 *...Indian gift-exchange ways.* See NFP/ENJ, 1877, entry #3, list of supplies, which mentions that he carried several small gifts as part of his expenses.

p.65 *...his trap line.* Certain conflicts between Ed's updated short record of this trapping trip in his 1879 notes, and the notes recording Garrett's arrival in the back of the 1877 journal lead me to believe that this trip took place during the fall of 1880.

p.65 *...place at Gladstone.* In his 1879 journal, Ed renders the family's name as Whitford.

p.65 *...Whitmore's in March.* See NFP/LDF, Statement Sworn before S.S. Taylor and A.C. Rutan. The apparent discrepancy between Ed's account and the location of the houses as they appear on McLatchie's 1885 map of the homesteads (PAM, Cartography Division, Field Notebook #4177) can easily be explained by assuming that the brothers ran their initial boundary survey westward from survey station 8, at the northwest corner of the HBC grant.

p.65 *...Dauphin, Manitoba.* See A.S. Little, *Dogtown to Dauphin* (Winnipeg: Watson & Dwyer Publishing, 1988), pp.19-22.

229

Notes to Chapter 6

p.69 ...*then at Flat Creek.* Flat Creek was located in Section 19, Township 9, Range 23 west of the First Meridian, near the modern town of Griswold, Manitoba.

p.70 ...*old Traders's Road.* Thompson (p.86) presents an excellent map of the routes the cart trails followed across Canada during the late 1880's.

p.70 ...*Qu'Appelle River valley.* I am grateful to Frances Kimpton and Mrs. Tess Nagle-Shirer for making Ed's lost 1882 journal available to me. Without it this chapter could not have been written.

p.70 ...*Big Arm River.* After July 24 Ed is keeping a daily journal.

p.70 ...*name of Madick.* I can find no other references to this surveyor named Madick.

p.71 ...*Four Mile Coulee.* Macoun calls this Six Mile or Cottonwood Coulee.

p.71 ...*south of the border.* The others were Forts McLeod, Calgary, Edmonton, and Carlton.

p.72 ...*surveyed every 36 miles.* The finest work on early Canadian surveying is D.W. Thompson's two volume set, *Men and Meridians* (Ottawa: Department of Mines and Technical Surveys, 1966). See Vol. 2 pp. 1 - 60 for information relating specifically to surveys on the western plains. Macoun (pp.661-78) also gives a short description of surveying for the benefit of potential settlers.

p.73 ...*Commissioner of Lands.* I have not been able to find other contemporary references to Sir A.T. Calf, but believe that Bridges must be Burgess, B.C. Commissioner of Lands at that time.

p.74 ...*freezing blizzards of 1907.* In early October Ed lost track of the date, By mid-October it is difficult to be certain which dates apply to individual journal entries.

Notes to Chapter 7

p.77 ...*which he had not claimed,* There seems to have been several reasons why Ed had not claimed the money, at least one of which concerned the fact that he was too impatient to remain at Rock Forest until his 21st birthday. He seems to have been extraordinarily anxious to get beyond the reach of his father's control.

p.77 ...*received his reply.* G.J. Nagle to Ed Nagle, 28 February 1883.

p.79 ...*Government Salary* Parker had taken over Gerrard's old job as Agent for Crown Lands and Forest at Saint Hyacinthe.

p.80 ...*hearing and credence.* See Bob Beal and R. Macleod (pp.72ff.) for the story of Reed's rise to power.

p.82 ...*Pictou Academy.* For more information on Hislop's family and childhood see Hector Center Trust Archives (Pictou, Nova Scotia) Pictou Co. Census, Vol. 1, A.25/89; and the *Pictou Advocate*, 13 May 1911, p.10.

p.83 ...*his father's next overture.* G.J. Nagle to Ed Nagle, 7 August 1883. Only the first page of this letter has survived.

p.85 ...*a man named Stark* There is no way of telling whether or not this was Jack Stark, who later became a noted Barren Lands wanderer and gave his name to Stark Lake, which lies near the east arm of Great Slave Lake.

p.86 ...*in the priest's vestments.* In a letter to the parents of the murdered priest Father Farfard (Saint Albert Archives des Missions, Tome XXIII 1885, pp.417-30, 27 aout 1885), Bishop Grandin notes that at least 15 Indians danced wearing vestments of cloth-of-gold and silver.

p.87 ...*the boats were not watertight.* See p.20 of "General Strange's Alberta Field Force," in H. Fryer's *Alberta: The Pioneer Years* (Langley, B.C.: Stagecoach Publishing Co. Ltd., 1977), for diagrams of the boats. Beal and Macleod (p.283), mention the trouble the soldiers had accepting that the boats were seaworthy.

p.88 ...*this terrible war.* This coup stick was displayed as one of the artifacts in the Glenbow Museum's Métis Exhibition in 1985. Along with the rest of the Nagle Collection, it has recently been accessioned as a permanent part of the Glenbow collections.

p.88 ...*called Frenchman Butte.* Beal and Macleod (p.286) have noted that the engagement commonly called the Battle of Frenchman Butte actually took place on a hill five kilometers north of that landmark.

p.89 ...*in Middleton's wake.* Although Ed eventually got a Fenian Raid medal, he was never given the bar that should have indicated his Northwest Rebellion service. And when he filed for hazardous duty pay, his request was refused.

Notes to Chapter 8

p.92 ...*should be executed.* Beal and Macleod (pp.296-305) develop what is certainly one of the finest and most insightful analyses of Riel's trial proceedings. Their whole presentation of the rebellion — its causes, personalities, battles, and results — is required reading for anyone interested in the early phases of western Canadian history.

p.93 ...*(also known as Shot)* Various postulations have been advanced as reason's for Villeneauve's taking the nickname "Shot" (see, for example, D.J. Comfort, pp.197-206), and I offer yet another. Among the Métis who prided themselves on their ability to dance, Shot was an acknowledged standout. Since his name is sometimes spelled Schott, and one of the favorite Métis dances was the Schottische or Red River Jig, it may be that this oft noted and colorful character took his name from a dance at which he was particularly adept. (Julliete Champagne — personal communication 29 April 1990 - tells me that Shot is listed on the mission records and the 1886 land claims records as Louis Fosseneuve.)

p.94 ...*at Athabasca Landing* I can find no document specifically mentioning that Hislop was, in fact, at The Landing during the winter of 1886-87. However, an inscription in an English grammar book donated by Pierre Mercredi to the Northern Life Museum and Heritage Center in Fort Smith, suggests that Hislop may have had regular contact with The Landing from as early as 1884. It reads, "P. Mercredi; Hislop Service Outfit. P. Mercredi, June 1884, N.W.T., Athabasca."

p.94 ...*reloaded their scow.* The only written mention of the Athabasca River petroglyphs that I have found appears in C. Mair, (pp.128-29). However, a photo of them entitled "Totems at Grand Rapids, Athabasca River" is part of the photo collection at the Provincial Archives of Alberta (AEPAA, photo album #1492).

p.96 ...*above Lake Athabasca.* See Ted Nagle and Jordan Zinovich, *The Prospector: North of Sixty* (p.31), for Ed's comments to his son about the Ambarra River.

p.98 ...*in various ways.* Although the Church did not actually trade for furs, it did accept furs as offerings or as payment for services.

p.98 ...*at Fort McKay.* McKay is pronounced McKie, as in pie.

p.100 ...*shared a drink with them.* See *MWPA,HBCA,* B.242/e/3, fo.1, "Athabasca Landing Report, 1889." In reading this it should be remembered that during the 17th and 18th centuries the HBC actually traded liquor to the natives. Secord can not be accused of having traded liquor.

p.101 ...*Ed and Aubrey.* It is not clear whether Frank Oliver merely made a mistake in calling Aubrey "McGee" in the fall of 1889 (see EB, 2 November 1889), or whether Ed and Aubrey temporarily parted. By early 1890, however, both the *Bulletin* (15 March 1890) and Ed's journal (1890) indicate they were again working together. My research leads me to belive that Ed and Aubrey stayed together throughout 1889-90, and Oliver was in error.

p.102 ...*Ed's 1889-1890 journals* Although two of the journals have survived that Ed kept between 1889-90, only one of them can be dated with any accuracy: "Trapping on the Pembina and Athabasca, 1890."

p.102 ...*more traditional deadfalls.* See *Appendix 1* for recipes for the baits he used to trap different furbearing animals.

p.102 ...*about $205,* I have arrived at this figure by comparing the outfit list Ed compiled in the back of his journal (see "Camp Outfit") with the "cost landed" prices for HBC goods

at Smith Post, Slave River (see MWPA/HBCA, B.39/2/2, fos.84-93), and the "cost landed" and "selling prices" of the principal articles at Athabasca Landing (MWPA/HBCA, B.68/2/2, fos.1-10).

p.102 ...*between $220 and $300.* To arrive at this estimate I have priced every fur Ed listed in his 1890 journals according to the prices the HBC offered Colin Fraser for his fur that year, and the general values suggested in the HBC circular "Fur Valuation Tarriffs from Outfit(s)" 1883-1898 (MWPA/HBCA, D.27/6).

p.103 ...*trapping and trading.* Fur trade historians call trapping and moving among Indian camps to trade the "en derouin" system. For an accurate description of it see H.I. Innis (pp.269 and 357). For descriptions of the lives the transient trapper-traders lived see Peter Baker. After the Northwest Rebellion Ed had tried to avoid trading powder to the Indians, but he and Secord had some in their outfit.

p.104 ...*closely with Hislop,* Between 1 January and 22 April 1890, Hislop and Secord exchanged at least 14 letters, none of which appear to have survived.

p.104 ...*Hislop's operation.* Keane claims that by this time Hislop had sold his operation to Colin Johnson, and is working for Secord. In spite of his apparent success against the HBC, during the first four months of 1891 Hislop appears to have sent Secord only two lots of fur.

p.104 ...*at his trading post.* Between March and early June of 1891 Hislop consumed at least seven gallons of overproof hard liquor and one barrel of bottled beer. His binge continued well into September, when he arrived at Edmonton for three days of serious drinking before returning to The Landing.

p.104 ...*north to its posts.* This early outfit, and some of the others that Secord put together over the next few years, so closely approximated the HBC outfits that Ed and Jack would find themselves carrying the same unsalable stock as the Company had.

p.104 ...*for the downriver trip.* Hislop charged them $100 for the boat, which suggests that it was a scow, not a York Boat.

Notes to Chapter 9

p.105 ...*Indian groups there.* Properly speaking, until 1906 Forts Smith (which lies at the northern end of Smith Rapids) and Resolution (which lies just west of the Slave River Delta) were considered by the Hudson's Bay Company Head Offices to belong within the boundaries of the Athabasca District. However, because of their geographical position below Smith Rapids, for conceptual purposes I suggest considering them as already belonging to the more northerly Mackenzie District; as they would after 1906.

p.106 *...or regional bands* This is not the place to get involved in the anthropological debate re. the applicability of these designative terms. For further information see J. Helm, "Bilaterality in the Socio-Territorial Organization of the Arctic Drainage Dene," in *Ethnology*, Vol.4, 1965, pp.361-85 and bibliography.

p.108 *...a major obstacle* D. Smith claims that Roman Catholic Bishop Taché pioneered the Athabasca River route in 1868-69, and that when the free traders followed him the HBC reacted. He quotes G.R. Rae (p.158). While Smith's analysis may be correct, it appears that the HBC actually cut the Athabasca Landing Trail and developed The Landing.

p.108 *...would be abandoned.* Donald Smith, who financed the C.P.R. and in whose honor both Smith's Rapids and Fort Smith were named, became Governor of the Hudson's Bay Company in 1889, and probably had something to do with the shift from steamboats to the railroad.

p.108 *...as Smith Portage,* See C.S. Mackinnon, "Portaging on the Slave River (Fort Smith)," *Musk Ox*, no.27, winter 1980, pp.20-35, for an excellent history of Smith Portage.

p.110 *...in his area.* See Appendix II for a more detailed description of some of the actual differences in pricing goods and furs that had developed at various posts.

p.110 *...cost of its transportation.* See / HBCA, B.39/d/153, and B.200/e/23 to get some notion of the practice. According to the 1892 Fort Simpson Report, when Ed and John Secord started down north the HBC tariffs were still being calculated according to the old system, whereby 33 1/3% and 20¢/ pound were added to the Winnipeg price.

Notes to Chapter 10

p.112 *...Hislop's trading post.* It is not clear whether or not Hislop had sold his post to Colin Johnston by this time. However, on the maps numbered 83.376/1467 and 83.376/1470 in the AEPAA collections it is designated as Johnston's post. From Richard Secord's journal notes, it is plain that Hislop and Secord are working closely together.

p.112 *...for Ed and Jack,* According to Comfort, the $100.00 Hislop accepted as payment for his work was approximately the cost of a sturgeon head. Flatboats cost $50, and Yorkboats about $300.

p.114 *...90-pound "pieces"* Ninety pounds was considered the standard load for one man.

p.115 *...in that direction.* According to MWPA/HBCA, B.39/a/57, Fraser had been forced to work for George Elmore at least once during the years between 1887 and 1891.

p.116 *...near Great Slave Lake.* Ed became fascinated with Pike, and when he finally reached Great Slave lake in 1893, he carried a copy of Pike's *The Barren Lands of Northern Canada* with him. That copy remains with the Nagle Collection of papers, artifacts, and photographs.

p.116 *...musk ox robe.* It was unusual for musk ox robes to get as far south as Fort Chipewyan.

p.116 *...without their bulk.* E.H. "Ted" Nagle first described the unborn musk-ox trade to me. In the Nagle Collection (now with the Glenbow Foundation in Calgary, Alberta) there are two garments made from unborn musk-ox fur

p.116 *...unborn musk-ox pelts.* Both Caspar Whitney (pp.251-52), and David Handbury, (p.27), mention the unborn musk-ox trade.

p.117 *...sturgeon-head upstream.* It was unusual for river scows to be used more than one season. Normally, when they reached their northern destinations they were broken up for lumber. In this instance, however, Ed and Jack appear to have decided to use their scow a second season.

p.118 *...on Fort Good Hope,* Unfortunately for Edmontonians, the raffle was not sufficiently advanced by the time Ed was prepared to return north. As a result, he sold his musk ox robe to a man named W.S. Edmiston.

p.118 *...trip to Chipewyan.* It is likely that during this downriver trip, the free traders found some way to use the HBC tramway at Grand Rapids Island. By 1893 the HBC had realized what they were doing, and were complaining to the head office that the tram was in need of repair.

p.118 *...George Martin.* According to Inspector W.H. Routledge (see *Canada Sessional Papers 14 to 15*, Vol. XXXIII, No.12, 1899, Paper #15, Pt. II, "Patrol, Fort Saskatchewan to Fort Simpson," p.89), as of 1899 "... George Martin ..., an American by birth, being a native of the State of Ohio, ...has been in the far north for the past three years." Routledge goes on to say, "This man served in the American [Civil?] war, and was at MacLeoud [*sic*] in the early days of 1871 and 1872, before the advent of the police, with Healey, Emerson, Akers and other traders of that time.

p.118 *...fur back upstream.* This strategy had also been employed by the traders who first struck at the posts below Smith's Rapids in 1888.

p.118 *...new outfits for the others.* There is some doubt as to what Richard Secord did when Jack Secord, and Martin and Nagle left Chipewyan. Leonard's assertion that he went as far north at Fort Smith appears based on a misreading of a *Bulletin* article published 2 November 1892. Although Secord may have

ENDNOTES

accompanied Martin and Nagle north to scout a route through Smith's Rapids, it is also possible that he accompanied his brother to Fond Du Lac in order to help him set up the new post there.

p.120 ...*at Smith's Landing:* Smith's Landing would soon be renamed Grahame Landing, although locals would continue calling it Smith's Landing until 1910, when it was renamed Fort Fitzgerald.

p.122 ...*portages that lay ahead.* With the assistance of the Alberta Historical Resources Foundation (AHRF), during the summer of 1986 I attempted to establish exact locations for the portages on the east bank. Mr. James Darkes, a boatman from Fort Fitzgerald, was my guide and the sketch that follows is a combination of my findings (see my report to the AHRF, 19 September 1986, "Smith Rapids" - unpublished), and several other descriptions of the east bank portage route. Interested readers should consult [Sir] John Franklin; C.S. MacKinnon, "Portaging on the Slave River (Fort Smith)," *loc. cit.*; the 1881 journal of A.E. Morris (MWPA/HBCA, E.78/1, fos.87d-91); NFP/ENJ, 1906, 1908, 1909, and 1910 (now at the Glenbow Foundation, Calgary, Alberta); and Frank Russell,(pp.61-64). Although I have made my narrative and maps as accurate as possible, I must add a cautionary note. These are among the most dangerous rapids in Canada. Attempting to boat through them without the assistance of a guide would be foolhardy, and possibly life threatening.

p.122 ...*that catastropic descent.* James Darkes, personal communication, 4 July 1986.

p.123 ...*a torrential cascade.* When viewing the walls of this channel and chute today, James Darkes suggests remembering that since the Bennett dam was built on the Peace River, the water level in the Slave has dropped approximately seven feet.

p.123 ...*block-and-tackle.* During my 1986 field trip I managed to locate the remnants of the frame to which the Cassette Portage block-and-tackle was attached. At that time I believed a capstan had hauled the scows from the water. A photo by C.W. Mathers in the Ernest Brown Collection (AEPAA, B.2981), plainly shows the lines running from the block and tackle to the water.

p.123 ...*"bull-dogs" attacked.* The information that bull-dogs are attracted to dampness and salt is courtesy of Louis Menez and E.H. Nagle.

p.124 ...*below Cassette Portage.* In my AHRF report I have called Cassette Portage "Split Rock Portage," after the rock that has tumbled from the left side of the channel and forms the cataract into the basin.

p.124 ...*ancient log jam.* James Darkes claims that this is the Ambara Portage mentioned by Alexander Mackenzie.

p.126 ...*Ed and Martin would follow.* James Darkes tells me that several years ago, before the forest overgrew the bottom of the portage trail, he was shown the location of the graves.

p.128 ...*the Laundry River,* Father Louis Menez, O.M.I., tells me that before linguistic evolution collapsed the name, Laundry River was known as La Rivier André.

p.128 ...*between Martin's post,* Mulkins was permanently established at Fort Resolution, and Ed was using Martin's post as his base of operation.

p.128 ...*Fort Resolution,* A note in the front of Ed's copy of W. Pike's *The Barren Ground of Northern Canada* reads: "Edmund Nagle, Resolution, G.S. Lake, January 16, 1893.

p.128 ...*breed them himself.* It is not clear exactly when Ed began his breeding program. However, the idea seems to have come to him quite early during his tenure in the far north

p.129 ...*had been badly frozen.* The loss of this hunter and the extreme difficulties faced by the parties on the Barrens are enshrined in Dog Rib oral history. The hunter who died was the grandfather of Mr. Louis Mackenzie of Rae-Edzo, N.W.T. (Elizabeth and Louis Mackenzie, personal communication 25 June 1986).

p.129 ...*discouraging summer hunts.* The action was well reasoned. The musk ox were beginning to get overhunted, and summer robes did not have the fine underwool that grew during the fall and early winter.

p.130 ...*waiting for them.* I can find no evidence to support Leonard's claim (p.48) that Hislop came up river from Fort Resolution to meet Secord.

p.130 ...*$7,500.00 for it.* Secord's journals regularly record the credit notes and debts owed to him. When he claims he "sold" an outfit, he does not appear to have extended it on credit.

Notes to Chapter 11

p.131 ...*south to Fort Resolution* These were wood bison, not the animals Ed had hunted on the prairies south of Manitoba.

p.131 ...*came upon Ed Nagle first.* Russell spells the name Lafferté. However, since both the Hislop and Nagle records and the present family spell the name Lafferty, that is what I use.

p.131 ...*engaged the Laffertys* There is no way of knowing why the Laffertys were chosen. It may be that they had met George Martin when he traded for the HBC, and that he contacted them again during the winter of 1892-93.

p.131 ...*or country French.* For more information on the fur-trade languages in the Mackenzie District see R. Slobodin (pp.13ff.); A.D. Cameron (p.35); and P.C. Douaud.

p.131 ...*both learned Cree,* Hislop's contact with the interpreters at Battleford leads me to think that he may have started learning it there.

p.131 ...*were mostly Yellowknife,* B. Gillespie, "Yellowknives: Quo Iverunt?" (*The 1970 Annual Meeting of the American Ethnological Society,* Seattle: University of Washington Press, 1970, pp.61-71), lists the many scholars who have noted that the Yellowknife Indians spoke a dialect of Chipewyan, and suggests that they should be considered Chipewyan Indians.

p.132 ...*subsist off the land.* Although I have not found the Hislop and Nagle supply lists, in the Fort Rae Journal (MWPA/HBCA, B.171/a/2) Joseph Hodgson mentions discovering that Hislop is much better provisioned that he is. Since Hislop and Nagle arrived too late in the season to gather much country produce before freezeup, it is reasonable to assume they carried their provisions with them. Certainly, that was Ed's strategy when he first trapped and traded with Jack Secord in 1891.

p.132 ...*Fort Rae trade.* It is worth noting that in 1893 he had his wife and son with him at Fort Rae.

p.133 ...*near their trapping grounds.* Mr. Vital Thomas, Mrs. Elizabeth Mackenzie, and Mr. Louis Mackenzie — all of whom are Rae-Edzo old-timers — tell me that Lafferty guided Hislop to the north arm at Dogrib insistence. E.H. Nagle supports their statements, and claims that Hislop and Nagle actually asked a Dogrib council to allow them to establish Hislop's post. Since Emile is said to have worked for the Catholic priest, Father Roure (Russell, p.82), it may be that the priest also had a hand in helping to locate Hislop's post.

p.133 ...*all came together there.* Dr. June Helm stresses that locating trading posts in Dogrib territory had no effect on the boundaries of the regional boundary hunting territories.

p.135 ...*reach the HBC post.* Dr. Helm's informants also told her that the Dogribs had asked the HBC to move its post to the place Lafferty was guiding Hislop, and the request had been refused.

p.135 ...*a tripper named Bouvier.* The HBC had tried developing a system of tripping at Great Slave Lake, but had discontinued the practice in 1888. The HBC officers had felt that the natives entrusted with the outfits had tended to favour their fellows in the trade exchange.

p.135 ...*and skin preparation.* For a detailed but somewhat disorganized introduction to the practice of buying and trading furs, see A.R. Harding's *Fur Buyer's Guide.*

p.135 ...*current market values.* Ever since his early days as a trader Secord had made an effort to circulate prices to the men with whom he traded. Other buyers competing with the HBC were also beginning to post their buying prices regularly in the Edmonton *Bulletin* (see, as examples, "James McMillan and Company's fur circular," EB, 10 January 1895; "London Fur Sales," EB, 24 January 1895; and "London Fur Sales," EB, 25 February 1895).

p.138 ...*of the northern year.* MWPA/HBCA, B.172/a/2, fos.24d-25. Published with the permission of the Hudson's Bay Company Archives.

p.139 ...*sons of Anak* At this point Hodgson notes, "I fear we must look on the above expression in light of poetical licence (printer note)."

p.143 ...*drew them back.* The entry reads "Grand Rapids," but must refer to Smith Rapids.

p.144 ...*flintlock guns,* These items are among those listed as unsaleable at Forts Chipewyan and Vermillion at the beginning of the decade.

p.146 ..."*Yes,*" *the journalist replied.* See Whitney (p.317) for a description of the emotional impact this conversation had on the journalist.

Notes to Chapter 12

p.149 ...*before a roaring fire.* For the Nagles' own story of their near catastrophic honeymoon trip see "Trip to the Far North," EB, 17 December 1905.

p.150 ...*at Liard River.* Boniface Lafferty was originally the H.B.C. interpreter at Fort Simpson.

p.150 ...*late fall of 1896,* J.G. MacGregor claims that Secord and McDougall did not become partners until 1897.

p.150 ...*important to the fur trade.* Although the Game Act became effective in 1896, the legislation was enacted two years earlier, in 1894.

p.151 ...*at The Landing* One especially important component of a tracking outfit was the supply of moccasins. Each man was supplied with as many pairs as he needed during the river journey.

p.151 ...*and Fort Smith.* McLeod was the son a a Hudson's Bay Company trader. Connor was working with or for the Ross brothers, of Edmonton.

p.151 ...*an ex-pugilist.* Marsh was born at Clarksburg, Toronto 18 June 1866, and began his missionary service at Fort Liard 1 July 1892. When he settled at Hay River he was still a deacon. He was not ordained a priest until 1900.

p.154 ...*burn off moose range.* Moose feed on the new growth and shoots of the plants that survive the fires.

p.157 ...*supplies down north;* That spring the HBC actually shipped at least 250 tons of supplies north.

p.157 ...*a mordern Eldorado,* According to J.G. MacGregor, *(The Klondike Rush Through Edmonton,* p.21), that occurred in May.

p.157 ...*Fort Smith staging centre.* Apparently, Hislop and Nagle never operated an actual trading post at Fort Smith, although they had an agent there.

p.157 ...*second week in August.* The Edmonton *Bulletin*'s special Klondike Issue was published on August 12, 1897.

p.159 ... *'God forsaken,'* Actually, the word is of Cree origin and appears to mean either "where there are reeds," or "meeting place of many waters."

p.159 ...*readable only by the natives.* The letter must have been written in Cree Syllabics, and could have been about anything.

p.160 ...*reminisce in a letter* For more of the text of the letter see Nagle and Zinovich, pp.73-74.

p.160 ...*Teddy Roosevelt was shooting.* Later in his life, Jones did indeed travel twice to Africa.

p.163 ...*from Arnprior, Ontario.* Charlie Nagle is the man Leonard refers to when mistakenly claiming that Ed set off for the Klondike (p.71).

Notes to Chapter 13

p.168 ...*cared and provided,* Madeline Zoe and Vital Lafferty (Rae-Edzo Dogrib elders), personal communication, 25 June 1986. Dogrib oral history establishes Mrs. Zoe as Jim Hislop's daughter, and Vital Lafferty mentions young Jim Hislop, who was apparently drowned at Willow River while still a boy. E.H. "Ted" Nagle cannot recall the Hislops having any children.

p.168 ...*at the Mission School.* Louis Menez says that many northern men got wives in this fashion.

p.168 ...*Dogrib, and French.* As near as Louis Menez and I could determine, she spoke at least these languages, and possibly English as well.

p.169 ...*was a woman.* It was not Mrs. Craig. She and her husband had moved on to Hay River in April.

p.170 ...*at Great Slave Lake.* W.J. McLean had once been a Hudson's Bay Company post factor.

p.172 ...*take out and have assayed.* There are conflicting reports on the condition of the Indians at the east end of Great Slave Lake that winter. Routledge claims that caribou were scarce and they were starving. McLean claims that caribou were plentiful.

p.173 ...*for $2,000;* Secord bought the Sparrow on 7 November 1898.

p.174 ...*calling it Nagle Channel.* For examples see the maps in NAC, RG 45, Vol.299, Robert Bell Journals.

Notes to Chapter 14

p.177 ...*when he returned to Resolution.* Ed Nagle writes that Hanbury appeared on 6 October 1901, but according to Hanbury's own memoir (pp.15-16), the accident appears to have happened in September of 1899.

p.178 ...*famous throughout the north.* Louis Menez says that when he first arrived at Fort Resolution, in 1945, Mackenzie Valley Huskies were still the best sled dogs a traveller could get. Although they were plentiful then, now the animals can only be found in the teams of the Indians from Roché River Village, on Great Slave Lake.

p.178 ...*Klondiker named Charlie Bunn.* The best descriptions of Bunn will be found in J. McGill's *Northern Adventure: The Exploration of Great Bear Lake - 1900* (Cobalt, Ontario: Highway Bookshop, 1976).

p.179 ...*resident northern priests* Father Albert Lacombe, who was travelling with the 1899 commission, was influential in helping the half breeds to change the Commissioner's initial stance.

p.180 ...*on which the Resolution post sat.* Father Louis Menez informs me that in 1988 the Fort Resolution community council regained control of the land where the Hislop and Nagle post was situated. It is slated to become the site for a new community center.

p.182 ...*signed it over to her husband.* Nancy Hislop did not transfer her scrip until 1903.

p.183 ...*that had previously been accorded them.* The incidents surrounding the musk ox hunts and the Fort Rae trader in 1892 (see Chapter 10) are a case in point.

p.184 ...*modern repeating rifles.* According to Ted Nagle, after the Klondike rush ammunition calibers were standardized in the Mackenzie Region. The traders had satisfied many special orders, only to have the shells remain unused on their post shelves. The caliber chosen for hunting rifles was 30-30 (see Nagle and Zinovich, p.31, and fn.).

p.184 ...*preserved as emergency supplies.* According to the surviving Nagle children, the caribou were butchered where they were killed then freighted back to to be stored in the Fort Resolution ice house. In 1904, E.H. Nagle observed a similar operation at Willow River (see Nagle and Zinovich pp.183-86).

p.185 ...*several photos of Ed.* Most of Mathers' photographs are now housed with the E. Brown Collection in the holdings of the Provincial Archives of Alberta.

Notes to Chapter 15

p.187 ...*catastrophes at Great Slave Lake:* I am unable to discern whether or not Ed is the author of this letter. It is possible.

p.189 ...*horse kind so far north.* Louis Menez claims that horses reached Resolution earlier than this. See Nagle and Zinovich, p.65, and fn.

p.193 ...*government exams,* George Phillips was his examiner.

p.193 ...*the SS Cariboo* This is the registered spelling of the boat's name.

p.193 *from Connor* The Hislop and Nagle boats were eventually registered at Kenora (previously named Rat Portage).

p.193 ...*the Northwest Territorial Assembly.* Secord had become a candidate for the North West Territorial Assembly in April of 1903, and was elected to a seat.

p.194 ...*lip of the North Saskatchewan valley.* It was located on the west side of what is now 115th Street, about 100 meters south of the junction with Jasper Avenue.

p.195 ...*world renowned Huskies.* Fitzgerald appears to be referring to the Eskimos, not their dogs.

p.195 ...*steamer to come back in.* Whittacker was a Church of England man.

p.196 ...*furs they had ever collected.* The Edmonton *Bulletin* ("Fur Export will Reach a Large Figure," 13 January 1905) suggests $101,000.00 as an overall value for the Hislop and Nagle furs collected during the winter of 1903-04.

p.197 ...*in front of each of its sleds.* See "Mails for the North," EB, 16 November 1904; and "Arctic Mail Service," EB, 10 December 1904. Strangely, although records in the National Archives of Canada verify that Ed was the first Fort Resolution postmaster, they maintain that the mail service was not instituted until 1910.

Notes to Chapter 16

p.201 ...*at Hislop's backdoor.* Mr. Vital Thomas, Mr. and Mrs. Louis Mackenzie, and Mrs. Madeline Zoe, personal communication, 25 June 1985. Stefansson (AMNH/AA, journal transcripts 1906-08, pp.17 and 42) also claims that the Mackenzie District was finally being enlarged to include Forts Smith and Resolution within its scope.

p.201 ...*Hislop and Nagle furs to London.* The sale of McDougall and Secord's merchandising and retail enterprises is an extremely complex action, for which no satisfactory chronological sequencing has been presented. Different interpretive versions of it and its effects appear in H.A. Innis (pp.368ff.); J.G. MacGregor, (ET, p.242); and D. Leonard (pp.126ff).

p.202 ...*one's story came out.* Ed kept a detailed journal of the trip.

p.202 ..."*uninhabited" on its maps.* The Stefansson letters and journals in the AMNH, AA are the best source of information about the part of the journey the anthropologist shared with Ed.

p.202 ...*After his wife's accident,* I have not been able to discover what happened to Mrs. McKinlay.

p.203 ...*at the New Portage.* The Mathers photographs indicate that the New Portage had been abandoned sometime before 1901, possibly during the Klondike Gold Rush.

p.204 ...*trailing behind the Eva.* The whaleboat eventually proved a sound investment, though Ed does not appear ever to have believed that.

p.204 ...*several conflicting accounts,* The Roman Catholic Church, the R.C.M.P., and the Nagle family all have their own versions of the story. For the Catholic version I consulted the Billy Clark file in the Oblate Provincial House at Fort Smith (research notes, 8 and 9 July 1986). For the R.C.M.P. version see NAC, RG 18, Accession 83-84/068, file G.516-197. Ted Nagle told me the Nagles' version, personal communication, January 1985. I have combined elements from all three versions in the presentation that follows.

p.204 ...*with the priest at Simpson.* When I saw it, it was in the collection of documents at the Roman Catholic Provincial House at Fort Smith (which may, by now, have been transferred to Saint Albert, Alberta).

p.206 ...*over to Hislop and Nagle.* See Leonard, *op. cit.,* p.126. My research notes (AEPAA, December 1985) indicate that when McDougall and Secord sold to the Revillon Freres they retained their Hislop and Nagle connection. I believe the *Bulletin* is my source.

p.208 ...*a knoll overlooking the Slave.* There is a photograph of the grave in the Nagle Family Collection. Natives in the Northwest Territories still surround graves with picket fences to keep bad spirits away.

p.210 ...*and fixed my mosquito bar.* What Ed calls a "mosquito bar" is now known as a mosquito net.

Note to Chapter 17

p.215 ...*reached Resolution in 1913,* There are some photographs of the trip in the Nagle Family Papers.

BIBLIOGRAPHY

Published Material

Asch, M. "Impact of Changing Fur Trade Practices on the Economy of the Slavey Indians." *Proceedings of the Second Congress, Canadian Ethnology Society*, Vol.2 (Ottawa: National Museum of Man Mercury Series, #28, n.d.).

Baker, P. *Memoirs of an Arctic Arab*. Yellowknife: Yellowknife Publishing Company Ltd., 1976.

Beal, Bob and R. Macleod. *Prairie Fire*. Edmonton: Hurtig, 1984.

Belcourt, G.A. "The Buffalo Hunt." *The Beaver* (December 1944).

Bell, J.M. *Far Places*. Toronto: Macmillan Company of Canada, 1934.

_____. *Report on the Topography and Geology of Great Bear Lake: and of a Chain of Lakes and Streams thence to Great Slave Lake*. Ottawa: Geological Survey of Canada, 1901.

Bell, R. "Mackenzie District," Annual Report, Geological Survey of Canada (New Series), Vol. XII, 1899, Report A. Ottawa: Geological Survey of Canada, 1902.

Bergeron, Leandre. *The History of Quebec: A Patriot's Handbook*. Toronto: New Canada Press Ltd., 1971.

Brown, Dee. *Bury My Heart At Wounded Knee*. New York: Bantam, 1975.

Brown, H.M. *Lanark Legacy: Nineteenth Century Glimpses of an Ontario County*. Perth: the Corporation of the County of Lanark, 1984.

Cameron, A.D. *The New North*. New York: D. Appleton and Co., 1910.

Campbell, F.W. *The Fenian Invasions of Canada of 1866 and 1870: and the operations of the Montreal Militia Brigade in connection therewith*. Montreal: John Lovell & Son, Ltd., 1904.

Camsell, C. *Son of the North*. Toronto: Ryerson, 1956.

Canada Directory For 1857-58, The. Montreal: John Lovell, 1857.

Comfort, D.J. *River of Water and Steamboats North*. Canada: n.pub., 1974.

Concise Dictionary of Canadianisms, A. Toronto: Gage Educational Publishing Ltd., 1973.

Dary, D.A. *The Buffalo Book*. New York: Avon Books, 1975.

Debrett's Peerage and Baronetage .... Great Britain: Debrett, 1977.

Dion, J.N., et al. *Des Vies, des siecles, Une Histoire : 1757 a Aujourd'hui*, Vol.1. Saint Hyacinthe: Chapitre 1480 des Femmes Moose de St. Hyacinthe, 1984.

Douaud, P.C. *Ethnolinguistic Profile of the Canadian Métis*. Ottawa: National Museum of Man, Mercury Series, Canadian Ethnology Services, Paper No.99, 1985.

Fenian Raids, 1866-1870, Missiquoi County, The. Sherbrooke: Missiquoi County Historical Society, 1967.

Franklin, John. *Narrative of a journey to the shores of the polar sea in the years 1811, 1812, 1813, and 1814*. London: 1824.

Fryer, H. "Murder in the Cypress Hills." In *Alberta: The Pioneer Years*. Langley, B.C.: Stagecoach Publishing Co. Ltd., 1977.

Fumoleau, R. *As Long As This Land Shall Last*. Toronto: McClelland and Stewart Ltd., 1973.

Gillespie, B. "Yellowknives: Quo Iverunt?" In *Proceedings of the 1970 Annual Meeting of the American Ethnological Society*. Seattle: University of Washington Press, 1970.

Gray, J.H. *Red Lights on the Prairie*. Winnipeg: Signet, 1973.

Handbury, David. *Sport and Travel in the Northland of Canada*. New York: Macmillan Co., 1904.

Harding, A.R. *Fur Buyer's Guide*. Columbus, Ohio: A.R. Harding Publishing Co., n.d.

Helm, et al. "The Contact History of the Subarctic Athapaskans: An Overview." In *Proceedings: Northern Athapaskan Conference, 1971*, Vol.1. Ottawa: National Museum of Man Mercury Series, #27, 1975.

Helm, J. "Bilaterality in the Socio-Territorial Organization of the Arctic Drainage Dene." *Ethnology* 4 (1965).

_____. "The Dogrib Indians." In M.G. Biccheri (ed.) *Hunters and Gatherers Today*. New York: Holt Rinehart, and Winston Inc., 1972.

Historic Winnipeg Restoration Area, The (pamphlet). Manitoba: n.p., n.d.

Hutchison, Bruce. *The Unfinished Country*. Toronto: Douglas and McIntyre, 1985.

Inman, H. *Buffalo Jones' Forty Years of Adventure*. Topeka, Kansas: Crane and Company, 1899.

Innis, H.A. *The Fur Trade in Canada*. Toronto: University of Toronto Press, 1984.

Keene, Irene. "In the Historian's Corner: James Hislop." *Edmonton Daily Capital*, 3 May 1913.

Kretch, S. "The Trade of the Slavey and Dogrib at Fort Simpson in the Early Nineteenth Century." In *The Subarctic Fur Trade*. Vancouver: U.B.C. Press, 1984.

Leonard, D. *A Builder of the Northwest: The Life and Times of Richard Secord*. Edmonton: Richard Y. Secord, 1981.

Little, A.S. *Dogtown to Dauphin*. Winnipeg: Watson & Dwyer Publishing, 1988.

Lovell s Canadian Dominion Directory for 1871. Montreal: John Lovell & Son, 1871.

MacDonald, J.A., Cpt. *Troublous Times in Canada: A History of the Fenian Raids of 1866 and 1870*. Toronto: W.S. Johnson and Coy., 1910.

MacGregor, J.G. *Edmonton Trader*. Toronto: McClelland & Stewart Ltd. 1963.

_____, J.G. *Father Lacombe*. Edmonton: Hurtig, 1975.

_____, J.G. *The Klondike Rush Through Edmonton*. Toronto: McClelland and Stewart Limited, 1970.

Mackay's Montreal Directory, 1862-63. Montreal: Owler and Stevenson, 1863.

MacKinnon, C.S. "Portaging on the Slave River (Fort Smith)." *Musk Ox* 27 (winter 1980):20-35.

MacLeod, M.A. "The Bard of the Plains." *Beaver* (Spring 1956).

Macoun, J. *Manitoba and the Great North West*. Guelph, Ont.: The World Publishing Company, 1882.

Mair, C. *Through the Mackenzie Basin*. Toronto: William Briggs, 1908.

Maltby, Peter L. and Monica "A New Look at the Peter Robinson Emigration of 1823." *Ontario History* 55, #1 (March 1965).

Mathers, C.W. "A Trip to the Arctic Circle." *Alberta Historical Review* (Autumn 1972):6-15.

McGill, Jean S. *Northern Adventure: The Exploration of Great Bear Lake - 1900*. Cobalt, Ontario: Highway Bookshop, 1976.

_____. *A Pioneer History of the County of Lanark*. Bewdney: Clay Publishing Co., 1977.

McRae, A.O. "Edmund Nagle." In *History of the Province of Alberta*, Vol.1. Alberta: Western Canada Historical Company, 1912.

Menonite Settlement. Manitoba: Historic Resources Branch, 1985.

Mitchell's Canada Gazetteer and Business Directory for 1864-65. Toronto: W.C. Chewet and Co., 1864.

North, Dick. *The Lost Patrol*. Anchorage, Alaska: Alaska Northwest Publishing Company, 1983.

Pascal Breland. Manitoba: Historical Resources Branch, 1984.

"Patrol, Fort Saskatchewan to Fort Simpson." *Canada Sessional Papers 14 to 15*, Vol. XXXIII, No.12, 1899, Paper #15, Pt. II.

Pike, W. *The Barren Ground of Northern Canada*. London: MacMillan and Co., 1892.

Rapport du Commissair Des Terres de la Couronne du Canada pour l'Annee 1856. Toronto: Stewart Derbishire and George Desbarats, 1857 (Appendice D).

Rapport du Commissair Des Terres de la Couronne du Canada, 1861. Quebec: Hunter, Rose, et Cie (en francais).

Ray, A.J. *Indians in the Fur Trade: their role as hunters, trappers, and middlemen in the lands southwest of Hudson's Bay, 1660-1870*. Toronto: University of Toronto Press, 1974.

Report of the Commissioner of Crown Lands of Canada for 1868 and 1872. Quebec: Daily Mercury.

Russell, F. *Explorations in the Far North*. Iowa City, Iowa: University of Iowa Press, 1898.

Seaton, E.T. *The Arctic Prairies*. New York: Charles Scribner's Sons, 1911.

Silver Heights. Winnipeg: Manitoba Historic Resources Branch, 1985.

Slobodin, R. *Métis of the Mackenzie District*. Ottawa: Canadian Research Center for Anthropology, 1966.

Smith, D. *Moose-Deer Island House People*. Ottawa: National Museum of Man Mercury Series, #81, 1982.

Somerset, H.S. *The Land of the Muskeg*. London: Wm. Heinmann, 1895.

Spry, I.M. *The Palliser Expedition*. Toronto: The Macmillan Company of Canada Ltd., 1963.

Steele, S.B. *Forty Years in Canada*. London: H. Jenkins, 1915.

Stefánsson, V. *Hunters of the Great North*. London: 1923.

_____. *My Life With the Eskimo*. New York: Collier Books, 1971.

_____. *The Friendly Arctic: The Story of Five Years in the Polar Regions*. New York: 1921.

Stegner, W. *Wolf Willow*. Toronto: Macmillan of Canada, 1977.

Stewart, E. *Down the Mackenzie and Up the Yukon in 1906*. Toronto: Bell and Cockburn, 1913.

Stranger, J.W. "Dawson Route." *Western People* (a supplement to *The Western Producer*) (3 May 1984).

Taylor, Elizabeth. "A Woman in the Mackenzie Delta." In *Tales of the Canadian Wilderness*. Secaucus, N.J.: Castle, 1985.

Thompson, D.W. *Men and Meridians*, two volumes. Ottawa: the Queen's Printer, 1967.

Tuttle, G.A. *Our North Land*. Toronto: C. Blackett Robinson, 1885.

Tyrrell, J.B. (ed.). *The Journals of Samuel Hearne and Philip Turnor*. Toronto: The Champlain Society, 1934.

Whalley, George. *The Legend of John Hornby*. Toronto: Macmillan of Canada, 1962.

Whitney, J. Caspar. *On Snow Shoes to the Barren Grounds*. New York: Harper and Brothers, 1896.

Zinovich, Jordan and Ted Nagle. *The Prospector: North of Sixty*. Edmonton: Lone Pine Publishing, 1989.

Newspapers

Calgary Daily Herald.
Chicago *Inter Ocean*.
Courrier de St. Hyacinthe.
Edmonton Bulletin, 1884-1913.
Edmonton Daily Capital.
Edmonton Journal.
Le Métis.
Pictou Advocate.
Winnipeg *Daily Free Press*.

Unpublished Material

Abbreviations employed:
Alberta Historical Resources Foundation, Calgary (*AHRF*).
American Museum of Natural History, Anthropology Archives (*AMNH/AA*).
Archives Nationales du Quebec, Quebec (*QQA*).
City of Edmonton Archives (*AEEA*).
Ed Nagle Journals (*ENJ*).
Ed Nagle Letters (*ENL*).
Hudson's Bay Company Archives (*HBCA*).
Lake Dauphin File (*LDF*).
Nagle Family Papers (*NFP*), now housed at the Glenbow Archives in Calgary, Alberta.
National Archives of Canada (*NAC*).
National Library of Canada (*OONL*).
Oblates of Mary Immaculate (*O.M.I.*)
Peter Robinson Papers (*PRP*).
Provincial Archives of Alberta (*AEPAA*)
Provincial Archives of Manitoba (*MWPA*).
Richard Secord Journals (*RSJ*).
Ted Nagle Letters (*TNL*).
Upper Canada State Papers (*UCSP*).

AEEA, Frank Oliver File, "Wonderful Journey of the Canadian Minister of the Interior."
AEEA/RSJ, 1890-1913.
AEPAA, 70.387, MR 3/4, Saint Peter's Mission Journals.
AEPAA, 71.369, Diary of Victor Mercredi.
AEPAA, 83.1/1872, court dockets; H.C. Taylor's report; 83.1/1873.
AEPAA, MR 110/17.
AEPAA, MR4, 3/4, Saint Peter's Mission Journals.
AMNH/AA, V. Stefánsson journal transcripts 1906-08.
Archives de la Societe d'Histoire regionale de Saint Hyacinthe, Cadastre Abrege de la Seigneurie de Dessaulles-Propre, No.53, Canada, B.C. Procedes sous l'Acte Seigneury de Saint Hyacinthe, suivant titre du 23 September 1748, Sec.B/Series 1/Das 22.
HBCA, A.12/FT, Miscellaneous, 1233; A.12/FT341/[1]; /[10].
HBCA, A.1/198.
HBCA, B.152/a.
HBCA, B.171/a/2; /4; B.172/e/1.
HBCA, B.181/a/18; 20; B.181/e/2; (report); /4.
HBCA, B.200/d/266; B.200/e/23; /24.
HBCA, B.220/e/23; /24.
HBCA, B.242/e/3.
HBCA, B.307/a/4; B.307/e/3.
HBCA, B.348/e/2; /4.
HBCA, B.39/a/57; B.39/d/153; B.39/e/13; /14; /19; /21; /23; B.39/z/2.
HBCA, B.68/z/2.
HBCA, D.27/178; D.27/1A; /1B; D.27/2/1; D.27/6; D.27/a.
HBCA, E.78/1, Journal of A.E. Morris, 1881.
HBCA, Finding Aid.
HBCA, G.1/300.
Hector Center Trust Archives (Pictou, Nova Scotia) Pictou Co. Census, Vol. 1, A.25/89.
NAC, 84/8054/KI-KL/770, "Report No. 9, War Claims Commission, Winnipeg."
NAC, MG29,A11,Vol.1, dossier 1894-1903.
NAC, MG30, E82, Vol.9.
NAC, RG12/ Vol.1453, "Masters and Mates Competency Certificates, Inland and Coasting," #4256.
NAC, RG12/Vol.3038.
NAC, RG18, Accession 83-84/068, file G.516-197.
NAC, RG45/Vol.299/Number 1, Robert Bell Journals, Great Slave Lake.
NAC, RG85/Vol.572, File 273.
NAC, RG85/Vol.574, dossier 323; RG85/Vol.664, File 3910; RG9, II A5, Vol.3, p.88.
NAC, RG9, II F6, Vol.2, "Militia on Actual Service, Pay List from 24 May 1870 to 31 May 1870."
NAC, RG9, II F6, Vol.2, "Saint Hyacinthe Infantry Co., No.1, Monthly Pay List for April."
NAC/Library, COP/YSI Sessional Papers 1898, #15, Vol.XXXIII, No.12, 1899.
NAC/PRP - on microfilm - B885.
NAC/UCSP RG1, E.3, Vol. 41A.
Nagle, E.H. "The Pioneer Woman, Eva Nagle, 1875-1954."
Nagle, E.H. and Jordan Zinovich, "An Historical Sketch," 1984.
NFP, genealogical material (courtesy of Frances Kimpton and Mary Nagle-Gallagher).
NFP/ENJ, 1874, 1877, 1879, 1882, 1889-1890, 1906-1911, 1914, 1916-1917, 1919.
NFP/ENL
NFP/ENP, "Agreement of Sale, The McMurray Registered Townsite Co. Ltd. - to - Edmund Nagle."
NFP/ENP, "Last Will and Testament of Edmund Nagle."
NFP/ENP, "Plan of the Subdivision of Hislop and Nagle Estate."
NFP/ENP, "Receipt for lot at Fort Smith," marked Resolution - Ft. Smith, August 13/98 (courtesy of Frances Kimpton).
NFP/ENP, Certificate from the Commission Appointing Edmund Nagle of Fort Resolution a Justice of the Peace, dated 9 April 1902.

NFP/ENP, F.J. Fitzgerald to E.B. Nagle, 1 February 1904.

NFP/ENP, Joseph Hodgson to Ed Nagle, Dease River, Great Bear Lake, N.W.T., June 12, 1911.

NFP/ENP, steam boiler copybook.

NFP/LDF (compiled by Sam Katayama and Frances Kimpton).

NFP/necrology for G.J. Nagle (***Courrier de St. Hyacinthe,*** 29 fevrier 1884).

NFP/TNL

NFP/traditional oral history.

O.M.I. Diocesan Archives, Fort Smith, Northwest Territories, "In the District Court of the District of Athabasca," from the file of the Estate of Mrs. James Hislop.

O.M.I. Diocesan Archives, Fort Smith, Northwest Territories, Cabinet Drawer 4 (Proprietes-Statistiques Finances Smith-Bulletins Paroissiaux/Estate Mrs. James Hislop).

OONL, "Canada Sessional Papers 15 to 17, Vol. XXXII, No.12, 1898," (Ottawa: S.E. Dawson, 1899), "Appendix L - Police Patrol, Athabasca District, Winter of 1896-97."

OONL, COP/CA1, "Canada Statutes, 1894, 57 Vic, Chapter 31."

QQA/Department des Terres de la Couronne, Bois et Forets (***DTC,BF***)/Registre de lettres recues (***RIr***), 1853-93, E-21, Art.806-26 (5A00-000A).

QQA/E-21, Art.806-26, loc. 5A00-000A.

QQA/Terres et Forets, E-21, Art.360-805.

Rae, G.R. ***The Settlement of the Great Slave Lake Frontier, Northwest Territories Canada From the Eighteenth to the Twentieth Century***. Ann Arbor: University of Michigan, unpublished Ph.D. dissertation, 1963.

Registre des Actes des Baptemes, Mariages set Sepultres, faits et celebres en l'eglise paroissials Notre-Dame-du-Rosaire de St. Hyacinthe (Reg. 1854, Fol. 218, No. S-102.)

Research notes from Dr. June Helm (1970).

Research notes from ***MWPA*** (Ketchison Collection).

Research notes from the O.M.I. Provincial House Archives, Fort Smith, 8 and 13 July 1986.

Research notes from the Societe d'Histoire Regionale de Saint Hyacinthe.

Saint Albert, Archives des Missions, Tome XXIII 1885.

Saint Joseph's Mission Church Registry, Fort Resolution.

Saint Joseph's Mission Codex Historicus, Fort Resolution.

Societé d'Histoire Regionale de Saint-Hyacinthe, Repertoire des Mariages (Catholiques), Mariages de Sherbrooke - Cathdrale St. Michel 1836-1950.

St. Joachim Parish Register, 19 September 1895.

WMPA, Cartography Division, McLatchie's 1885 map of the homesteads (Field Notebook #4177).

WMPA, D22, 1132; "Red River Route Map Shewing Land, Roads, and Navigable Sections between Thunder Bay, Lake Superior and Fort Gary [sic], Red River Settlement," (Traced by W. Eustace Maxwell, February 1875, Indian Branch No. 2790).

WMPA, MG3, D.1. (Riel 620); George H. Young, "The Second Riel Uprising or Alleged Fenian Raid, October 1871."

WMPA, MG9, A76; "Introduction to John Norquay's Account of the Buffalo Hunt," and "Buffalo Hunting, by John Norquay."

WMPA, MG10: G.F. Reynolds, "The Man Who Built Portage and Main."

WMPA, MG12, B1.

WMPA, MG12, B2; Alexander Morris Letters (Ketchison Collection).

Zinovich, Jordan. "A Catalogue of the Artifacts in the Nagle Collection," 1984.

Zinovich, Jordan. Report to the ***AHRF***, 19 September 1986, "Smith Rapids."

Interviews and Personal Communication:

Juliette Champagne (Edmonton).

Alec Charlot (Rae-Edzo Dogrib elder).

James Darkes (Fort Fitzgerald, N.W.T.).

C.H. "Punch" Dickins (Victoria, Toronto).

Dr. June Helm (Iowa City, Iowa).

Frances Kimpton (Invermere, B.C.).

M. Lucien Lefrançois (Saint Hyacinthe, P.Q.).

BIBLIOGRAPHY

Elizabeth Mackenzie (Rae-Edzo Dogrib elder).
Louis Mackenzie (Rae-Edzo Dogrib elder).
Father Louis Menez, O.M.I. (Fort Resolution, N.W.T.).
E.H. "Ted" Nagle (Kimberley, B.C.).
Richard Y. Secord (Edmonton).
Tess Nagle-Shirer (Kimberley, B.C.).
Dr. J.G.E. Smith (New York City).
Mrs. S.A.S. Smith (Winnipeg).
Vital Thomas (Rae-Edzo Dogrib elder).
F.W. "Ted" Watt (Victoria).
Madeline Zoe (Rae-Edzo Dogrib elder).

INDEX

INDEX

245

ABOUT THE AUTHOR

PHOTO BY ADELE J. HAFT-ZINOVICH

This is Jordan Zinovich's second biographical work about a member of the Nagle family. His previous work, also published by Lone Pine Publishing, is *The Prospector: North of Sixty*. It is a biography of Ed Nagle's son Ted, who was a prospector and a key player in the race to own the north's vast mineral resources.

Jordan currently lives with his wife, Adele in New York City. He is editing a critical, theoretical and aesthetic survey of Canada which Semiotext(e) intends to publish in the fall of 1993. He is also working on a novel set in Canada and Crete.